Schooling Citizens:
The Struggle for African American
Education in Antebellum America

Schooling Citizens: The Struggle for African American Education in Antebellum America

HILARY J. MOSS

THE UNIVERSITY OF CHICAGO PRESS   CHICAGO AND LONDON

HILARY J. MOSS is assistant professor of history and black studies at Amherst College.

The University of Chicago Press, Chicago 60637
The University of Chicago Press, Ltd., London
© 2009 by The University of Chicago
All rights reserved. Published 2009
Printed in the United States of America
18 17 16 15 14 13 12 11 10 09   1 2 3 4 5

ISBN-13: 978-0-226-54249-2 (cloth)
ISBN-10: 0-226-54249-1 (cloth)

Library of Congress Cataloging-in-Publication Data

Moss, Hilary J.
    Schooling citizens : the struggle for African American education in antebellum
America / Hilary J. Moss.
        p. cm.
    Includes index.
    ISBN-13: 978-0-226-54249-2 (cloth : alk. paper)
    ISBN-10: 0-226-54249-1 (cloth : alk. paper)   1. African Americans—Education.
2. Racism—United States—History—19th century.   3. Educational equalization—
United States.   4. Discrimination in education—United States.   I. Title.
LC2741.M688 2009
371.829'9607309034—dc22

                                                                2009010015

TO MIKE, A PARTNER IN ALL THINGS

Contents

List of Figures and Tables

Acknowledgments

Researching the educational experiences of others has made me profoundly grateful for the teachers in my life. I owe the greatest debt to my parents, Stephen and Abigail Moss, who read to me nightly, showed me the joy to be found in teaching others, and pushed me to do what I love no matter what. They made possible my own education, and for that I am grateful. This book would not exist without their support. When I was an undergraduate at Northwestern University, Carl Smith introduced me to the nineteenth century, made me love American history, and gave me the best piece of advice I have ever received: Go to Brandeis.

There I met my adviser, Jackie Jones. Jackie taught me that what matters most is hard work. Under her supervision, I completed my first research paper, a study of African American literacy in the antebellum South. I had no idea that this project would become my dissertation and now a book. I cannot remember how many times I entered her office with a jumble of ideas and left with focus and inspiration. She had a way of teasing out the best of what I gave her and then making me think those ideas were my own. Even now, when I am no longer her student, Jackie remains the best mentor I have. When I think about the kind of teacher I want to be, she is the model that comes to mind.

The students I met at Brandeis have become the scholars I depend upon most in my professional life. I could not have asked for a more encouraging, engaged, and energetic cohort. Jason Opal kept me on my toes and tutored me patiently. Benjamin Irvin deciphered the rituals of the American Revolution and kept me laughing throughout. Molly McCarthy read more drafts of the same chapter than anyone should ever have to. Emily Straus shared my fascination with educational opportunity and along with Lindsay Silver demystified the twentieth century. Paul Ringel, Jeff Wiltse,

Eben Miller, Amy Dahlberg Chu, Alexis Antracoli, William Walker, and Jessica Lepler read multiple chapters in inchoate states. Along the way, Greg Renoff became one friend whom I consider family. I cannot express how much I appreciate all he adds to my life.

Several other professors graciously shared their time and insight. John Brooke hired me to help with his book after my first year, a daring decision by any account. I hope he will see how much he taught me, particularly about the importance of a good research assistant. As a member of my dissertation committee, Jane Kamensky provided indispensable lessons on writing and life. Her Narrative Strategies course remains the one educational experience I return to the most. Joanne Pope Melish taught me the importance of what to leave out. Joyce Antler, Sharon Feiman-Nemsar, Marya Levenson, and Ted Sizer showed me the joy to be found in educational research.

As if a steady stream of friends and mentors was not enough, Brandeis also offered five years of financial assistance. I am grateful for the Rose and Irving Crown Fellowship, the Graduate School of Arts and Sciences Dissertation Year Fellowship, and the University Prize Instructorship. The Spencer Foundation gave me a dedicated year to research and write. I also benefited greatly from residential fellowships at the Gilder Lehrman Center for the Study of Slavery, Resistance, and Abolition at Yale University and the Virginia Historical Society. Finally, Amherst College made it possible to finish this book. A Trustee Faculty Fellowship funded an invaluable sabbatical year. I am grateful as well to the H. Axel Schupf '57 Fund for Intellectual Life, the Amherst Academic Internship Program, which is financed by the Andrew W. Mellon Foundation, and the Office of the Dean of the Faculty. Janet Tobin deserves special thanks for steering me through the complex world of faculty resources.

My colleagues in the history department at Amherst have been unfailingly supportive and have taught me much. Over five years of lunches, Monica Ringer, Trent Maxey, Rick López, and Celso Castro Alves have raised my spirits more times than I can count. Martha Saxton, my compatriot in the nineteenth century, has never ended a conversation without words of encouragement. Catherine Epstein continues to astound me with her love of writing and her ability to plan. Gordie Levin, John Servos, Jerry Dennerline, and Sean Redding helped me believe I could finish this book. Frank Couvares instructed me in Catholic history. Kevin Sweeney and Margaret Hunt taught me about weaponry, knowledge that did not come in handy for this project but might at some point. Finally, Marni

Sandweiss introduced me to a gift that keeps on giving: Ancestry Library. I hope she will see how much her efforts improved this book.

My colleagues in Black Studies have been equally encouraging. I spent my sabbatical year writing in my departmental office, something against which many people warned me. I cannot express how much I appreciate the steps they took to enable me to write. My neighbor Rowland Abiodun cheered me on every morning and reminded me to go home every night. David Wills saved me from several research mistakes. Andrea Rushing never failed to ask how I was doing each time we met. Rhonda Cobham-Sander sharpened my prose with challenging advice. Jeffrey Ferguson pushed me daily without wavering in his support. Celso Castro Alves inspired me with his intensity. Mitzi Goheen kept me together and keeps all of us on track. It is a rare thing to be part of a department that considers itself a family. I am especially grateful to Karla Keyes, who makes my life better in ways too many to count.

A number of other colleagues enriched this book. Special thanks go to Benjamin Justice, who provided skilled and copious commentary on the entire book. As part of a Faculty Work-In-Progress Seminar funded by the Dean's Office at Amherst College, Martha Umphrey, Rhonda Cobham-Sander, Marisa Parham, Lucia Suárez, Martha Saxton, Karen Sánchez-Eppler, and Marni Sandweiss shared their own work and gave expert advice. I owe particular thanks to Karen for reaching out to me and for bringing us together in the first place. As part of the Five College Education Studies Writing Group, Meg Gebhard, Kristen Luschen, Lenore Carlisle, Laura Wenk, and Lucy Mule provided thoughtful feedback on chapter 3. Rachel Remmel, Heather Barrow, Elizabeth Fraterrigo, Michael Innis-Jimenez, Anthony Raynsford, Christopher Miller, and Michael McCoyer provided equally valuable commentary as part of the Urban History Dissertation Group. Joseph Cullum, Charlotte Haller, Stephanie Dunson, Marty Rojas, and Molly McCarthy gave chapter 1 a rigorous read. To this day, Molly remains one of the readers whom I trust the most.

Commentators and audiences provided invaluable feedback as well. I would like to thank James Anderson, Ron Butchart, Jack Dougherty, Carl Kaestle, Ira Katznelson, Marybeth Gasman, John Rury, Vanessa Siddle Walker, and David Tyack for their expert advice. I am equally appreciative of the many suggestions I received from audiences at Amherst College, the Boston Area History of Education Working Group, Brandeis University, Connecticut College, the New Haven Historical Society, Historic Deerfield, the University of Maryland Law School, the History of

Education Society, the Organization of American Historians, Trinity College, Smith College, the Virginia Historical Society, Wellesley College, and Yale University. The History of Education Society in particular has energized my work. Nancy Beadie, Barbara Beatty, Ron Butchart, Adah Ward Randolph, Carl Kaestle, and Jack Dougherty especially have guided me through the early phase of my academic career. Emily Straus, Charles Dorn, Bethany Rogers, David Gamson, John Spencer, Judith Kafka, Michael Clapper, Margaret Nash, Tracy Steffes, and Benjamin Justice have become friends I look forward to seeing every year.

Several other individuals have strengthened the substance of this book. In addition to reading the introduction, Kate Masur provided critical insight on nineteenth-century notions of citizenship. James Brewer Stewart happily tutored me on Benjamin Roberts. Seth Rockman shared a love for all things Baltimore and, most importantly, gave me his manuscript at a critical point. Tracy Steffes scrupulously read the introduction. Kate Tranbarger coached me in statistics. Steve Rivkin taught me about sampling and helped me with quantitative research. Adam Honig tutored me in quantitative analysis as well. I am hoping he will permit me to complete the course. Sami Alpanda saved me from a key mistake. Andrew Dole steadied me throughout the writing process. I am particularly indebted to Andy Anderson, who spent days teaching me geographic information systems and came to my rescue when those lessons failed to take.

As intrepid research assistants, Marie Cyndy Jean, Matthew Mendoza, Erin Sullivan, and Christopher Tullis logged in more hours than I can count. Claire Rann came to my rescue multiple times. Heather Wilson stayed with this project for nearly two years. I cannot express how much I appreciate the time she spent transcribing census schedules, translating addresses, and making maps. Without Heather this would be a much lesser book.

Many curators, librarians, and archivists also provided invaluable research support. I am particularly indebted to the librarians at Brandeis and Amherst, who gave me sacred research space, tracked down an infinite number of interlibrary loan items, and answered a stream of research requests. In addition, I would like to thank archivists at the American Antiquarian Society, Boston Public Library, Connecticut State Library, Connecticut Historical Society, Beinecke Rare Book and Manuscript Library, Maryland State Library, Maryland Historical Society, Baltimore City Archives, and Massachusetts State Archives. Edwin Schell at the Lovely Lane Museum in Baltimore, Elizabeth Bouvier at the Massachusetts State Archives, and Bill Holsey at the New Haven Historical Society deserve special mention for their efforts.

Portions of chapter 2 appeared previously as "Education's Inequity: Opposition to Black Higher Education in Antebellum Connecticut" (*History of Education Quarterly* 46 [Spring 2006]: 16–35). Parts of chapter 6 appeared previously as "The Tarring and Feathering of Thomas Paul Smith: Common Schools, Revolutionary Memory, and the Crisis of Citizenship in Antebellum Boston" (*New England Quarterly* 80 [June 2007]: 218–41). I would like to thank both Blackwell Publishers and MIT Press for their permission to reprint.

At the University of Chicago Press, my editor Robert Devens held my hand through every step of the publication process. I remain in awe of his unremitting dedication to authors and books. In addition to providing expert editorial advice, Robert secured swift and skillful readers. Adam R. Nelson and Shane White returned exhaustive commentaries in record time. I hope they will see how much I took their suggestions to heart. Emilie Sandoz and Anne Summers Goldberg provided excellent editorial assistance. Sharon Brinkman sharpened my prose and saved me from countless mistakes. My cartographer, Harry Johnson, created beautiful maps.

For more than two decades, Deborah Becker and Rachel Singer have been my foundation. Raina Uhden has become my in-case-of-emergency phone call and keeps me happy with laughter and with soup. Arthur Horwich, David Horwich, and Martina Brueckner deserve special thanks for giving me even more reason to love New Haven. Ron Wilson, Sharon Seidel, Kate Ball, Maxine Horwich, Walter Horwich, Annie Horwich, Mackenzie Young, and Wally Young have been with this project from the beginning. Aubrey and Jason Metakis never fail to ask when the book will be out.

My husband, Michael Horwich, to whom this book is dedicated, deserves a coauthor credit. He has read every word multiple times, designed the tables, and helped make the maps. He is the best friend I could hope for and the love of my life.

Introduction

On July 4, 1835, in bustling cities and in small towns, Americans assembled to celebrate their nation's fifty-ninth birthday. In Canaan, New Hampshire, a village on the northwestern boundary of the Connecticut River Valley, townspeople also came together on this day. But the purpose that united these citizens bore no resemblance to the ideals of the founding: justice, tolerance, or equality. After a raucous public assembly, some seventy white Canaanites paraded through town. They marched toward Noyes Academy, an institution that provided advanced literary instruction to young men and women, white and African American. "No day like 'independent day' for demolishing a school house," one editorialist castigating the mob commented sarcastically.[1] The crowd encircled the institution it had come to destroy, when a voice called out from inside the building identifying the assailants by their full names. The mob dispersed, only to return six weeks later, triggering the explosive violence that would mark one of the most spectacular episodes of white opposition to black education in American history.[2]

On August 10, 1835, approximately one hundred white inhabitants of Canaan and its surrounds once again gathered at the gates of the integrated academy. With around ninety-five yoke of oxen, they ripped the schoolhouse from its foundation, dragged it for half a mile, and then dumped the building into a swamp.[3] The school had been open for just more than a year, created by individuals sympathetic to antislavery and eager to make higher education accessible to African Americans.[4] As George Kimball, a white Canaan resident and academy founder observed, despite an expansion in public schooling throughout the North, black and white children still possessed disparate access to education. "It is unhappily true," Kimball noted, that "the colored portion of our fellow citizens, even in the free

States, while their toil and blood have contributed to establish, and their taxes equally with those of whites, to maintain our free system of Education, have practically been excluded from the benefits of it."[5] At Noyes Academy, in contrast, black and white students could study an array of literary and vocational subjects: bookkeeping, geometry, algebra, trigonometry, surveying, navigation, astronomy, grammar, logic, and philosophy.[6]

At the time of its demise, the institution enrolled approximately forty-two pupils, fourteen of whom were African American. Three of these students, Alexander Crummell, Thomas Sidney, and Henry Highland Garnet, had trekked "four hundred and more miles" to reach the school in 1834. Crummell remembered the trip from New York City to Canaan as grueling, largely because racial segregation made travel arduous, if not impossible, for African Americans. "On the steamboat from New York to Providence no cabin passage was allowed colored people," he recalled, "and so [they were] exposed all night, bedless and foodless, to the cold and storm." The trio moved by stage coach for the next leg of the journey. "[R]arely would an inn or a hotel give us food, and nowhere could we get shelter," Crummell recollected. Sick even before he left New York, the journey took the greatest toll on nineteen-year-old Garnet, who had spent much of his childhood enslaved in Maryland. Crummell never could forget his companion's "sufferings—sufferings from pain, sufferings from cold and exposure, sufferings from thirst and hunger, sufferings from taunt and insult at every village and town, and oft times at every farm-house, as we rode, mounted upon the top of the coach through all this long journey."[7] Thankfully, the trustees could not have selected a more splendid site in which to study: "The climate is remarkably healthy; the water excellent; and the soil, though thin and rocky, well-suited to such pasturage," according to one visitor.[8] These weary travelers could not have imagined what would transpire in this serene setting one year later. As Crummell would recall, "Fourteen black boys with books in their hands set the entire Granite State crazy!"[9]

That second Monday in August 1835, as the crowd gathered on the school grounds, town historian William Wallace spied a number of white men brandishing "bars and axes" as a "wagon loaded with chains" rolled through town.[10] He described the next set of events in real time: "The team is attached. Ninety-five yoke of cattle. It is straightened. The chains break. They try again and again the chains break! Almost in vain do they try. Thermometer ranges at 116 in the sun. At half past 7 they had succeeded in drawing [the schoolhouse] into the road, when they adjourned till next day." At night while the oxen dozed, someone attempted to set the schoolhouse on fire but it would not burn. "I need not tell you of the band of earnest philanthropists—men and women—who met together in secret that dark night and wept and prayed because of the destruction that had befallen their beautiful hopes," Wallace mourned.[11] Inside their boarding-house, pupils fashioned bullets in anticipation of the assault. Just before midnight, the sound of horses and hooves rang through the air. Someone shot into the students' residence, at which point Garnet returned fire, re-pelling the onslaught for a time.[12]

As the sun rose the following morning, the crowd went on the offensive again. "This day was hotter than the preceding," Wallace reported, "yet with redoubled ardor these men persisted in their crime, until they hauled the house on to the corner of the Common, in front and close by the old church. They arrived upon the spot just at dark, so completely fagged out, both oxen and men, that it was utterly impossible to do anything further." There they left the schoolhouse, "shattered" and "mutilated" "beyond reparation."[13] In so doing, Canaanites had made a mockery of their revo-lutionary heritage, according to one commentator. The ruins of Noyes Academy stood "not like the monument on 'Bunker's Heights,' erected in memory of those *departed spirits*, which fought and fell *struggling for liberty*, but as the monument of the *folly* of those living spirits, who are struggling to destroy what our fathers have gained."[14]

This book seeks to understand what inspired individuals like Garnet, Crummell, and Sidney to endure so much for an education and what moved others—like the villagers of Canaan—to oppose them.

*   *   *

The central objective of *Schooling Citizens* is to make sense of the wide-spread, often violent, white opposition to African American education that erupted in northern and southern communities in the early 1830s, a period that coincides with the birth of public education—the so-called rise of the common school—in America. With the onset of insti-tutional segregation and a series of attacks against black schoolhouses, like that which occurred in Canaan, some whites sought to deny educa-tion to African Americans at the same time that many others, includ-ing white women and immigrants, were ushered into these "public" institutions. In this book I ask why public schooling and white opposi-tion to African American education expanded simultaneously. Drawing from an in-depth examination of three distinct antebellum cities—New Haven, Baltimore, and Boston—this study strives to resolve this apparent paradox.

According to school reformers in the antebellum period, common schools were intended to provide children from disparate social, religious, and economic backgrounds with a common set of values and experiences. That shared understanding, in turn, would inspire students to shed their diverse, if not divergent, personal loyalties for a national identity. Public schools, to put it plainly, could teach children to become Americans. The stakes of this educational philosophy felt particularly pronounced as tensions over immigration, slavery, urbanization, industrialization, and westward expansion compelled individuals to work out for themselves what it meant to be American.[15]

But despite its promise to expand educational opportunity, this particular rationale for public schooling held unsettling implications for black people, whose place in the body politic remained contested and uncertain. By advancing an argument for universal education that privileged citizenship instead of equality, school reformers inadvertently reinforced efforts to deny black people access to public schooling; in other words, by invoking civic inclusion rather than social justice to promote public education, they implicitly justified denying African Americans, as noncitizens, equal educational opportunity.

Likewise, the marriage between public schooling and citizenship also informed and complicated black educational activism in this period. While the meaning of citizenship was inchoate in the early nineteenth century, many free blacks acutely understood its relationship to suffrage, property rights, jury service, and military participation. Most importantly, citizenship offered the only sure way to escape the tentacles of slavery.[16] That realization felt especially pronounced after 1850, when the Fugitive Slave Law simultaneously empowered masters to claim ownership over black residents of free communities and stripped accused fugitives of their right to a trial by jury.

In this context, public schools became a particularly charged site for Americans, white and black, to work out questions of civil rights and civic identity. Some African American educational activists, for example, contested school segregation not simply—or even primarily—because they believed black children learned less in separate institutions, but from a desire to capitalize on the linkage between schooling and citizenship as articulated by school reformers. Black activists' efforts to claim this elusive identity through entry into the public schools, in turn, raised troubling questions for African American parents, eager to shield their children from white abuse, and for black educators, uneasy with placing politics above pedagogy and hesitant to jeopardize the existence of all-black institutions and, by extension, their own economic security.

To my mind, in-depth comparative history—history defined not by flat regional contrasts but rich in nuance and rooted in archival documentation—is ideally suited to elucidating the relationships between race, citizenship, and educational opportunity. Because I am concerned with how ideas about race and citizenship evolved as Americans created public school systems, I selected cities that supported public schools in the early nineteenth century. As most American communities did not finance and sustain educational institutions until after the Civil War, it is impossible to include every locality in this account. To do so, one would have to ground this history in the postbellum period; in the process, one would miss a critical moment when many of Americans' most deeply held ideas about public education took root.

Although I discuss New Haven, Baltimore, and Boston independently, this book advances chronologically. It opens in 1827, as white opposition to black education emerged in New Haven, and closes in 1855, when Boston desegregated its public school system. Each chapter focuses on a distinct theme: "whiteness," higher education, labor, self-education, segregation, and American identity. Part 1 charts the onset of white opposition to black education in New Haven through a detailed examination of two episodes: an 1827 debate over the African Improvement Society and the local uproar four years later in response to the effort to build the nation's first black college. Part 2 similarly employs intensive local analysis to understand a larger question: what factors contributed to Baltimore's tolerance of black religious, classical, and vocational education? Finally, part 3 explores black Bostonians' educational activism against the backdrop of the common school movement by querying the city's conflicted commitment to public education and racial segregation and by tracing the relationship between black efforts to desegregate public schools and to claim citizenship in the aftermath of the Fugitive Slave Law (1850).

Of these three communities, some readers might anticipate slaveholding Baltimore to have been the most hostile to African American education; yet, in actuality, black schools in this southern seaport encountered little resistance from the white community. Unlike many other slaveholding states, Maryland passed no antiliteracy laws and few Baltimoreans ever took to the streets to shut down a school for black children. Baltimore's educational history becomes particularly striking when one examines the free black community's dramatic success at self-education. Despite their exclusion from public schools, African Americans in Baltimore constructed and sustained a number of private schools during the antebellum period. At the same time, white residents of "free" New Haven avidly, and often violently, opposed higher education for African Americans. Similarly, while many regard Boston as the birthplace of public education, its commitment to educational opportunity broke down in the face of white enthusiasm for racial segregation.

By no means, however, should readers leave this brief discussion with the impression that Baltimore was a utopia for black people. In contrast to their counterparts in Baltimore, African Americans in New Haven and Boston retained important civil rights: to own property; to establish churches; to enter into contracts; and to testify in court.[17] By extension, African Americans in the two New England seaports also had greater access to schooling than their counterparts in slaveholding Baltimore, as New Haven and Boston provided at least some public education to black children. Baltimore, in contrast, simultaneously excluded African Americans from its public schools *and* taxed black people for these institutions. Thus, because regionalism in and of itself does not explain access to education in this period, I look to different factors, including emancipation, immigration, labor, and ideas about citizenship and American identity. I also examine themes that suffuse scholarship on race and citizenship in antebellum America: print culture, violence, the market, religion, and gender, among others.[18]

In all three cities, slavery and freedom are both paramount to understanding the relationship between race, citizenship, and educational opportunity. Residents of antebellum New Haven, Baltimore, and Boston experienced emancipation differently. Whereas Massachusetts eradicated slavery with a judicial decree in the aftermath of the American Revolution, Connecticut's legislature did not decree the death of slavery until 1848. Although slavery had largely vanished from the state by this time, this disappearance took decades to play out.[19] Maryland, in contrast, did not outlaw slavery until after the Civil War, yet because of the popularity of gradual manumission agreements, whereby a master promised freedom to a slave after a predetermined term of service, thousands of African Americans enslaved in Baltimore became free around the turn of the nineteenth century.[20] In fact, by 1830 the southern seaport contained the nation's largest free black community and a small enslaved population relative to other southern cities.

This observation may lead some readers to wonder whether Baltimore, located on the boundary between North and South, should be considered southern. Most historians now reject the notion of a single, monolithic South, or a monolithic North for that matter, for a more expansive understanding of regional identity that allows for a multiplicity of experiences.[21] At the same time, however, slavery's infectious existence distinguished Baltimore from northern cities like Boston and New Haven, where emancipation had largely run its course by 1830. Even as Baltimore's enslaved population was small and shrinking after 1830, slavery's presence loomed large. As Seth Rockman points out, to hold a slave in Baltimore was to possess an individual who could be converted into cash, should the need or inclination arise.[22] Because of slavery's invidious influence over Baltimore's political, social, and economic institutions, I believe this city can be understood as part of the South while also recognizing its differences.

In recounting this history, I hope to communicate the profound significance of education to black parents, pupils, teachers, and activists, many of whom came of age under slavery. Several issues African Americans grappled with during this period will likely feel familiar to readers versed in contemporary debates about educational equality. How should African Americans balance the educational needs of individuals with their collective political priorities? What role should children play in movements against slavery and racial prejudice? Should parents allow—or encourage—their sons and daughters to sacrifice their own security for other people's liberty? Which strategy—moral suasion, militancy, or accommodation—would best advance African Americans' civil rights? Yet even within dialogues as disparate as these, certain ideas about education appeared beyond dispute. In all three cities, African Americans valued schools not just for their potential to benefit themselves and their families but also for their promise to advance the civil rights of all black people. And while occupational segregation prevented many African Americans from realizing a vocational benefit from their literary abilities, black parents remained committed to their children's schooling. Finally, most African Americans approached the concept of educational opportunity from a profound sense of shared responsibility. Few lost sight of how their achievements might affect black people still held in slavery.

Because few primary accounts detailing African Americans' educational experiences survive from this period, this book reads people's actions as speaking for their intentions. In Boston, for example, I argue that free blacks choreographed their educational activism deliberately, invoking the memory of the Revolution to claim citizenship and to assert their American identity. In contrast, free black Baltimoreans, living within a slaveholding society, could not express their intentions as overtly. In Baltimore more than in Boston and New Haven, I rely upon nonnarrative sources: census records, city directories, apprenticeship contracts, and help-wanted advertisements, for example. To paint the fullest possible picture of education in this period, this investigation peers beyond the schoolhouse and explores a range of other institutions including apprenticeship, the family, the workplace, benevolent associations, and the church. Such an expansive conception of education is essential because so many antebellum African Americans received instruction outside the classroom.

An additional point of clarification: when making comparisons across locales I often employ the phrase "educational opportunity." My use of this term relates more to issues of access than quality. This distinction is driven largely by the particular sources that document black instruction in the antebellum period, most of which resist easy conclusions about educational outcomes. For example, my examination of census records details that, in 1850, a greater proportion of African Americans—68 percent—attended school in Boston than in Baltimore, where just 17 percent of black children received formal instruction at some point in the year. These numbers say little, however, about the kind of education these children received once they passed through the schoolhouse doors.

Although I situate education at the center of my study, I did not set out to write an educational history. Rather, I began this project with the belief that Americans have historically made known their beliefs about civic inclusion and national identity through educational opportunity. In other words, the choices that individuals and communities made about schooling their children—about whom to include, whom to exclude, and who should get priority—speak to much larger questions about inclusion, exclusion, and equality within American society. By extension, public schools in particular were uniquely important institutions in which antebellum Americans debated, decided, and contested questions of political inclusion and national identity.[23] For these reasons, I sought to make sense of how, as communities, New Haven, Baltimore, and Boston decided whom they would—and whom they would not—educate and, by extension, whom they would admit into nominally public schools.

While scholars have mined African American history and the expansion of public education in the antebellum period, no study before this one has united these two histories.[24] In his sweeping survey of common school reform, for example, Carl Kaestle asserts that the common school movement arose primarily from three factors: republicanism, Protestantism, and the development of capitalism.[25] Yet if one integrates African American history into this narrative, the importance of a fourth factor—race—becomes apparent. Incorporating the black experience into the triumphal story of the rise of the common school shatters any pretensions we might have about the democratic and progressive origins of public education in America.

Specifically, as greater numbers of white people availed themselves of public schooling, some white people also sought to deny access to their black neighbors because it was a mark of the very citizenship they sought to withhold from African Americans. The more that schooling came to be preserved for whites only, the more its racial exclusivity increased its perceived value. In the process, common schools became a powerful filter that both promoted and protected access to citizenship. For the purposes of this study, I use the term the citizenship to connote a broad spectrum of civil rights necessary for individual liberty and for collective engagement with political power. At times, I also employ the concept more loosely to articulate a kind of cultural identity, a sense of inclusion, equality, or equal opportunity.[26] For this definition, I have looked to scholars like Linda Kerber and Evelyn Nakano Glenn, who are particularly attuned to the relationship between civic inclusion and categories of difference like race, gender, and ethnicity.[27]

Common school reform gave white children from all classes and ethnicities the opportunity to become citizens or, at the very least, to feel a part of the larger society; yet, at the same time, it also reinforced a conception of citizenship becoming increasingly synonymous with whiteness, in which black Americans, enslaved or free, could not participate. Along the way, white opposition to black education became a critical component in a much larger movement to remove—figuratively, if not physically—black people from the body politic. By extension, many African Americans sought to integrate public schools, not from any desire to be closer to white people, but rather from the recognition that inclusion in these Americanizing institutions was necessary to secure citizenship—

legal recognition of their full and equal membership in civic society with all the "privileges and immunities" such standing guaranteed to their white counterparts. That designation, black activists understood, was necessary to exercise freedom: to vote, to hold property, and to live without fear of slavery.[28]

I also began my research with the premise that white opposition to African American education was never a foregone conclusion. In fact, in the seventeenth and eighteenth centuries, many white citizens, slaveholders included, tolerated and even encouraged African Americans' literary, religious, and vocational instruction. Particularly in New England, where biblical literacy was central to Puritan and Protestant theology, many ministers worked to bring enslaved and free black people into their spiritual fold. Beyond religious instruction, the apprenticeship system served as another avenue for African Americans to obtain literacy and vocational instruction in the eighteenth and early nineteenth centuries. Apprenticeship contracts are perhaps the best documentation of this tradition as they reveal the legal, social, and personal expectations apprentices and masters carried into these arrangements. In addition to a trade, apprenticeship contracts frequently specified that masters were to teach black men to read, write, and cipher, while they were to instruct black women in the art of reading and the mystery of housewifery. The apprenticeship system served this function until the early nineteenth century, when the nature of the institution began to shift from instruction to control. After this juncture, some states allowed masters to withhold literacy from black apprentices specifically.

At the same time, African Americans independently increased their educational opportunities. Particularly in the urban North, free black communities created and sustained an array of educational institutions including reading clubs, debating societies, lyceums, infant schools, Sabbath schools, and academies. These efforts often stemmed from the expansion of African Americans' religious institutions in the early nineteenth century. African American adults embraced self-improvement with equal enthusiasm.[29] Around the late 1820s, however, whites in both northern and southern communities began to oppose these activities with a singular intensity.

Despite a crazy quilt of sporadically enforced antiliteracy laws, no state had legislated against free black schooling before 1829.[30] But in the aftermath of David Walker's *Appeal,* which sanctioned violence to eradicate slavery, white southerners began to criminalize providing literacy to black

people. In the North, whites spurned black calls for self-improvement, segregated their public schools, and, in the case of Connecticut, proscribed
African Americans from entering the state for literary instruction. In fact,
between 1831 and 1839, whites in New Hampshire, Washington D.C.,
Philadelphia, New York City, and Boston undermined black education
through protest and petition and, in some instances, through violence
(Figure 1). At the same time, many of these municipalities crafted their
common school systems. To avoid racial integration, they created separate
schools specifically for black children. As of 1830, towns including Providence, Rhode Island, Portsmouth, New Hampshire, Portland, Maine, and
Salem, Massachusetts sustained at least one "African" school with public
monies, while Boston, New Haven, New York, and Philadelphia supported
multiple primary schools for black students.[31]

White attitudes toward black improvement thus became mired in a
strange paradox: many whites, living and laboring against the backdrop
of gradual emancipation, complained about the fictive ignorance of the
free black population and the burden it imposed upon the republic. At
the same time, many also resisted efforts to elevate African Americans to
equality. As enslaved people slowly became free in the aftermath of the
Revolution, whites responded with a multitude of measures, symbolic and
actual, to limit African Americans' liberty. The demise of African Americans' voting rights in the early-nineteenth-century North is perhaps the
most telling expression of this transformation. Prior to the late eighteenth
century, suffrage was contingent upon gender or property holdings, but it
was never dependent upon race. In the early nineteenth century, however,
several northern states began to delineate voting privileges along racial
lines. While Massachusetts did not deny suffrage to black men, its neighboring states, including New York and Connecticut, moved to do so when
they expanded voting privileges for white men.[32]

Whites who were uncomfortable with African American forays into the
public sphere through parades, celebrations, or print similarly attempted
to imagine black people out of the polity by depicting them as inarticu-
late, unintelligent, and, most notably, uneducated.[33] Popularized around
1816, the "Bobalition broadside" epitomized these impulses, as northern
white pamphleteers lampooned black efforts at self-improvement and
civic engagement by publishing "black" speech with egregious spelling
and grammatical mistakes and malapropisms. In one such broadside, for
example, "Cesar Crack-Em-All" raised a glass to "De Africum School."
"Bress dare little souls," he decreed, "how fass dey do larn Mattymattacks

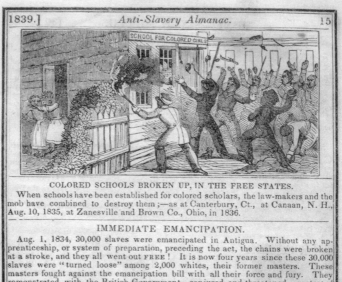

COLORED SCHOOLS BROKEN UP, IN THE FREE STATES.

When schools have been established for colored scholars, the law-makers and the mob have combined to destroy them ;—as at Canterbury, Ct., at Canaan, N. H., Aug. 10, 1835, at Zanesville and Brown Co., Ohio, in 1836.

IMMEDIATE EMANCIPATION.

Aug. 1, 1834, 30,000 slaves were emancipated in Antigua. Without any apprenticeship, or system of preparation, preceding the act, the chains were broken at a stroke, and they all went out FREE ! It is now four years since these 30,000 slaves were "turned loose" among 2,000 whites, their former masters. These masters fought against the emancipation bill with all their force and fury. They remonstrated with the British Government—conjured and threatened,—protested that emancipation would ruin the island, that the emancipated slaves would never work—would turn vagabonds, butcher the whites and flood the island with beggary and crime. Their strong beseechings availed as little as their threats, and croakings about ruin. The Emancipation Act, unintimidated by the bluster, traversed quietly through its successive stages up to the royal sanction, and became the law of the land. When the slaveholders of Antigua saw that abolition was *inevitable*, they at once resolved to substitute immediate, unconditional, and entire emancipation for the gradual process contemplated by the Act. Well, what has been the result? Read the following testimony of the very men who, but little more than four years ago, denounced and laughed to scorn the idea of abolishing slavery, and called it folly, fanaticism, and insanity. We quote from the work of Messrs. Thome and Kimball, lately published, the written testimony of many of the first men in Antigua,—some of whom were among the largest slaveholders before August, 1834. It proves, among other points, that

EMANCIPATED SLAVES ARE PEACEABLE.

TESTIMONY. " *There is no feeling of insecurity.* A stronger proof of this cannot be given than *the dispensing, within five months after emancipation, with the Christmas guards, which had been uninterruptedly kept up for nearly one hundred · years*—during the whole time of slavery.

"I have *never head of any instance of revenge* for former injuries." *James Scotland, Sen. Esq.*

"Insurrection or revenge *is in no case dreaded.* My family go to sleep every night with the doors unlocked. There is not the *slightest* feeling of insecurity —quite the contrary. Property is more secure, *for all idea of insurrection is abolished forever.*" *Hon. N. Nugent, Speaker of the House of Assembly.*

"There has been no instance of personal violence since freedom. I have not heard of a single case of even *meditated* revenge." *Dr. Daniell, member of the Council, and Attorney for six estates.*

"Emancipation has banished the *fear* of insurrections, incendiarism, &c." *Mr. Favey, Manager of Lavicount's.*

"I have never heard of an instance of violence or revenge on the part of the negroes." *Rev. Mr. Morrish, Moravian Missionary.*

FIGURE I. Colored schools broken up in the free states. *The American Anti-Slavery Almanac,* 1839, 13. Printed text. Courtesy of Manuscripts, Archives and Rare Books Division, Schomburg Center for Research in Black Culture, The New York Public Library, Astor, Lenox, and Tilden Foundations.

and Combomblifications."[34] At Fourth of July and other nationalist celebrations, northern working-class whites drove free blacks from public spaces in an attempt to cast them out as political "others."[35] "Warnings-out," a process in which town leaders ordered outsiders to leave their community to prevent them from claiming poor relief, and mob violence also increased in frequency and intensity. White efforts to expel black people from the body politic were not just figurative, they were also literal, as white enthusiasm for African American "repatriation" attests. Founded in 1817, the American Colonization Society aspired to send all black people "back to Africa."[36] The intended message of such varied forms of exclusion was clear. In the midst of slavery's demise, some whites sought to remove all black people from the polity and, in so doing, to link whiteness with American identity.

Those familiar with the history of public schooling may have learned that the antebellum era was the age of the common school, when reformers like Horace Mann stumped for democracy, building schools to serve every child. But, as this book makes clear, that ideology did little to ensure that black people would be included—let alone included equally—in public schools. The common school movement, in consequence, empowered white children, regardless of their religion or ethnicity, to claim citizenship, but it also reinforced white efforts to withhold civil rights from African Americans.

As foreign immigrants arrived en masse into northern port cities later in the nineteenth century, native whites responded with a systematic language of prejudice that aimed to make them appear less white, or, alternatively, less American, than themselves.[37] At the same time, common school reformers appealed to nativism by asserting public schools' power to assuage social, religious, and ethnic distinctions. It was in these institutions, school boosters contended, that all children, no matter their birthplace or social standing, could enter as individuals and exit as Americans. The expansion of public schooling and white opposition to black education thus was not coincidental. To the contrary, they were part and parcel of a larger impulse to expel black people from the polity in the early nineteenth century.

PART I

Education's Inequity: New Haven, Connecticut

Notwithstanding the fame which Connecticut has acquired in distant lands, for intelligence and liberal feelings, in no part of the Union are the people more prejudiced against persons of colour.[1] —John Brown Russwurm, 1827

In 1638, several hundred settlers left Massachusetts Bay to form a new colony. Eager to create a community pious and profitable, Englishmen John Davenport and Theophilus Eaton had selected the site a few months before: a flat plain bounded by two rivers, the Quinnipiac and the West, on the shores of Long Island Sound. Set on a large harbor on the southern edge of the Connecticut River Valley, the area appeared especially well suited for agriculture and commerce. With fertile soil and navigable waterways, the landscape foretold a future of abundant harvests and prolific trade. Colonists anticipated that the location, midway between Boston and New Amsterdam, would encourage a vibrant coastal exchange, while its proximity to Long Island Sound would facilitate connections with merchants in Europe and the Caribbean.[2]

These new arrivals soon discovered the site was not as ideal as it appeared. The harbor was too shallow for their livelihood to depend upon the sea. It would take decades for laborers to dredge its basin and build a wharf long enough for ships to enter and exit without difficulty. Colonists had more success shaping the interior than the shore. They planned a settlement—initially called Quinnipiac and later named New Haven—on a neat grid of nine squares. On its southern corner lay the harbor, fed by two small creeks that spilled onto the southeastern and southwestern edges of town. They reserved the middle square for a public green and divided the eight remaining sections into household lots. The buildings they erected upon the common embodied their shared priorities. At its center they set a meetinghouse to accommodate political and religious assemblies. And on its northwestern edge they built a schoolhouse to look after the next generation's spiritual, civic, and commercial capabilities.[3]

New Haven's early legislative efforts similarly attest to the importance of educational opportunity in this nascent community. In 1645, town authorities heralded that "For the better training vpp of youth in this towne, that through Gods blessinge they may be fitted for publique service hereafter, either in church or commonweale, it is ordered, that a free schoole be sett vp."[4] Their use of the term "free" school in this context requires clarification. While public money funded the institution, students paid a modest tuition. Instructors also expected students to be literate prior to admission. Finally, the school served boys exclusively. There was no public provision for schooling girls. Such limitations suggest that access to public education in New Haven was less diffuse than it appeared. Students desiring advanced instruction could attend the local private school, which offered lessons in penmanship, arithmetic, and bookkeeping—critical skills for any young man who might one day run his own business or manage the accounts of his employer.[5]

Like their Puritan neighbors in Massachusetts, many colonial New Haveners believed that every individual, irrespective of his or her race, gender, or social standing, should be able to read the Bible. To this effect, in 1656 New Haven ordered households to provide all children—enslaved and free, black and white, boys and girls—with sufficient literacy to "read the Scriptures, and other good and profitable printed Books in the English tongue, being their native Language, and in some competent measure, to understand the main grounds and principles of Christian Religion necessary to salvation."[6] Legislators further commanded all townships larger than fifty families to sustain a school that offered lessons in reading and writing. By 1690, Connecticut—which had united with New Haven Colony in 1665—sent annual visitors to ensure families were educating their children and apprentices properly; noncompliant households could be penalized a shilling.

Colonial New Haveners not only expected schools to prepare boys to fulfill their future spiritual and commercial responsibilities, they also anticipated these institutions would instruct them to exercise citizenship's sundry rights and responsibilities. This purpose took on especial importance in the aftermath of the American Revolution. As one member of the Connecticut legislature articulated in 1831, "The importance of educating every child in the state, so far, as to enable him to transact the ordinary business of life, is readily conceded." But Connecticut, he asserted, had created common schools with a "higher destiny" in mind: to initiate soon-to-be citizens into "the principles of our Government."[7] In 1795, the state had established a permanent school fund to this end, appropriating over $1,000,000 from the sale of western lands to finance public education.[8]

New Haven's early enthusiasm for educational opportunity should not be mistaken for a commitment to racial equality. To the contrary, whites participated in and profited from chattel slavery from their first days in the region. Theophilus Eaton, town founder and New Haven's first governor, owned slaves, as did several other prominent religious and political officials.[9] While Connecticut never codified chattel slavery, by the late seventeenth century legislators had enacted a number of measures to limit black people's liberty. After 1690, "Negroes and Indians" could not travel after nine at night, nor could they pass beyond their town's borders without their master's written consent.[10] In 1702, Abda, the son of a black New Haven bondswoman and a free white man, sued his master, Thomas Richards, for freedom. The General Court refused Abda's appeal on the grounds that "such persons as are born of Negro bond women are themselves in like condition, that is born in servitude."[11] Thereafter, slaveholders in Connecticut had legal precedent to claim all children born to enslaved women.

In contrast to other New England seaports including Boston, Massachusetts, and Newport, Rhode Island, New Haven never became a significant node in the trans-Atlantic slave trade, largely because its harbor was too shallow for slaving vessels. This is not to say, however, that white New Haveners did not aid the slave trade indirectly. Ships constructed along its harbor later spirited slaves to America from Africa and the West Indies.[12] White townspeople also participated directly in the domestic slave trade, as evidenced by the announcements local newspapers carried describing "Negroes" for sale. In 1779, for example, Elizabeth Thompson informed *Connecticut Journal* readers that she had "a Variety of Houshold Furniture, of every Kind" and "a young Negro Wench" available for purchase.[13] New Haven papers also assisted masters in their efforts to recover runaways. In 1771, Ralph Isaacs placed a notice in the *Connecticut Journal,* hoping to locate his "two Negro Fellows" Peter and Primus, who had escaped the evening before. Peter, "a stout Fellow," had taken a "light Suit of Cloth Clothes, and many other Articles of Apparel." Primus, Isaacs reported, "has lost one of his Toes, has pretty long Hair for a Negro" and had fled once already. Isaacs also informed readers that Primus "will probably change his Name to Charles; is a handy Fellow, a pretty good Carpenter, and most likely has a Pass."[14] Such predictions spoke to Isaacs' familiarity with his bondsmen, a likely consequence of the close quarters and frequent interactions typical of New England slavery. In 1783, Josiah Burr offered a twenty-dollar reward to anyone who helped him recover "a Negro Man named Sam." Burr not only provided a physical description of Sam, "a tall, stout, well built Fellow," he also included details of Sam's particular educational history: "He speaks pretty good English, but with something of the Dutch Accent, which Language he has some little Knowledge of, having been brought up in a Dutch Family on Long-Island."[15]

In the aftermath of the Revolution, like other New England states, Connecticut took tentative steps to eliminate chattel slavery. But while enslaved African Americans were transitioning into free men and women, whites began to resist their demands for education with a newfound intensity. In fact, no northern state witnessed more upheaval over African American schooling in the antebellum period. As chapter 2 details, in September 1831, white townspeople in New Haven ended an interracial campaign to open the nation's first black college. But a year and a half after the college movement collapsed in New Haven, the Connecticut legislature enacted its infamous "black laws" which precluded any "school, academy, or literary institution" from enrolling African American students from outside the state.[16] Such legislation did little to mollify white animosity toward African American education. In response to white teacher Prudence Crandall's refusal to close her boarding school for black girls, whites in Canterbury, Connecticut, clogged her well with manure, shattered the school's windows, and attempted to set the building on fire. Violence against black schools continued to break out sporadically for several years. In 1833, a dozen white students attending Middletown's Wesleyan University threatened to use "forcible means" if two black students did not withdraw immediately.[17] In 1835, whites in Norwich, Connecticut, assailed Giles Buckingham's academy for "Negroes."[18] Four years later, whites in Brookfield raided a Sabbath school after it increased its student body by one black child.[19]

The following chapters set out to explain why black schools became targets of white hostility, particularly in a city like New Haven, which had historically embraced educational opportunity. One can trace the beginnings of this transformation back to the 1827 debate over the African Improvement Society (AIS): an association of white men in New Haven who pledged to improve the intellectual, moral, and spiritual condition of free people of color. Just a short time after the AIS celebrated its inauguration, an otherwise unidentified editorialist named Aristides authored a trio of essays disparaging the society and its intentions. As far as I can ascertain, Aristides' editorials represent the first published diatribe against black schooling in New England.

As chapter 1 details, when African Americans expanded their educational opportunities in the early nineteenth century, whites generally viewed their efforts with indifference. But around 1827 this forbearance began to wane. As the abolition movement supplanted the colonizationist campaign to send black people "back to Africa" in the late 1820s, the political objectives underlying African American education reflected this change. Opponents of slavery now championed black schools not for their power to remove African Americans from America by preparing them to "return" to Africa but for their potential to advance black people's civil liberties at home. As chapter 2 narrates, both movements—for emancipation and equal rights—informed the interracial effort to open a black college in New Haven. White resistance to this effort demonstrates how gradual emancipation, the transformation of abolitionism, and African American calls for citizenship combusted in 1831 to ignite white opposition to black higher education.

For another window into the thorny relationship between African American education and civic inclusion, consider the debate surrounding Connecticut's black laws that played out in 1834, three years after the college campaign collapsed in New Haven. The statute's opponents argued it violated the constitutional expectation that states treat all citizens with equanimity. Defenders of the law rebuffed such claims by asserting that African Americans were not citizens and that, as such, these protections did not extend to them.[20] Andrew T. Judson, the prosecutor in the case against Prudence Crandall, charged the jury with deciding whether "persons of color are *American citizens*."[21] The answer to such a question, he believed, was easy, for citizenship depended upon white identity. As he defined it, the term referred to "a white man who can enjoy the highest honors of a republic, the privilege of choosing his rulers, and [the privilege of] being one himself."[22] David Daggett, the judge presiding over Crandall's case, concurred. In his ruling against Crandall, he upheld the constitutionality of Connecticut's black laws by pointing to places where the Constitution affirmed that people of color were not citizens. Enslaved men and women were not taxed as full persons, he commented, nor could they intermarry with the white population. "God forbid that I should add to the degradation of this race of men," he concluded, "but I am bound by my duty to say, they are not citizens."[23]

As the dialogue surrounding Connecticut's black laws attests, more lay in the balance in this dispute than whether black children from outside the state might study in Connecticut. Samuel J. May, a vocal white opponent of the antieducation statute, sized up the situation perfectly: "The question between us is not simply whether thirty or forty colored girls shall be well educated," but rather, "whether the people in any part of our land will recognize and generously protect the 'inalienable rights of man,' without distinction of color."[24] It was precisely this question that led people to fight so intensely over black schooling. The issue at stake, as May suggested, was not whether African Americans had the right to an education but whether, in fact, they possessed any rights at all.

CHAPTER ONE

The Emergence of White Opposition to African American Education

On Friday evening April 13, 1827, an assembly congregated in New Haven's North Church for the unveiling of a new association: the African Improvement Society (AIS), dedicated to elevating black people's "moral, intellectual, and religious condition."[1] The society's origins stretched back two years, when Center Church minister Leonard Bacon hosted a gathering for friends uneasy with both the growth of southern slavery and the North's free black population. Unsure how its efforts might be received, the group kept its weekly meetings quiet, at least for a time. Members included Theodore Dwight Woolsey, Edward Beecher, and Alexander Twining, individuals with ties to Yale, New Haven's Congregationalist churches, and the Federalist power base of the city.[2]

Made up largely of whites who opposed slavery and championed colonization, the AIS embodied the inherent contradictions of the early nineteenth century's "benevolent empire."[3] Its founders believed it was their duty to uplift people of color, yet doubted their moral and mental capacity. As one AIS supporter demurred, "Whether or not they are capable of a degree of intellectual improvement equal to that of ourselves is foreign to the present subject."[4] It sponsored an array of institutions for African Americans including a day school, an evening school, a savings bank, a temperance society, and a library.[5] Members aspired to spread the staples of capitalist and Protestant theology: an appreciation for hard work and thrift, temperance, and literacy, lessons that were not revelations to the seaport's small black community.[6]

African American New Haveners likely bristled at the racist assumptions the AIS's platform advanced, yet being pragmatic about the practical and symbolic value of education, they accepted its assistance. They understood that literary instruction would supplement the sparse education New Haven's segregated public schools provided; and spiritual training might bring all black people closer to salvation, or at the very least, increase their knowledge of biblical Christianity. And not only would the AIS augment educational opportunities for African Americans within New Haven, word of its activities might inspire black people outside the city to secure education for themselves and their families, which would, in turn, undermine racist and proslavery ideology. AIS institutions attracted students easily: children and adults, men and women. One man left Long Island for New Haven upon learning of the society "to find advantages here for learning to read."[7] He was far from alone in the lengths he would journey for literacy.

Newspaper coverage also confirmed broad support for the AIS within New Haven's white community. The *Connecticut Journal* considered its efforts "worthy of a Washington or a Franklin."[8] Editorialists at the *New Haven Chronicle* endorsed the AIS more cautiously, observing that "we do not wish [African Americans] to become statesmen and legislators—we do not wish them to become our companions and admit them to our drawing rooms, but we do wish to see them becoming a useful, intelligent and industrious people—a blessing and not a curse to our city." With those limitations in mind, they bid the AIS "God Speed."[9] And so, it seemed, a consensus had formed; so long as the AIS did not facilitate racial integration or African Americans' political elevation, it was welcome in New Haven.

Then, but one week after the North Church celebration, the *New Haven Chronicle* printed a scathing, if not hyperbolic, attack against the AIS. Under the alias "Aristides," an otherwise unidentified editorialist castigated the association as "alarming" and "dangerous" and urged members to "weigh well the results" of their mission. He wrote,

> . . . I put it to the sober judgment of every person in this community whether, if the objects of this society are attained, they will not prove the direct positive cause of a rapid and extensive increase of our coloured population. I ask then

this society to pause, to weigh well the results of a project fraught with so much mischief. Let them pause and ask themselves whether they are willing that their children should be the victims of so dangerous an experiment in extending and perpetuating an evil, the existence of which every good citizen laments. Ameliorate the condition of our present coloured population, and you offer a bounty to others whose circumstances are less tolerable, to fell to this as to a city of *refuge*—every step you take you assuredly will strike the roots of evil deeper into our soil.[10]

While his invective filled two vertical columns, each argument Aristides advanced about the dangers of black education—to white laborers, to the republic, and to the mythic history of a free, white New England—circled back to the same contention: education encumbered white efforts to remove black people from America. Word of the association would draw people of color into the community. Any expansion in the seaport's free black population would come at the expense of the white working classes, laborers and domestics, whose wages would decline from increased competition. Finally, by encouraging, and even acknowledging, the very presence of African Americans in New Haven, the AIS gave the lie to assertions that the sin of slavery had skipped over New England. Despite claims from some New Englanders that their forefathers had never participated in chattel slavery, the institution remained legal in Connecticut until the mid-nineteenth century. The most pressing problem New Haven's townspeople faced, argued Aristides, was not "how shall we render this degraded class of beings more tolerable" but rather "how shall we remove them."[11]

As local support for the AIS confirmed, prior to the late 1820s, white New Haveners largely tolerated African Americans' literary and religious instruction. But as radical abolition eclipsed colonization, educators began to aspire not to deport African Americans but to affirm their place in the polity.[12] Aristides, in turn, rejected *any* effort to instruct black people that did not require removal, even one supported by proponents of colonization. By 1831, when abolitionists lobbied for a black men's college in New Haven, many of their most vocal opponents—most notably Yale professor Benjamin Silliman and Leonard Bacon—had been members of the AIS in 1827. Differences between the AIS and the proposed college abound, and one must be careful not to conflate them under an undifferentiated banner of "education." Yet, if one wants to understand why white tolerance for black schooling deteriorated in New England around 1830, it is useful to listen to Aristides. His appearance signified a new period in the history of African American education: a time of opportunity and a time of opposition.

*   *   *

New Haven experienced dizzying transformations in the early nineteenth century: the demise of slavery and the disenfranchisement of African Americans. Enslaved men and women had labored in the seaport from the middle of the seventeenth century, tilling the soil and tending to crops, caring for children, and preparing meals. The rhythms of their labor followed the turning of the seasons. Bondsmen planted in the spring, harvested in the fall, and performed a hodgepodge of agricultural and household tasks throughout the year. Bondswomen's duties varied similarly. Cleaning, cooking, spinning, and sewing, they spent much of their time laboring inside the home under their mistress's watchful eyes.[13] Outside the household and off the farm, bondsmen could be found in nearly every industry, on land and on sea, including fishing, whaling, leather tanning, blacksmithing, rope making, and shipbuilding. Africans and their descendants often worked along the waterfront, carting the goods and constructing the ships that connected Connecticut to the rest of the Atlantic world.[14]

With some exceptions, slaves were scattered thinly throughout Connecticut. Other than several large landowners on the colony's eastern shore, slaveholders usually held one or two enslaved laborers. The small holdings typical of slavery in New England deterred many masters from residing apart from their human property, as was customary on large plantations. Instead, enslaved blacks often lived inside white homes in whatever space was available. Such arrangements encouraged frequent, and often uneasy, interactions between white and black people. As historian Joanne Pope Melish points out, while the number of slaves in the region never reached that of the Chesapeake or the Carolinas, in performing tasks that would have otherwise occupied their masters, slaves freed white people to pursue other intellectual and commercial interests, thereby facilitating New England's transition to capitalism.[15] By the onset of the Revolutionary War, more than 6,000 black people lived in Connecticut, which was second only to Massachusetts as the largest slaveholder in New England.[16]

In the aftermath of the Revolution, like other New England states, Connecticut began the long process of gradual emancipation. After March 1, 1784, children born into slavery would be free upon turning twenty-five;

subsequent statutes lowered the age to twenty-one and prohibited slave-holders from selling children beyond state lines. But as slavery dissipated, Connecticut's free black population climbed. In 1790, approximately 2,700 free blacks lived in the state; by 1810, that number increased almost three-fold, to around 6,500. Free African Americans gravitated to Connecticut's urban centers, Hartford, New London, and New Haven, in search of em-ployment and community. At the turn of the nineteenth century, for ex-ample, census takers counted 248 black inhabitants of New Haven (166 free, eighty-two enslaved). But two decades later, 624 African Americans (622 free, two enslaved) lived in the seaport, making up about 7.5 percent of New Haven's total population (8,327).[17]

Within the city, black people labored in positions that promised lengthy hours and a dismal wage. While most black women worked as servants and domestics, African American men in New Haven more often labored out of doors, driving hacks and carting loads as stevedores, or as seamen on vessels sailing to and from the West Indies. A large percentage of Af-rican Americans sustained themselves in service to whites, as waiters, barbers, and bootblacks, while some worked as independent artisans.[18] A few owned businesses that employed other African Americans. Scipio C. Augustus, for example, ran a boarding house for "genteel Persons of Colour."[19] William Lanson similarly operated an "African Boarding House."[20] He also supplied and supervised laborers (willing to submerge themselves in "mud and cold water" up to their "middle") who helped to construct Long Wharf and dredge the Farmington Canal.[21]

But as African Americans rejoiced over slavery's disappearance from New Haven, black men of property like Augustus and Lanson simulta-neously mourned the loss of their own civic privileges. In the seventeenth, eighteenth, and early nineteenth centuries, Connecticut's African Ameri-can freeholders had possessed full and equal voting privileges. But in 1814, the General Assembly inserted the word "white" into its definition of "freeman." Four years later, in 1818, Connecticut amended its constitu-tion, eliminating the property requirement necessary to vote and linking suffrage to white identity.[22] As suffrage often operated as a synecdoche for citizenship in the early nineteenth century, denying black people the right to vote was tantamount to denying them a place in the polity. As Evelyn Nakano Glenn points out, Americans have historically utilized citizen-ship "to draw boundaries between those who are included as members of the community and entitled to respect, protection, and rights and those who are excluded and thus not entitled to recognition and rights."[23] The very notion of a white identity taking shape during this period began to connote a range of economic, social, and political privileges. By denying suffrage specifically to African Americans and linking that right to whiteness, Connecticut's General Assembly attempted to mark black people as distinct and dependent and to increase the value of citizenship for white Americans.[24]

To add insult to injury, while the 1814 and 1818 statutes denied African Americans the benefits of citizenship, they did not relieve them of its responsibilities. Connecticut continued to demand a poll tax from black people even after it drove them from the polls. The spitefulness of this practice did not escape Lanson and other disenfranchised African Americans. In 1815, a year after they lost suffrage, Lanson and fellow black New Havener Biars Stanley petitioned the General Assembly to not only exempt African Americans "from taxes on their polls" but to release them from "all taxes whatsoever on their property and occupations."[25] They tapped into the rhetoric of the Revolution both to spotlight their familiarity with American history and to draw attention to the hypocrisy of the state's action. They recalled that "when the rights of *white* men were in jeopardy from the encroachments of the Parliament of England this Honorable Legislature declared publicly and solemnly before God and Man that the right of representation was inseparable from the liability to taxation." They averred that they were not asking the legislature to reconsider ("submit[ting] thus to be disfranchised without any fault on their part"). And given their understanding of just how "strong . . . the feelings and prejudices of this community" were against them, it is unlikely Stanley and Lanson expected to be exempted from taxation.[26] Rather, as self-described "free and natives of the State of Connecticut," "property owners," and "persons of a quiet behavior and civil conversation," they were utilizing one of the few avenues for political expression still available to them to display their capacity for citizenship and, in the process, to mock the foolishness of the state's decision. Independent, well-educated, virtuous, and reverential, Lanson and Stanley each embodied the good citizen: "one who rules and is ruled in turn."[27]

In 1824, a decade after the General Assembly denied their petition and one year before the AIS's North Church inauguration, Lanson, Stanley, and Augustus collaborated again, this time to launch the African Ecclesiastical Society, dedicated to "improving the morals, promoting the piety, and increasing the religious knowledge" of "the descendants of Africans, of different religious denominations."[28] At the time, black people who desired to attend religious services in New Haven usually patronized either Center Church or North Church, both of which confined them to segregated pews in the balcony. Within a year, the group, assisted by white Congregationalist minister and engraver Simeon Jocelyn, attracted twenty-one members, seventeen women and four men, and secured a small wooden building for their meetings (a "rough-looking thing... in a very unfinished state," as one visitor described it).[29] One year later, Temple Street, now the first black church in Connecticut, comprised one hundred congregants. As was customary of black churches during the antebellum period, Temple Street quickly became a locus of African American literary and religious education in New Haven. In its first four years, it more than doubled the number of black schools in the city.[30]

Before Temple Street's opening, local opportunities for black people to obtain primary and religious instruction were modest at best. The first schoolhouses for African American children in New Haven had opened around 1810. In later years, the city funded one public school for black boys; a charity school for black girls relied upon white female volunteers. By the early 1820s, New Haven funded four public schools for white girls and eleven for white children of both sexes; yet it maintained just two schools open to African American children, no matter where they resided in the city. Each of these institutions provided rudimentary instruction in reading, writing, and mathematics.[31] In 1825, the city opened a second school for black students, but both institutions remained open less than half the year. Statistically, the ratio of schools per white student was the same as the ratio of schools per black student, but as was typical of many segregated public school systems in the early nineteenth century, black children could attend school for fewer days and, within those days, for fewer hours.

By 1829, Temple Street housed a Sabbath school with eighty pupils, a day school with sixty, and a women's evening school, which attracted more than thirty attendants regularly (Figure 2). One can only imagine what such instruction must have meant to these women, who braved the night's darkness and the chill of New Haven's winter twice a week, many after a long day of domestic labor. Their instructor confirmed his students' uncommon dedication to their studies. Never had he "attended a school where so much interest was manifested and so much punctuality and engagedness in improving their opportunities for acquiring knowledge," he noted.[32] The city helped to fund Temple Street's day school, supporting it six months of the year. For the remainder of its expenses, black parents

AFRICAN SABBATH SCHOOL.

Come thou with us, and we will do thee good.--Num. x. 29.

merits and receives
this certificate as a token of approbation for the
kindness shown to
by introducing   into the African Sabbath
School.

Superintendent.

NEW HAVEN,   183

CERTIFICATE OF MERIT

Presented in the 1830's to anyone who persuaded a Negro child to join the African Sabbath School of New Haven. Pictured on the New Haven Green are the two Congregational churches which sponsored the school. The original certificate is printed in three colors and is to be found in the New Haven Collection of the Sterling Memorial Library at Yale University.

FIGURE 2. Certificate of merit. From Robert Austin Warner, *New Haven Negroes: A Social History* (New York: Arno Press and the New York Times, 1969), 83.

provided what they could and benevolent societies like the AIS contributed the rest.

News of the AIS and its efforts to expand African Americans' access to education quickly spread beyond New Haven. In the summer of 1827, New Yorker John Brown Russwurm, editor of the newly formed black newspaper *Freedom's Journal*, learned about the association and its efforts to improve black people's literary abilities. He extolled the society, believing the "benevolent exertions of the age could not be better directed." "What can be more ennobling to the dignity of man," Russwurm wondered, "than to enlighten his fellow man—to convince him that education and good conduct are all which ought to distinguish one man from another." "Surely," he determined, "their labour is one of love, which should meet the cordial support of every Christian."[33]

Himself an educator, Russwurm had devoted a great deal of his own energy to expanding African Americans' literary abilities. Born in 1799 in Port Antonio, Jamaica, to an enslaved African mother and a white American father, Russwurm embodied the Atlantic world nexus that connected people of color throughout Africa, the Americas, and the Caribbean. At his father's behest, the young Russwurm had emigrated from Jamaica to Quebec, Canada, and then to Maine for his early education. In 1819, he graduated from Portland's Hebron Academy. In 1821, at age twenty, he accepted a position as an instructor at the Smith School, a segregated public school for black children in Boston. He remained at the post for three years, until 1824, when he relocated to Brunswick, Maine, to attend Bowdoin College. Customary of higher education in the early republic, Russwurm's studies concentrated on the classics: Greek and Latin, history, and philosophy.[34] He finished two years later, and in so doing, he became one of the first African Americans to graduate from college. Upon receiving his diploma, Russwurm left Brunswick for New York City, where he accepted Samuel Cornish's invitation to help launch *Freedom's Journal*. Its inaugural issue appeared on March 16, 1827, one month before Aristides appeared in New Haven (Figure 3).

Russwurm contended that an independent press could do a great deal to increase African Americans' educational opportunities and in so doing to expand their civil liberties. In its very first issue, the *Journal's* "Prospectus" stressed this expectation: "As education is what renders civilized men superior to the savage; as the dissemination of knowledge is continually progressing among all other classes in the community, we deem it expedient to establish a paper, and bring into operation all the means with

JOHN B. RUSSWURM

FIGURE 3. John B. Russwurm. n.d. Print. Courtesy of the Photographs and Prints Division, Schomburg Center for Research in Black Culture, The New York Public Library, Astor, Lenox and Tilden Foundations.

which our benevolent Creator has endowed us, for the moral, religious, civil and literary improvement of our injured race."[35] Under Russwurm's leadership, the *Journal* publicized an array of educational activities available to African Americans including libraries, literary societies, reading clubs, and lyceums.[36] Philanthropos, a contributor to the *Journal,* stressed to readers the value of these institutions: "Here, we have the privilege of communicating to each other, the little store of knowledge, which we have industriously acquired; at one and the same time, supplying ourselves and imparting to others, from the same common fountain."[37] Comments like his reveal how the *Journal* both reflected African Americans' actual educational opportunities in the early nineteenth century and projected what its editor Russwurm, a collegian, a writer, a scholar, and a teacher, wished they would be. The *Journal*, Russwurm imagined, would serve as a display, a physical embodiment of black literacy and culture, and as tangible proof of African American engagement with the printed word. Such roles took on special importance in light of white efforts to expel black people, figuratively and literally, from the cornerstones of the public sphere: print culture, parades, party politics, and public schools.[38]

This particular understanding of education typified the political philosophy popular among members of the African American middle and upper classes before 1840 known as moral suasion. In the early nineteenth century, as northern racism escalated in frequency and intensity, elite and middle-class blacks increasingly complained about whites' conflation of skin color with character. Despite their industry and prosperity, they contended, whites continued to use any evidence of black misconduct to justify racism against them. Hoping to disconnect ideas about race from images of black disorder in the white imagination, moral suasionists like Russwurm posited that just as whites had used black misconduct to justify discrimination, African Americans could use evidence of their good behavior to discredit white claims against them. It was precisely this faith in the mutability of racial prejudice that led Russwurm to rally around the AIS, despite its hostile depictions of African Americans.[39]

The past year had been a whirlwind for the twenty-eight-year-old editor. Russwurm could not have arrived in New York City at a more tumultuous time. In 1799—a decade after Connecticut began the gradual emancipation process—New York's legislature set slavery's drawn out demise in motion. Bondsmen and bondswomen born before July 4 of that year would be enslaved for life; but from that day forward, those born into slavery would become free, at least eventually. Enslaved men would be emancipated upon their twenty-eighth birthday, and enslaved women upon turning twenty-five. Nearly two decades later, in 1817, the legislature decreed July 4, 1827, to be the day slavery would end in New York. For the next ten years, from 1817 to 1827, whites braced themselves for black liberty, and African Americans did all they could to hasten its arrival.[40] In 1821, as Connecticut's General Assembly had done before, New York also conflated citizenship with skin color by eviscerating African American suffrage and expanding white voting privileges.[41] But in 1827, when Russwurm settled into New York and Aristides appeared in New Haven, both cities were abuzz with talk of abolition. Throughout the spring and summer of that year, black New Yorkers rejoiced and "return[ed] thanks" to the "ALMIGHTY."[42] In New Haven, African Americans paraded through the streets and then assembled for "public exercises" at the African church "in unison with their [New York] brethren."[43]

Just weeks after emancipation arrived in New York, Russwurm boarded a Hudson River steamer bound for New Haven. On July 20, 1827, Samuel Cornish, coeditor of *Freedom's Journal,* informed readers of Russwurm's departure. He had embarked upon "a tour to the Eastward," a month-long journey through the northeast to drum up support for the fledgling publication.[44] At seven o'clock in the morning, the young editor's boat, "crowded with passengers," pushed off into the fog. But by 11:00 A.M., Russwurm reported, the clouds had cleared, "leaving all above sunshine and all beneath waters." Throughout the voyage, Russwurm ruminated on his commitment to educational opportunity. "So entirely am I devoted to the cause of Education," he wrote to his readers, "that all others seem to me of minor consequence; and while in meditation upon it, all others are forgotten." His passage also reminded him of just how much white racism stole from him and every other African American. Despite his "wearied frame," he could not secure a "birth" [*sic*] on the boat "though nearly all were unoccupied."[45]

Thankfully, the trip from New York to New Haven took less than one day. At five o'clock that evening, Russwurm "safely landed" in New Haven.[46] Nestled between two large bluffs, East and West Rock, the small seaport spilled onto a plain that skirted a large bay, just four miles from Long Island.[47] Should Russwurm have strolled through the streets surrounding the harbor, he might have spied white and black workers loading and unloading ships, building boats, and making sails. Should he have continued to amble, he might have taken note of the distance most African Americans lived from the town center, in neighborhoods whose names revealed the pervasiveness of residential segregation: New Liberia, New Guinea, and Poverty Square.[48]

The morning after his arrival, Russwurm went to work, spreading word of the *Journal* to the city's "most respectable" citizens. New Haven's African Americans, he reported, "immediately saw the great advantages likely to arise" from the paper, and the "necessity and expediency that we should possess such an engine." Recognizing that the *Journal's* survival depended upon broad patronage, Russwurm also set out to meet with the most "distinguished" white men of New Haven: Congregationalist minister Simeon Jocelyn, Yale professors Timothy Dwight and Benjamin Silliman, and wordsmith Noah Webster. After his meeting with Jocelyn, Russwurm reported back to *Journal* readers about the intensity of Jocelyn's devotion to New Haven's African American community. "Little did I think to find Mr. S. S. J. so great a philanthropist, and so warm a friend to the improvement of our brethren," Russwurm recounted. "He is a practical and active philanthropist; not one, who wishes well to us, and would be willing to do his part, if others would aid; but one, who feeling the importance of that admirable precept of our LORD, 'do unto others, as ye would that others should do unto you,' strives all in his power to walk in the footsteps of his Lord and Master." But despite breaking bread with Jocelyn and several others eager to uplift African Americans, the person Russwurm "had the greatest desire to see" was none other than Aristides: the author of "three essays . . . against the views and designs of the African Improvement Society of New Haven."[49]

And so it was that John Brown Russwurm came to sit face to face with Aristides, the most vocal opponent of the AIS in New Haven. The details of this meeting are maddeningly enigmatic. The only traces of the conversation that remain are the few lines Russwurm jotted down to share with *Journal* readers. Apart from those, one is left to imagine what the young editor thought of this man who took the time and had the inclination to denounce black education, who fantasized about a white republic, and who had so many misconceptions about African Americans. Nor do any details survive that speak to Aristides' assessment of Russwurm, an individual whose very existence refuted so many of the editorialist's specious claims about African Americans.

One might anticipate Russwurm to have dismissed Aristides' character from his racism alone. From the way that Russwurm characterized his unpleasant encounter with Noah Webster (quipping, "I hope the word politeness will be properly defined in Mr. W's forthcoming Dictionary"), it is clear he did not feel compelled to censor his impressions.[50] And given that Aristides had his pseudonym to protect him, one can assume that had Russwurm felt Aristides personally affronted him, he would have intimated as much to his readers. Yet despite Aristides' racist opinions, Russwurm described him respectfully. If one takes Russwurm at his word, it is clear that something about Aristides, whoever the man behind the pseudonym was, impressed him. In his letter to the *Journal,* Russwurm asked rhetorically, "who is Aristides?" the same question, no doubt, which vexed many of his readers. Yet electing to respect an editorial tradition that allowed for anonymity, he did not violate the sanctity of his pseudonymous identity. He revealed only that Aristides was a man of "considerable respectability" and "considerable property, acquired by his own individual exertions." Despite Aristides' hostility toward black people, Russwurm had found something to recommend him: "the redeeming part of his antipathy against us," Russwurm reported, "is that Aristides is willing to hear what we have to say in our defense against his views." Moreover, Russwurm assured his readers, Aristides was not only "a man of sound sense" but also a "subscriber to the *Freedom's Journal.*" In the end, the two men spent but a short time together, for as Russwurm reported "time on neither side permitted" a longer conversation. No doubt, Russwurm left the meeting hostile to Aristides' position. Still, he appreciated Aristides' willingness to engage him. At some point, he hoped, they might continue the conversation in a public forum, when "some champion among our brethren might be found, who would be willing to enter the arena against him."[51]

So what is one to make of Aristides, a man who agreed to sit down with Russwurm on his visit to New Haven, who on the one hand subscribed to the *Freedom's Journal* and on the other penned a trio of lengthy diatribes against black education? Beyond revealing to his readers that Aristides subscribed to the *Journal,* Russwurm disclosed little about his identity. In some respects, apart from a temptation to solve this historical mystery, it is not necessary to know Aristides' real identity to make sense of his opinions. In fact, Aristides likely used a pseudonym to stress the universality of his position. Editorialists during this period frequently assumed a classical identity to appeal to antiquity and to the Founding Fathers, who had popularized the practice during the Revolution.[52] Adopting a persona suggestive of republican virtues like objectivity, independence, and disinterestedness empowered an author like Aristides to appear above the political fray; yet it also allowed him—for writers were often white men of standing—to lessen the social space separating himself from his readers with an anonymous and therefore universal identity. Anonymity further enabled Aristides to lob personal jabs at his opponents and to advance unsavory political opinions without risking public condemnation or personal retribution. A counterweight to the baseness of the vitriol one advanced, a well-chosen alias signaled an editorialist's own education and demanded the same of readers who wished to decipher a writer's full intentions.[53]

The pen name "Aristides" appeared with some regularity in the eighteenth and early nineteenth centuries. Many editorialists selected the pseudonym for its association with truth, objectivity, and justice. Readers from this period would easily have recognized the allusion to Aristides the Just, the Athenian general renowned for fairness whom Plutarch had canonized in his *Lives*.[54] According to Plutarch, Athenians bestowed the ancient Aristides with the moniker "the Just" because of his famed reputation for honesty. In one legendary act of self-sacrifice (and likely, the action that led the nineteenth-century editorialist to assume this specific identity), Aristides the Just sacrificed his social standing for his integrity. According to Athenian tradition, a popular vote determined whether a citizen would be sent into exile. During one such "election" in 482 B.C., a man who could neither read nor write approached Aristides, unaware of his identity, and asked him to inscribe the name "Aristides" on his behalf. Aristides pushed the man to explain his selection but did not reveal his own identity. While he did not know Aristides personally, the man informed him, he had grown weary of hearing about his honesty. Without further inquiry, Aristides assented. At the end of the day when the results were announced, the Athenians had exiled Aristides from their community.[55]

Whoever the individual behind the alias, it is likely New Haven's editorialist selected the pseudonym both for its connotation of impartiality and because of the specific circumstances with which the Athenian had garnered such acclaim. Aristides the Just had treated an illiterate man honestly, even when his lack of education, or ability to make a well-reasoned decision, came at Aristides' own expense. No doubt Aristides the editorialist assumed his readers would get the reference. He too was engaging in an act of justice, telling the truth to the uneducated blacks of New Haven and, by extension, to those foolish whites of privilege who sought to "uplift" them, even if he ostracized himself in the process.

Given the immediate, unforgiving response Aristides engendered among other columnists in New Haven, it is unsurprising he sought anonymity and feared ostracism. His diatribe triggered a brief but bitter debate over black "improvement," which ultimately came out in favor of African American education. As mentioned, Aristides' editorials represent some of the first evidence of white resistance to black education budding in New Haven. Yet the arguments other editorialists levied against him also reveal how ideas about African American education were changing. A handful of individuals wrote in to defend the AIS, not from a desire to remove black people but rather to assert their place in the polity.

One week after Aristides appeared in the *Chronicle,* an unsigned editorialist mocked his audacity to assume a sobriquet synonymous with justice.

"Can a man be too just," he asked "to feel the woes of the injured?" After lobbing a flurry of personal assaults against Aristides, the columnist revealed his central point of contention. By suggesting that the AIS would "injure" New Haven's "native" population, Aristides constructed a definition of American identity that excluded black people. That assertion, his opponent challenged, contradicted the principles of the founding: tolerance, inclusion, and freedom. As this editorialist expounded, Aristides' assertion "that the white man is in all such cases to be preferred, and the other excluded, is a claim which God or nature never can agree." He questioned, "How does it agree with that part of the Declaration of American Independence, which holds these truths to be self-evident; 'That they are endowed by their Creator with certain unalienable rights; and that among these rights are life, liberty, and the pursuit of happiness?'"[56]

Affirmations of African American citizenship appeared even more boldly in the anti-Aristides editorials to follow. In the *Chronicle*'s May 22, 1827, edition, two more columnists, "Clarkson," no doubt a nod to Thomas Clarkson, the famed British antislavery activist, and "T.Z." wrote in to support the AIS and to denounce Aristides. Both T.Z. and Clarkson agreed Aristides' most troubling assertion was that black people were not citizens. Clarkson similarly tapped into the memory of the Revolution by contending that to deny African Americans their place in the body politic was to "proclaim war against the first sentence of what we call the charter of our freedom."[57] T.Z. used similar rhetoric to denounce Aristides' support for colonization: "The plan of operation by which [Aristides] would exterminate the people of color from our city," he affirmed "violate[d] all principles of republican right and liberty."[58]

Unwilling to cede an inch of rhetorical ground, Aristides replied in the *Chronicle*'s next edition. He mocked the two men's "illiberal conjectures" and "absurd conclusions." Yet he agreed with their assessment of the real distance between them. Their dispute did not revolve around whether or not African Americans should be uplifted, he maintained. Rather, they split over whether black people were, or would ever be, citizens. To Aristides' mind, "the intelligent and virtuous" white "freemen" of Connecticut had settled this issue when they expelled African Americans from civic institutions. Here he alluded to Connecticut's disenfranchisement of African Americans. People of color, observed Aristides, were not permitted to "vote into our ballot boxes" or to "wield the sword in defense of our country." Denied those "peculiar rights and privileges" that "appertained only to our citizens, our free white citizens," African Americans did not possess that identity, Aristides contended.[59]

It was here that Aristides revealed precisely why he opposed the AIS, an association, after all, composed largely of colonizationists who agreed that blacks were not citizens. He understood the real stakes of the coming contest over African American education. Referring to himself in the third person, Aristides had "questioned the expediency of measures adopted by the African Improvement Society, believing them calculated to *extend and perpetuate* the evil, which they proposed to remove." In other words, he suggested, while AIS founders believed they could uplift African Americans and then remove them, Aristides knew otherwise. He understood that black education by definition would make such a solution impossible. Not only would schools draw black people into New Haven, their existence would sustain assertions that African Americans were American citizens. And while Aristides denied that he was "gifted with the spirit of prophecy," many New Haveners would again likely find it difficult to believe him: it was precisely this strategy abolitionists articulated when, four years later, they proposed to open an African college in New Haven.[60]

Aristides' diatribe also revealed the impending rift between colonizationists and advocates of African American education. Where many white-run schools in the 1810s and 1820s had linked education to emigration, the AIS did not. Even though its members endorsed colonization, they concentrated on improving educational opportunities for black people within New Haven. Larger intellectual and socioeconomic transformations in New England would soon exacerbate this shift: declining white enthusiasm for African "repatriation," the radicalization of an abolition movement that reached out to African Americans and women, and growing black demands for equal rights and political inclusion. By the early 1830s, some white New Englanders attempted to repel each of these movements by resisting efforts to provide higher education to African Americans.

In the early nineteenth century, however, some white northerners sympathetic to colonization had sustained schools for African Americans. Typically affiliated with religious denominations, these institutions attempted to prepare African Americans to become Christian missionaries in Africa and the Caribbean. They offered classical, religious, and literary instruction to free blacks, far more than what most public schools provided at the time. Most waived tuition, and some provided a small stipend.

Even so, these schools struggled to enroll students. Few black pupils, it seemed, were willing to pay the price of admission: exiting America upon graduation.

One of the first such institutions, established by white Presbyterians from the Synod of New Jersey, opened in 1816 in Parsippany, New Jersey. The school's supporters hoped to give African Americans the "rudiments of education" and access to the gospel.[61] Parsippany trustees understood their endeavor to improve black people's literary capabilities as part of a larger effort to temper the social disruptions portended by emancipation. While New Jersey did not fully outlaw slavery until the onset of the Civil War, its legislature did begin to discuss abolition as early as 1778. And several states to its north had elected to move forward with emancipation, contributing to white uneasiness with free blacks in the region. Although it never possessed any significant enslaved population, Vermont outlawed slavery in 1777. Two years later, in 1779, Rhode Island passed a gradual emancipation statute similar to that which Connecticut later enacted.[62]

To put it plainly, Parsippany trustees did not create a school to integrate black people into American society. To the contrary, they lamented the process that "set [a former slave] loose upon Society to act for himself, with no qualifications but a freedom paper" and portended that without their intervention emancipation would be "dangerous" and "impracticable."[63] African Americans were, they asserted, "emphatically a separate people." As such, "They must be trained and educated by themselves."[64] The school's first students, Jeremiah Gloucester and William Pennington, arrived in 1817 from Philadelphia, Pennsylvania.[65] By 1820, four more enrolled: Gustavus Cesar, from Jamaica, Long Island; Mark Jorden, from New Brunswick; John Bartley, also from Philadelphia; and Joseph Michael, from Charleston, South Carolina. Yet the school failed to attract a sizable following; just eleven students entered in four years.[66] These pupils, all teenage boys, were required to complete a four-year course of study at minimum. Their curriculum encompassed subjects ranging from reading, writing, and spelling to philosophy and astronomy. In addition to attending class daily, students were required to reside in a house adjacent to the institution.

On the surface, these young black men from Charleston and beyond were quite fortunate: they received free tuition and board, a stipend of twenty dollars, and extensive tutoring in literature and religion.[67] But the school's white sponsors also anticipated that their investment would yield themselves a sizable return. Sustained largely with donations from the

New Jersey Colonization Society, the school's mission was to prepare men of color to be missionaries in Liberia and Haiti, who would, in turn, lead all black people "back" to Africa and to the Caribbean. As its board of directors advised, "Let [our students] so understand us—that we are instructing them not for our society—not to form our magistrates or legislators, but preparing them to go home."[68]

Despite its difficulty enrolling qualified—and willing—students, the Parsippany institution inspired a handful of similar efforts. In 1816, the same year that the school in Parsippany opened its doors, Congregationalist members of the American Board of Commissioners for Foreign Missions launched the Foreign Mission School in Cornwall, Connecticut. While the majority of its pupils were Native American, the school also enrolled students from as far away as Hawaii, Indonesia, and China. Akin to the Parsippany institution, the Foreign Mission School provided students with classical, vocational, and religious instruction in the hope that they would disseminate that knowledge to their home countries. In spite of the diversity of its student body, however, the Foreign Mission School did not enroll students of African descent.[69]

In 1826, in Newark, New Jersey, whites organized another society that also sought to use education to facilitate black people's exit from America, although it also struggled to attract students.[70] In 1830, the Washington, D.C.–based African Education Society reported that the "school in New Jersey has not received sufficient support, and has not always been able to find suitable subjects. The right plan seems to be, to receive the pupils almost in infancy."[71] The following year in 1827, at the same time that Aristides denounced the AIS in New Haven, a group of Connecticut Episcopalians organized another offshoot of the education-emigration exchange. Their African Mission School Society (AMSS) endeavored to create an institution to educate free people of color to be "Missionaries, Catechists, and School masters in Africa."[72] AMSS members agreed with their Parsippany predecessors that education could resolve many problems brought on by emancipation. As one of its white supporters, Jonathan Mayhew Wainwright, observed, blacks new to freedom would beget the "immediate destruction" of the "white population" if left to their own devices. "The colonizing of Africa is our only hope," he insisted. But for repatriation to succeed, Liberia needed missionaries able to Christianize its native population. Fearful that whites could not "endure the climate," Wainwright and fellow AMSS members set out to prepare newly emancipated blacks for the charge.[73]

Declaring Hartford's climate "healthful" and its "means of living" "cheap," the AMSS leadership selected the Connecticut cocapital to house their new institution. They hoped that nearby Washington College, soon to be Trinity College, would share its educational facilities. As in Parsippany, pupils at the Hartford school received broad-based classical and religious instruction to prepare them for emigration. They were required to be at least eighteen years of age and literate prior to admission. Once enrolled, they received lessons akin to their New Jersey counterparts in "the useful sciences and arts" and in subjects including "botany, mineralogy, [and] surveying." In addition, AMSS students obtained instruction in "agricultural and mechanical labor" with the hope that such training would enable them to bring "native tribes" closer to "civilization."[74]

As its curriculum suggests, the Hartford school shared many features of its Parsippany predecessor. Officials expected black students to live together. They also required them to devote most of their time to their studies, save two hours each day for manual labor. But while the school offered extensive instruction to African American pupils free of charge, upon completion of their studies, it also expected students to leave for Liberia.[75] In likely consequence of that arrangement, despite obtaining white support from Connecticut to South Carolina, the AMSS struggled to entice even a small number of black pupils.[76] Entrance requirements were admittedly steep, as students were required to be well educated prior to their admission. Samuel Cornish, coeditor of *Freedom's Journal,* believed the Hartford school would have had much more success if it had agreed to admit younger pupils.[77] Nevertheless, the collective failures at Hartford and Parsippany confirm that few, if any, free black people desired an education when deportation was required in return.[78]

Despite lackluster black interest in both the New Jersey and Connecticut institutions, white supporters of colonization continued to champion the marriage of African American education and emigration into the late 1820s. In 1829, a contingent of reform-oriented white men launched the African Education Society (AES) in Washington, D.C., with a parallel objective: "to afford to persons of colour destined to Africa, such an education, in Letters, Agriculture and the Mechanic Arts, as may best qualify them for usefulness and influence." While its ultimate goal of African repatriation resembled that of the societies in Connecticut and New Jersey, the AES envisioned an even more radical institution. While the two previous schools had elected to educate black students in early adulthood, the AES sought to isolate future missionaries at a much younger age. They hoped to select students in "early childhood" to separate them from potentially "idle and vicious companions." In so doing, they would shape black students' "whole character . . . such as it will qualify them to become pioneers in the renovation of Africa."[79] Such a philosophy suggests the AES believed that if it could reach African Americans at a young enough age, it could persuade them to repatriate voluntarily.

Just five years after its formation, the AES's membership roster would appear to be very strange indeed. Founding members included both staunch southern defenders of slavery and colonization, like Charles Fenton Mercer, Francis Scott Key, William Meade, and William H. Fitzhugh, as well as some of their soon to be most ardent abolitionist opponents: New Yorkers Gerrit Smith and Arthur Tappan. While AES activities centered in Washington, D.C., the organization enjoyed solid white support throughout Connecticut, including in the cocapitals of Hartford and New Haven. Ultimately, however, the AES's timing would sow the seeds of its demise. Despite its register of reform-oriented luminaries, the group failed to garner the funds necessary even to open an institution. Securing support for similarly colonizationist black schools would grow more difficult in the decade to come.[80]

In the late 1820s, many whites and African Americans also began to assail the American Colonization Society (ACS). Founded in 1817, the brainchild of New Jersey Presbyterian minister Robert Finley, the ACS had quickly amassed a devout constituency: religious, reform-oriented northerners eager to use blacks to deliver Africa unto the Christian fold and equally ambitious white southerners seeking a safe repository for the physical residuals of slavery. But a decade later, many white southerners intent on protecting the "peculiar institution" refused any "scheme" that might facilitate emancipation.[81] Similarly, northern advocates of immediate abolition rejected colonization's central claim: that racial prejudice was so inveterate blacks would not advance unless they returned "home."[82] They castigated the ACS for siphoning support from the antislavery movement and for providing individuals uneasy with immediate emancipation any excuse to delay. As William Lloyd Garrison commented, colonizationists maintained a "benevolent" façade by claiming that the source of black degradation was environmental and not inherent. But by articulating an apocalyptic vision for America's racial future, the ACS stymied slavery's demise. Colonization was, he contended, "a conspiracy to send the free people of color to Africa under a benevolent purpose" in the hope that southern "slaves may be held more securely"[83] by removing a population that could fuel and facilitate slave rebellion.

Black resistance to repatriation also undermined support for the ACS by bolstering charges that its plan was impracticable, if not impossible. Nationwide, colonization never succeeded in securing more than a slight following among African Americans, and, more often than not, they represented its most vocal opposition. In 1831, free blacks in Hartford condemned the ACS as the single "greatest foe to the free colored and slave population."[84] Black Bostonians concurred, calling colonization a "clamorous, abusive and peace-disturbing combination." In New Haven, black people rallied to reject one of colonization's central contentions: that Africa, not America, was their "appropriate home."[85] In fact, between 1816 and 1830, fewer than 1,500 African Americans made the trip back to Africa. Thousands more declared their intentions to remain.[86]

One notable exception to this trend, however, was none other than John Brown Russwurm. While in 1827, at the time of his meeting with Aristides, he had stridently denounced colonization, two years later, he had clearly changed his mind. On March 28, 1829, he resigned from *Freedom's Journal*. The following September with support from the ACS, he set sail for Liberia. Six months after his arrival, Russwurm penned a note to an alumnus of the African Mission School in Hartford, Edward Jones, expressing his hope that other black people would follow him across the globe. "I long to see young men, who are now wasting the best of their days in the United States, flocking to this land as the last asylum to the unfortunate," he confided to Jones.[87] In Liberia, Russwurm worked hard to resume the life he had known in America: teaching school and publishing a newspaper.[88] For those whom he left behind, however, Russwurm's decision to leave was nothing short of heartbreaking. "As his usefulness is entirely lost to the people," one *Liberator* editorialist lamented bitterly, "I sincerely pray that he may have the honor to live and also die there."[89]

Aristides also disappeared from New Haven as quickly as he had arrived, and he never did succeed in shifting support from the AIS. Yet despite his lack of rhetorical influence, his comments reveal volumes about how some white people were beginning to understand African American education. The arguments he advanced—his conflation of black improvement with citizenship, his conception of education as a zero-sum game, and his contention that uplift would thwart black removal—would soon become mantras in white diatribes against black schooling. If one listens closely to Aristides (whose Athenian namesake was renowned for honesty after all), it becomes clear why white attitudes toward African American education were transforming. The consequences of that evolution are the subject of the chapter to come.

CHAPTER TWO

Interracial Activism and African American Higher Education

Although African Americans' access to primary and religious instruction expanded in the early nineteenth century, with few exceptions, higher education remained beyond reach. Most high schools and academies refused to enroll black students, and even when African Americans secured the preparation necessary for advanced study, few colleges would accept them. In 1831, hoping to empower black people to access higher education independently, an interracial abolitionist alliance launched a movement to build the nation's first "African" college. Two ministers, one black, Peter Williams from New York, the other white, Simeon Jocelyn from New Haven, led the campaign. After much consideration, they selected New Haven to house the proposed institution, believing that in "no place in the Union" is the "situation [of blacks] so comfortable, or the prejudices of community weaker against them."[1] On September 5, 1831, college planners announced their intentions. Their timing could not have been worse if they had tried.[2]

A fortnight earlier, a tornado had twisted through the streets of New Haven. But the havoc it wreaked was nothing compared with the chaos that erupted in Virginia on the same day. On August 22, 1831, the literate enslaved preacher Nat Turner commenced his uprising against the white residents of Southampton. Gruesome reports about the educated black man who incited fellow bondsmen to rise "like blood hounds" in the name of "freedom" spread quickly throughout the country.[3] Details of the massacre reached New Haven on September 3, only two fateful days before Jocelyn and Williams publicized their "revolutionary" intentions.[4]

The idea of a college for black men championed by an interracial abolitionist alliance would have been controversial before Turner's rebellion, but in its aftermath it was downright insurrectionary. Upon learning of the proposal, New Haven's mayor, Dennis Kimberly, assembled an opposition in less than three days.[5] On September 8, he summoned a city meeting; that Saturday, over seven hundred white men swarmed city hall. "So great was the interest to hear the discussions," observed one attendant, "that notwithstanding the excessive heat and the almost irrespirable atmosphere of the room, the hall was crowded throughout the afternoon."[6] Townspeople disparaged the college with a zeal that was reminiscent of Aristides. After just a few hours of discussion, they rejected the proposal by a vote of seven hundred to four and determined to "resist the establishment of the proposed college in this place, by every lawful means."[7] Black New Yorker Thomas Van Rensselaer recalled his disappointment upon hearing the news: "My heart was made to rejoice once . . . when a school of this kind was contemplated in New Haven, but I was disappointed." He "had thought of making application for admission in it, had it not failed."[8]

By the first week in October, college backers withdrew their proposal. In the aftermath of Turner's rebellion, Jocelyn confided to his abolitionist ally William Lloyd Garrison, "It is very difficult to say anything . . . without the charge of blood shedding."[9] But despite acquiescence, unrest persisted. Weeks later, whites in New Haven continued to unleash their anger over the proposed college onto tangible symbols of their frustrations: a black-owned hotel, a black-owned home, and an abolitionist's summer residence. Black Philadelphian and college supporter James Forten considered the whole episode one of "the most discreditable things for a free state that [he had] ever heard of."[10] Debate and protest about the proposed institution lingered in local papers and on city streets for months after violence subsided in the city.

As this narrative attests, whites in antebellum Connecticut generally endorsed universal education—except insofar as it applied to African Americans. By 1830, the state ranked first in the nation in college matriculation per capita. And by 1840, it also boasted the nation's highest literacy rate, over 99 percent.[11] New Haven was no exception to this trend. As one visitor observed in 1830, "[It] is believed that there is no place in the United States, where greater facilities are offered, for acquiring in every respect, a literary education than there is in New Haven."[12] A decade later, another town booster offered an even more hyperbolic assessment of the city's dedication to education: "There is no place on the face of the earth where nature and art, religion and science are more beautifully harmonized or exert a more benign influence than in this community—this oasis in New England—the fairest section of the most enlightened nation in the known world," he affirmed.[13] In light of its reputation for educational enthusiasm, it is understandable that Williams and Jocelyn placed so much faith in New Haven; but as visionaries, they failed to recognize a host of white anxieties toward black aspiration bubbling beneath the city surface, many of which Aristides had articulated in 1827.

First, expanding access to collegiate education led many white elites to worry that the status of their degrees was diminishing; conferring diplomas on African Americans, they contended, would only speed up the declension process. Further, deteriorating public education, industrialization, immigration, and gradual emancipation led many white workingmen to fear for their socioeconomic stability; and for that apprehension, they blamed free blacks. Then, around 1830, the goals and tactics of the abolitionist movement transformed. Activists demanded immediate—not gradual—emancipation and reached out to a broad constituency, including African Americans and women. As the abolitionist movement radicalized and democratized, many whites in New Haven began to fear that a southern black migration loomed on the horizon. The twin traumas of Turner's rebellion and the African college would bring these tensions, once latent, to a boil.[14]

To comprehend white opposition to African American higher education, it is useful to explore the college proposal in detail. As previously stated, in the late 1820s, two circles, one in New Haven, the other in New York, independently formulated strategies to increase black opportunities to obtain classical and mechanical instruction.[15] Simeon Jocelyn had been working throughout the 1820s to expand African American access to literary and religious education inside New Haven, but, as he understood, advanced instruction continued to elude most African Americans. While white students had access to primary, grammar, and high schools, school committees in many northern cities often assigned black children to a single institution. Providence, Rhode Island, for example, funded schools for white students through age fifteen, but for black students through age ten.[16] The small number of black collegians in this period typically had exceptional access to education well before they entered advanced institutions.[17] Recall that John Brown Russwurm enrolled at Bowdoin in 1824 after completing secondary studies at Hebron Academy—studies he financed with an inheritance from his white father.[18]

African Americans' access to vocational instruction was equally bleak. As one New Haven newspaper observed, many of the city's free blacks "being without trades, and destitute of the means of acquiring them, have to seek employment in the capacity of servants, or labourers, or what is worse remain idle."[19] By 1830, most apprenticeships were closed to black youths, and for those without such training, so were most trades. Without vocational instruction, black girls and boys would spend their days toiling in the most grueling, worst paid occupations, laboring in a position of service to whites or performing a service whites could afford to avoid. And, by 1830, with the influx of immigrants willing to work in low-wage positions, free blacks were losing hold of even the least desirable professions.

In recognition of this educational and occupational crisis, Jocelyn articulated a vision for a black men's manual labor college in the fall of 1830. He imagined such an institution would connect "agriculture, horticulture and the mechanic arts, with the study of literature and sciences."[20] Garrison promised Jocelyn his full support. Arthur Tappan signed on just as eagerly. When Jocelyn approached Tappan with plans for the college, he volunteered $1,000 and later purchased land in southern New Haven for the campus.[21] A white New Haven merchant, Tappan had a long record of educational philanthropy. He had paid the tuition of one hundred white Yale students who wished to join the ministry. He was also a founding member of the Washington, D.C.–based African Education Society (AES), formed "to prepare, by a suitable education, young persons of colour for usefulness in Africa."[22]

As Jocelyn, Garrison, and Tappan discussed the college in New Haven, African Americans in New York pursued a similar objective. In 1830, a group composed of the city's black religious and entrepreneurial elite formed an "association for the purpose of establishing a high school."[23] Peter Williams, reverend of New York's St. Philip's African Episcopal Church, led these efforts. Like Jocelyn, he had a long history of commitment to African American education.[24] In 1828, he helped to organize a census to locate school-aged black children. That endeavor was part of a larger campaign led by Williams and Samuel Cornish, coeditor of *Freedom's Journal,* to boost attendance in New York City's African schools. Williams also served on the advising committee of the African Dorcas Association, a benevolent society that collected garments, hats, and shoes for poor schoolchildren.[25] Williams, Cornish, and their New York associates

appreciated the obstacles facing those with aspirations beyond rudimentary instruction. In the late 1820s, Williams attempted to secure college
admissions for two of his most gifted young black parishioners but found
that "the Colleges were all closed against them."[26]

To understand the import of an African college at the time, it is critical
to realize just how few students of any color received a collegiate education. In 1830, just over 1 percent of New England's white men aged fifteen
to twenty attended colleges. Still, such opportunities were expanding.
Over the previous three decades, several colleges including Middlebury,
Colby, the University of Vermont, Bowdoin, and Amherst had emerged to
educate the second sons of farm families. Far less expensive and exclusive
than Harvard and Yale, these rural institutions extended collegiate access
to indigent and middling white men. But while opportunities for higher
education were increasing by class, racial barriers remained impermeable.
Some institutions, like Bowdoin, Amherst, and Oneida, had accepted a
limited number of black students as early as the 1820s, but by 1831 less
than a handful had gained admission. Mindful of such restrictions, Williams and his New York associates requested a meeting with Jocelyn immediately upon learning of his plan.[27]

Beyond his initial interest, Williams approached the collaboration cautiously. When Jocelyn arrived in New York, he made it clear that while
he appreciated white assistance, African Americans were responsible for
their own education. "I insisted," recalled Williams, "that while they were
laboring to restore to us our rights, it was exclusively our duty to labor to
qualify our people for the enjoyment of those rights."[28] The New York
contingent further asserted that if such an institution were to be built,
they wanted African Americans to have an equal voice in its affairs. With
that understanding, Williams and his "association for an establishment of
a high school" agreed to forgo their efforts and turn their attention to the
New Haven campaign.[29]

In early June, college supporters unveiled their intentions to African
Americans from across the nation at the First Annual Convention of the
Free People of Color in Philadelphia. There, Jocelyn recognized New Haven's delegate, Scipio C. Augustus, immediately; one of Temple Street's
original founders, he ran a lodging house for "genteel Persons of colour."[30]
Delegates agreed the institution should provide classical and vocational
instruction to black men by combining physical work with study.[31] This
style of instruction, "manual labor education," had gained popularity in
the mid-1820s in white seminaries. By 1830, manual labor schools oper-

ated in New York, Tennessee, Kentucky, Maine, New Jersey, and Ohio.[32] Proponents of manual labor instruction anticipated it would extend access to higher education to poorer students. In addition, reformers worried students were becoming effete from spending too many hours studying indoors. As the *Connecticut Courant* articulated, "A lad is sent to college, and after a few months he returns, pale, emaciated, and puny." Physical labor would protect the "health and vigor of the body."[33]

While few black people could say their children suffered a life of too *little* labor, the financial benefits of such a scheme gave the philosophy broader appeal. Advocates also expected the school to break up the white monopoly on vocational education and, by extension, skilled labor. As Garrison maintained, "A good trade is better than a fortune, because once obtained it cannot be taken away."[34] The African college in New Haven, had it opened, would not have been the first black institution to employ such a strategy. Sometime around 1816, James Easton, a free African American owner of an iron foundry, launched a manual labor school for "young men of color" in North Bridgewater, Massachusetts. Students apportioned their time between classical and vocational study. The school most likely remained in operation through the early 1830s and then closed under the weight of prejudice and financial pressure. Easton's son, Hosea, attended the school for several years and served on the Boston branch of the African college's fundraising committee.[35]

Although planners dubbed the proposed institution a "manual labor" college, they emphasized both classical and vocational instruction. Garrison, for example, envisaged that the school's "students will be fitted to pursue not only the professions of Law, Medicine and Divinity, but mercantile, mechanical and agricultural employments."[36] College planners incorporated such an expansive curriculum to serve both students' individual needs and the larger demands of the race. While the school itself might educate only a handful of students, they would become ministers and teachers who, in turn, would expand access to advanced education exponentially. Planners also anticipated that the college would help to create a black professional class, whose existence would refute white assertions of African Americans' inferior intellectual capabilities. Along similar lines, antislavery advocates also endorsed the institution for its potential to weaken the rhetorical foundation of the colonization movement.

It was no secret that among the New England states, Connecticut contained colonization's most fervent following. As one New Havener remarked in 1836, colonization made up the North and South's "only common ground."[37] And if Connecticut was the locus for colonizationist sentiment in New England, New Haven undoubtedly had Connecticut's most colonizationist clime. White New Haveners launched the American Colonization Society (ACS) auxiliary, the Connecticut Colonization Society (CCS) in 1827. Annual CCS meetings rotated between Hartford and New Haven.[38] Visitors to the seaport frequently commented on local white enthusiasm for the association. As John Brown Russwurm observed during his visit in 1827, "The Colonization Society appears to have some few friends in New Haven."[39] The city's dogged white support for repatriation elicited even more caustic commentary as the nineteenth century advanced. In 1833, abolitionists and proponents of black education Elizur Wright and Beriah Green dubbed New Haven, "the very citadel of the *arch-episcopal* palace of High Church Colonization."[40]

To legitimize its efforts, the ACS relied on conceptions of African Americans' innate inferiority to support their contention that blacks could not advance amid a superior race and would succeed only if sent "home." If, through college education, African Americans could demonstrate that their intellectual and economic degradation was situational and not inherent, colonizationists could no longer maintain that their progress depended upon repatriation. As abolitionist supporters of the college recognized, colonizationist rhetoric opposed African American education with inherently contradictory arguments. Many asserted that uplift was futile because black people, by their very nature, could never *be* uplifted, and, moreover, all efforts would inevitably be disappointed because whites would never permit them to utilize whatever education they might obtain. African repatriation, then, was the most "munificent" means to release blacks from this double bind. As abolitionists correctly surmised, because of its uneasy dependence on assertions of black people's innate inferiority, colonizationist ideology was vulnerable. If free blacks could prove themselves to be educable and economically self-sufficient—the primary objectives of the African college—the "benevolent" veneer of the ACS would crack. Just as importantly, the slender ideological thread separating colonizationists from abolitionists would unravel. Dismantling the ACS was critical for the success of the burgeoning abolitionist movement, for the two contingents competed for many of the same reform-minded constituents—as well as for their donations. Consider, for example, that Arthur Tappan funded the colonizationist AES in 1828 and the abolitionist African college just three years later.

For African American supporters of the college, the institution similarly fulfilled a wide-ranging agenda. Throughout the 1820s and 1830s,
African Americans refashioned the Protestant ethos of reform and Jacksonian spirit of self-improvement into an ideology of uplift that encompassed the virtues of temperance, religion, and education. As Philadelphia
Convention delegates asserted,

> If we ever expect to see the influence of prejudice decrease and ourselves re-
> spected, it must be by the blessings of an enlightened education. It must be
> by being in possession of that classical knowledge which promotes genius, and
> causes man to soar up to those high intellectual enjoyments and acquirements,
> which places him in a situation, to shed upon a country and a people, that scien-
> tific grandeur which is imperishable by time, and drowns in oblivions [*sic*] cup
> their moral degregation.[41]

Under a platform of moral suasion, these activists contended that righ-
teous behavior could disprove the rhetorical justifications for southern
slavery and northern prejudice. But to achieve this end, African Americans needed to rise from their socioeconomic depression and embody
those virtues that their opponents charged they lacked. As Samuel Cornish affirmed,

> The further increase of prejudice, and the amelioration of the condition of
> thousands of our brethren who are yet in bondage, greatly depend on our
> conduct. It is for us to convince the world by uniform propriety of conduct,
> industry and economy, that we are worthy of esteem and patronage. But to
> obtain which, we must use diligence to form ourselves a virtuous and intelligent
> character. This will disarm prejudice of the weapons it has too successfully used
> against us.[42]

This strategy spoke directly to proslavery and colonizationist rationalizations and highlights African Americans' faith in the mutability of northern prejudice and the rationality of their oppressors. By the close of the
1830s, more overt political agitation replaced this style of activism in
most African American circles. Nonetheless, in 1831, penetrating the
fortress of higher education went to the heart of this tradition of activist
by example.

In a similar spirit, African Americans embraced the college for its potential to enable black people to infiltrate mental professions that promised

higher wages and greater status than physical labor. As *Freedom's Journal* editorialist Philanthropos pointed out, white people often trumpeted African Americans' lack of advanced education to justify excluding them from nonmanual professions: "We grant now, that the colour of the skin is made a sufficient objection to our employment in a merchant's counting-house; but until now, there has scarcely been an instance of a coloured man, a native of this country, possessed of qualifications necessary to his conducting a set of books," he asserted. "But, let education become general; and even this objection will be eventually removed."[43] In the absence of such training, however, a vicious cycle entrapped African Americans, within which they could perform only the least desirable labor that, in turn, degraded them by association. An independent college would train a fortunate few to escape a life of "nigger work" and become clerks, doctors, and lawyers; in an incipient "talented tenth" sensibility, college advocates believed these individuals would lift the race upward by their example.[44]

Such a philosophy also helps to explain why a community that abhorred segregation opted to create a separate institution. Not surprisingly, when abolitionists revived the college movement in subsequent decades, this point would spark the most controversy. In the early 1850s, for example, when Frederick Douglass attempted to secure support for a black industrial college, several African American Bostonians opposed the institution from the fear that it would undermine their efforts to desegregate public schools in their city. Black attorney Robert Morris informed Douglass that he "deprecated the establishment of a Manual Labor College in which white children were to be excluded" believing it did not differ much from Boston's "[separate] Smith School."[45] William C. Nell, another champion of school integration, similarly disparaged Douglass's proposed institution in a letter to George T. Downing, a leader of the movement to desegregate Providence's public schools. "If Colored Organizations can best promote the cause of Freedom and Humanity let them try, fallacious though I deem the theory to be," he confessed to Downing.[46]

Yet in 1831, before school desegregation campaigns had taken shape, college proponents did not debate over whether or not to accept white students in their proposed institution. In the aftermath of its demise, African college supporter Biars Stanley, who in 1815 had petitioned alongside William Lanson to be freed from taxation, informed white New Haveners that he never wanted an integrated college, even if such an institution were possible: "I did not favor the academy because I thought it would connect us any more with you (whites). I would to God that the white population did not connect themselves with the colored population any more than the colored population do with the white."[47] Emancipation and equal rights, college supporters believed, depended upon access to higher education. More exclusive than democratic, colleges also did not possess the same "Americanizing" potential that reformers and integrationists would later bestow upon common schools. In 1831, college planners emphasized the importance of mechanical training to African Americans' economic survival and believed classical learning was necessary to dismantle prejudice. These were unsavory compromises, but given the importance of higher education to African Americans' economic and political elevation, there seemed to be no other choice.

New Haven, college proponents believed, was the perfect city to accommodate such varied objectives. Jocelyn recollected, "New Haven was regarded as a good location for the college, and would still be such, were it not for the very unexpected excitement which has been got up against it, through the influence of prejudice and a slavery-accommodating spirit."[48] For students and professors, travel to and from the college would be easy. The seaport was conveniently sandwiched between New York, some seventy-five miles to the south, and Boston, about 130 miles to the north. Transportation networks around the city were improving daily. Work on a turnpike system had nearly finished by 1814; a year later, regular steamboat service connected New Haven with Manhattan; and by 1829, construction on the Farmington Canal was complete. Commercial activity bustled around the wharf, Custom House Square, and East Water Street, where an active West India trade fueled the local economy. Tradesmen could boast of a strong tradition of manufacturing; their clocks and carriages were reputed to be the best in the nation. College planners anticipated numerous opportunities for students to obtain mechanical training.[49]

Alternating with Hartford as the capital of Connecticut, the town provided the benefits of both a large, cosmopolitan city and of a small community intimately linked by ties of family and church. At the time of the college campaign, New Haven was the largest city in Connecticut. Between 1800 and 1830, its population had more than doubled. At the turn of the nineteenth century, approximately 5,157 individuals resided in New Haven. Three decades later the seaport housed 10,108 whites, 566 free blacks, and four slaves. Yet it was still small in comparison with the other eastern ports of Boston, Philadelphia, Baltimore, and New York. Baltimore's African American community alone, for example, was greater than the entire population of New Haven. Despite increased immigration, fewer than five hundred foreigners lived in New Haven County and the city proper. As its demography suggests, New Haven in 1831 was predominately Protestant, white, and native born.[50] New Haven also had a long history of racial progressiveness, particularly in comparison with other northern cities. As of 1825, the seaport housed five churches—two Congregationalist, one Episcopalian, one Methodist, and one Baptist—whose congregants generally championed temperance, colonization, and education.[51] The African Improvement Society (AIS), which had hired Jocelyn to instruct black New Haveners in the 1820s, exemplified such inclinations. Its existence likely helped to convince college planners that their institution would complement New Haven's larger commitment to religion, schooling, and reform.

After a day's "animated debate" over the college's location, every attendant at the Philadelphia convention save one endorsed the proposal.[52] While "some diversity of sentiment existed, as to the place of location," delegates soon rallied around New Haven. They acknowledged the city's reputation for tolerance and benevolence, observing that "its laws are salutary and protecting to all, without regard to complexion." Representatives further hoped the seaport's commercial ties to the West Indies would induce island residents with sufficient funds to send their sons abroad to the college.[53] Ultimately, the New Haven that college supporters encountered bore little resemblance to these expectations. College planners did not anticipate the perfect storm of opposition gathering as dormant white anxieties over black aspiration collided with news of Nat Turner's rebellion.

By 1830, college was becoming less the reserve of the intellectual and economic elite and more a means for ambitious men to enter the middle classes. Elite white New Haveners associated the African college with this disturbing trend in higher education. As mentioned earlier, from 1765 to 1820 eight colleges had opened in New England with student bodies far less affluent than Harvard's or Yale's. As more whites sought professions over farm life, these new institutions began to serve the aspiring poor. According to David Allmendinger, while just one in 6,495 people graduated from college in the 1790s, by the 1830s, one in every 2,560 individuals received a degree.[54] No doubt many elite white New Haveners worried that extending diplomas to African Americans would further decrease the status their degrees bestowed. In response, the image of "students of Yale" being "met by [black collegians] in all the pride of supposed equality" particularly troubled the college's elite white opponents.[55]

While white elites fretted about men from the middling ranks adulterating their colleges, members of the white middle and working classes were experiencing a sharp decline in the quality of public education. By 1830, common schooling in Connecticut was in disarray. The creation of a school fund from the sale of western lands provided a ready source of school funding, but it also freed citizens from the tradition of personally contributing to public education. Reluctant to supplement the dwindling fund with increased taxation, Connecticut residents watched their schools deteriorate. Statewide, the annual appropriation per pupil in 1831 averaged less than a dollar. And New Haven was no exception. Poor white children's educational prospects were not much better than their black counterparts. Overall, fewer than one in three white children between the ages of four and sixteen attended public schools in New Haven; demand far exceeded the space available. And even if those who attended private schools are taken into consideration, quality schooling for New Haven's white children was nowhere near universal. Thus New Haven's educational progressiveness was a bit of a chimera. Elites were reluctant to extend collegiate education to even the white middling classes, and neither constituency wished to support public education for the white working classes with their tax dollars.[56]

In contrast to its public schools, however, New Haven's private schools were blossoming. In addition to Yale, New Haven hosted three male academies, two female seminaries, and several boarding schools. Yet the tuition at these institutions effectively excluded the working classes. As of 1830, for example, it cost $200 annually to attend the New Haven Female Seminary. Expenses at Yale similarly ranged from $140 to $190 per year. In general, New Haven's private institutions typically serviced children of the elite, many of whom hailed from outside of town. Less than 50 percent of Yale's students came from Connecticut, for example, and 16 percent lived below the Mason-Dixon Line. In 1831, class as much as race dictated educational opportunity in New Haven.[57]

Accordingly, a commonplace complaint about the college was its promise to attract and educate African American interlopers. As one white New Havener complained, "The establishment of a College here would [...] hurry in the blacks, as bees to a hive."[58] Such a statement is somewhat ironic given white New Haveners' simultaneous pronouncement of black indolence and laziness. Further, college planners' audacity in recruiting not only southern but foreign black people particularly enraged local residents. Just eight months earlier, the *New Haven Advertiser* reported rumors of a free black uprising on Guadaloupe and Martinique that had caused island residents to sleep "with swords and pistols under their pillows."[59] With visions of Toussaint L'ouverture and Nat Turner possibly not far from their minds, white townspeople denounced the college planners' determination to seek out students from the West Indies and bring them to New Haven.

Concern over such educational disparities also exacerbated a deeper uneasiness among many white people with broader transformations in the socioeconomic landscape. The confluence of industrialization, immigration, and gradual emancipation convinced many working people that their own financial independence and social status were in jeopardy. In the early nineteenth century, tradesmen throughout the Northeast watched as a system of outwork and sweating removed the place of production from the independent craft shop. Under the outwork system, manufacturers subdivided and contracted labor out to low-wage workers, traditionally women. With sweating, industrialists dispersed work to a middleman, or sweater, who, in turn, distributed tasks to other laborers at a greatly reduced wage. Collectively, these early-nineteenth-century employment practices undermined the status and security of the independent crafts. The social standing once accorded to mechanical labor declined accordingly.[60]

The college's promise to provide black men with classical and vocational education amplified workingmen's fears over the precariousness of their position. As white workingmen complained to the state legislature in 1834, "Not satisfied with depriving us of our labor, [free blacks] are determined to become our Lawyers, Physicians, Divines and Statesmen." They continued,

> The white man cannot labor upon equal terms with the negro. Those who have just emerged from barbarism or slavery, have few artificial wants. Regardless of the decencies of life, and improvident of the future, the black can afford his services at a lower price than the white man. And as he is in a caste below the influence of public opinion, he seldom hesitates in supplying any contingent wants, without the ceremony of contracts or the efforts of toil. If native indolence should deter him from this course, he has no compunctions in supplying himself from the public store-house, as a legal pauper. Whenever they come into competition, therefore, the white man is deprived of employment, or is forced to labor for less than he requires. He is compelled to yield the market to the African, and, with his family, ultimately becomes the tenant of an alms-house, or is driven from the State, to seek a better lot in western wilds. Thus

have thousands of our most valuable citizens been banished from home, and kindred, for the accommodation of the most debased race that the civilized world has ever seen; and whom the false philanthropy of enthusiasts is hourly inviting, to deprive us of the benefits of civilized society.[61]

Here white working people in Connecticut contended that socioeconomic change was a zero-sum game where any black advantage necessarily came at their expense. As Aristides had made clear in 1827, "The *miser* has a much better prospect of *cheapening* the services of the black, than of the white man—he prefers him, therefore."[62] But in reality, few, if any, African Americans had actually displaced white men from their jobs; they were just safer targets than those elites actually profiting from industrialization. Instead, New Haven's African Americans traditionally dueled with foreign immigrants for positions with the least status and compensation, leaving native white workers to compete among themselves in the skilled and semiskilled trades. While native white workers publicly targeted African Americans, the real cause of their frustration was not impoverished black laborers but rather prospering white industrialists. Politically and economically marginalized, New Haven's free blacks served as likely objects for their aggression.

In the 1830s, as David Roediger has demonstrated, the phrase "nigger work" became synonymous with difficult, unskilled, and subservient labor. The real consternation of white working people's opposition to the college then was probably not African Americans' upward mobility but rather whites' declining occupational status, a status that would only diminish if displaced white workers were forced to toil in professions traditionally performed by black people.[63] Given their experience with the one college already in New Haven, it is no surprise that many whites came to this conclusion. In the 1820s, nearly one-third of Yale's graduates became attorneys, close to 20 percent became doctors, over 40 percent went into the ministry, and 7 percent worked in local government.[64] The notion that African Americans might have access to higher education convinced some New Haveners that free blacks would rapidly rise above poor whites. As the self-styled editorialist "One not ashamed of his color" portended, "How our streets would swarm with the children of philanthropy, laughing at the industrious white man who cuts wood and carries coal," while the black man ceases to be a hauler of water.[65]

Foreign immigration aggravated concerns over the consequences of industrialization. By 1830, many white New Haveners decried that "outsiders" were invading their "peaceable kingdom." Heavy westward migration depleting the city's "natural-born" numbers coupled with fast-growing transportation networks exacerbated anxieties over decreasing "homogeneity."[66] New Haven had opposed fare reductions for steamboat service to and from New York, fearing it would "bring throngs of idle boys, dissipated journeymen, and thriftless loungers" into their "peaceful" city.[67] Many whites were, at the very least, uncomfortable with black and immigrant outsiders. The *Connecticut Observer* lamented the influx of immigrants as an "alarming evil."[68] The *Connecticut Journal* decried free blacks as "a pest and burden to society."[69] Some white New Haveners worried these groups would burden town coffers and associated them with poverty and disorder.

But contrary to such perceptions, in 1831 New Haven was not under siege from outsiders either black or foreign. Both the absolute number of African Americans and their relative percentage had been declining for over a decade, despite a 20 percent rise in the town's total population. In 1820, around six hundred free blacks and two slaves made up 7.5 percent of the population. By 1830, this number fell below six hundred; African Americans now constituted just 5 percent of the city. And immigrants had yet to flood New Haven either. Despite the number of Irishmen who arrived to labor on the Farmington Canal in 1831, even African Americans outnumbered foreigners by about 2:1. The Irish population did not dramatically increase until later in the 1830s and 1840s.[70]

So what accounts for this incongruity between New Haven's actual and perceived demographic composition? While free black numbers diminished, so did the forces checking their social and economic elevation. By 1831, most black people in Connecticut had transitioned from enslaved to free men and women. To white dismay, the excruciating process of gradual emancipation that Connecticut began in 1784 had been steadily eroding the legal and occupational strictures that fixed blacks' physical, social, and economic mobility. Whereas, for example, the town government once could limit enslaved blacks' mobility by enacting curfews, it did not have the power to enact such restrictions on free men and women, regardless of their color. Whereas New Haveners could prohibit taverns from serving enslaved people "forbidden drink," they could not order free blacks to remain temperate.[71] And perhaps most importantly, whereas the government could prevent enslaved men and women from holding property and toiling on their own accord, free blacks out of economic desperation might accept less for their labor, forcing white workingmen to depress their wages to compete. In response, whites attempted to fashion alternative systems of control. As Alexis de Toqueville observed in 1831, "[T]he prejudice which repels the Negroes seems to increase in proportion as they are emancipated."[72] While masters instructed enslaved blacks to perform all sorts of occupations, free African Americans less often received vocational education and were rarely permitted to labor in profitable trades.[73]

Precise details of African Americans' exclusion from skilled trades within New Haven are difficult to obtain, as city directories did not classify entrants by skin color before 1840 and census records did not include detailed occupational information until 1850. *Patten's City Directory* for 1840, however, provides a useful illustration of the degree to which black New Haveners clustered in unskilled and service occupations nine years after the collapse of the college campaign. A word of caution with this analysis: because *Patten's* did not list servants living in white homes, it provides an incomplete picture of women's labor in the city. As of 1845, in fact, nearly one in four African Americans in New Haven resided in the same household as their white employer.[74] Of the black women *Patten's* did include, it listed twelve without any occupation. Next to Sarah Wilson's name, however, *Patten's* noted the word "school," suggesting Wilson probably worked as an educator in some capacity. The directory also listed three black washerwomen.

Patten's similarly highlights the infrequency with which black men in New Haven performed skilled and nonmanual occupations. Of the sixty-six "colored" entrants *Patten's* included, six black men worked as waiters, while it described eighteen simply as "laborers." On the other hand, *Patten's* noted just a few African American tradesmen: shoemakers George Frazer and Jefferson Way, bootmaker Richard Green, cobbler John Williams, and wig and toupee maker William C. Innis. A similarly modest number of black people operated businesses. For example, George Frazer ran an Oyster House, William Cisco managed an eating house, Laban Lason owned a clothing store, and Charles Coe supervised a boarding house, while Bradley M. Goodman and Ezekiel T. Scott worked as grocers.[75]

Census records from 1850 provide additional documentation of the extent to which black New Haveners remained concentrated in occupations with low wages and little security. Census takers counted 671 African Americans seventeen years of age and older who lived in the southern New England seaport. Of those individuals, 57 percent were listed with no occupation. Of the remainder, 109 worked as laborers; thirty-three supported themselves as sailors; and fifty-two worked as waiters. As in 1840, a minority of black men performed skilled trades. Census takers counted eight shoemakers; three blacksmiths; and two bookmakers, for example. An even smaller number performed nonmanual labor. Thirty-three-year-old Samuel Cook, thirty-two-year-old Samuel Gray, forty-three-year-old Charles Burch, and thirty-eight-year-old Amos G. Beman worked as clergymen, while thirty-two-year-old Pelman Williams was the only black teacher in New Haven, according to census takers.[76] For the majority of New Haven's free black community, however, achieving economic independence like this was nearly impossible. When African American William Grimes, for example, opened a "victualing" shop in the city, he was warned out of town. As Grimes lamented, "A poor man just gets agoing in business, and is then warned to depart." "The practice," he concluded, "is very cruel."[77]

At the same time, a rigid system of socio-occupational and residential segregation emerged to replace the boundary that demarcated enslaved from free. With some exceptions, black families clustered in ramshackle neighborhoods located some distance from the city center: Sodom Hill (now Wooster Square) on the seaport's southwestern edge; Mount Pleasant, abutting the harbor; and New Liberia, on New Haven's eastern border. African Americans with greater means owned homes on Negro Lane (now State Street), which dissected the northeast quadrant of the city.[78] In New Haven, as in the rest of Connecticut, the uneasy transformation from slavery to freedom was not quite complete. Scattered bondsmen and bondswomen continued to dot the landscape. As of 1831, approximately twenty-three enslaved blacks still labored in the state. Whites sold enslaved people on New Haven's Center Green into the 1820s, and papers still carried the occasional notice of a "servant" for sale. Perhaps more than any other New England state, the emancipation process moved slowly in Connecticut. At the turn of the century, close to one thousand African Americans remained in bondage. After 1800, the number of enslaved people dropped dramatically, suggesting the delayed impact of gradual emancipation. In 1810, 310 slaves lived in the state. That number decreased to ninety-seven in 1820, to twenty-five in 1830, and to seventeen in 1840. Connecticut would not complete the emancipation process until 1848.[79]

While many white townspeople distinguished their northern racial liberality from southern slaveholders' depravity, living without the protection of a slave code or system of black laws made most far more uncomfortable with the free black presence than their southern counterparts. One Virginian who attended Yale in the early 1830s observed the contradictions between white townspeople's professed racial liberalism and their simultaneous disdain for their free black neighbors. George McPhail wrote home,

> They seem determined to set our negroes free at all hazards, and raise them to a level with the white population and if possible a little above it, . . . If the Virginia people would collect together the inhabitants of . . . [the] free negro settlements in the state, and send them all to New England, we shall never hear any more of abolition after that, for the yankees would dread it five times as much as the people of the South. They talk of ameliorating *our* colored population, when they treat those they have among them with supreme contempt and indignity.[80]

As McPhail realized, white New Englanders could profess racial tolerance because their black population was comparatively minute. But if it were to increase, he expected they would learn they were not that different from their southern counterparts. The *New Haven Palladium* agreed with McPhail's assessment: "It is true that on the subject of immediate emancipation there is not one in a thousand north of the Potomac that would favor the measure, should even the southerners agree to it."[81]

Cries to expand emancipation and black education stoked such anxieties. In 1829, free black Bostonian David Walker released his *Appeal to the Colored Citizens of the World.* In this revolutionary text, Walker denounced colonization, championed education, and counseled enslaved blacks to use any means at their discretion, including violence, to secure their freedom. The *Appeal's* endorsement of black-on-white violence represented a dramatic departure from previous African American forays into print like *Freedom's Journal,* which usually rejected violence and espoused a gradualist doctrine of moral suasion. Unlike John Brown Russwurm, for example, Walker demanded education for free and enslaved African Americans and coupled it with an endorsement of rebellion.[82] Even Garrison admitted, "The south may be reasonably alarmed at the circulation of Mr. Walker's Appeal; for a better promoter of insurrection was never sent forth to an oppressed people."[83] A year later, in January 1831, his own radical periodical, the *Liberator,* appeared in New Haven. And like Walker, Garrison tied black education to slavery's demise. In the *Liberator's* first edition he observed, "Knowledge is power. A people generally enlightened cannot be enslaved."[84] Thus while gradual emancipation seemed to be decreasing white power over African Americans' socioeconomic mobility, "insurrectionary" texts like these exacerbated white fears over the power of education to undermine racial stability. By 1831, the demise of white support for colonization and the radicalization of the abolition movement as typified by Walker and Garrison's exegeses were eroding white tolerance for black education.

Then, in early September 1831, white New Haveners' worst fears of emancipation and education were finally confirmed. Local papers and the local imagination inextricably linked these two stories: Turner's rebellion and the proposed African college. In some cases, editors positioned articles about the college and Southampton side by side.[85] Local coverage of the rebellion also trumpeted Turner's education. The *Columbian Register*, for example, highlighted his literacy by observing that, "Nat is a shrewd fellow" who "reads and writes, [and] preaches."[86] The bondsmen's rampage in Virginia showed New Haveners the consequences of too much black enlightenment. When local whites responded to the African college proposal, they naturally invoked the lessons of Turner's uprising. For a community already uneasy about a free black population living, working, and seemingly multiplying unfettered in its midst, the shock of Southampton was too much to withstand. Turner's last casualty was to be the first African college.

Of all northern states in the antebellum period, Connecticut displayed the greatest hostility to both abolition and African American education. In the 1830s alone, whites attacked antislavery assemblies in Canterbury, Norwich, Hartford, Middletown, Plainfield, Danbury, Meriden, Brookfield, and New Haven. Yet even within this "desert of pro-slavery indifference and hostility," as one abolitionist referred to it, New Haven's racism and anti-abolitionism were striking.[87] In 1851, one black visitor to the seaport appraised these contradictions perfectly: "New Haven is the head quarters of Connecticut Religion, Literature, Politics, Colonization, Aristocracy, and Negro-hate" and "one of the most hopelessly pro-slavery places in New England." "There is no more abolition in that city," he affirmed, "than there is in Baltimore."[88]

PART II

Education's Enclave: Baltimore, Maryland

[T]he large colored population of Baltimore, now from thirty to forty thousand souls, have no sort of Public School provision made for them, by the city or state governments. They are left entirely to themselves for any education they may obtain.[1] —Noah Davis, 1859

Nestled near the Chesapeake Bay to the north of the Patapsco River, Baltimore's beginnings trace back to 1729, when a coalition of Maryland planters eager to expand tobacco production appealed to the colonial assembly for a charter.[2] For the next few decades, the town's economy and population grew at a measured pace. As they had in the seventeenth century, planters in Baltimore's hinterlands continued to hedge their fortunes on slavery. In 1664, Maryland had codified a labor system that enslaved Africans and their descendants from birth to death, heralding that "all Negroes and other slaves already within the Province and all Negroes and other slaves to be hereafter imported into the Province shall serve Durante Vita."[3] Thereafter, whites also claimed ownership of all children born to black parents. Anticipating a conflict between baptism and bondage, in 1671 Maryland's legislature decreed the religious rite did not proffer other privileges to people of color, most notably freedom.[4] By 1755, whites enslaved more than 4,000 black people in Baltimore County alone.[5]

Around the mid-eighteenth century, however, Baltimore's taste for tobacco began to sour. Unstable prices and shallow water routes made profiting from the cash crop difficult, if not impossible. Unlike other counties near the Chesapeake Bay that were awash in rivers, Baltimore's surrounding waters were too swift or too shallow to move tobacco.[6] Plummeting tobacco prices did little to entice settlers into the nascent community. By 1752, more than two decades after its founding, fewer than fifty families resided in the town, which itself "consisted of only about twenty-five houses, a tobacco inspection warehouse, a brewery, a tavern and a church."[7]

If Baltimore's origins lay in tobacco, the town blossomed because of wheat. As Pennsylvania's colonists pressed south and west, many entered northern Maryland already familiar with cereal production.[8] And as tobacco profits fell, grain prices edged higher, propelled by demand from Europe, where sporadic warfare had disrupted food production. Between 1765 and 1769, cereal exports from Baltimore's once sleepy port increased almost 50 percent, aided by the expansion of flour milling in the hinterlands.[9] Ships left stocked with flour and arrived flush with staples to sustain Baltimore's continued growth: timber from the Carolinas, sugar from New Orleans and the West Indies, and salted fish from the North.[10] Flour production energized industries inside the seaport, attracting workers in need of housing, food, and infrastructure and creating demand for more labor in turn. The Revolutionary War fueled even more expansion, as manufacturers capitalized on shrinking imports from Great Britain to strengthen their hold on textile, clothing, food, and metal production.[11] By 1790, more than 13,000 people resided in this boomtown, the fourth largest city in the new nation.[12]

The decline of tobacco juxtaposed with the rise of wheat also produced Baltimore's distinct racial demography: a large free black community coupled with a comparatively small enslaved population. For much of the year, a single family could tend to a wheat crop independently. While slavery had complemented tobacco planting, cereal cultivation neither required nor benefited from year-round workers; it employed a large labor force only at harvest time.[13] Upon abandoning tobacco for wheat, planters found themselves in possession of an enslaved labor force that was too costly to maintain.[14]

Masters responded to their surfeit of slaves in various ways. A number elected to manumit their slaves outright. Especially among Quakers and Methodists, antislavery sentiment gained momentum in the ostensibly egalitarian aftermath of the Revolution. As early as the 1770s, Quaker meetings began to advise members to abandon slavery.[15] Two years later in Baltimore, Quakers and Methodists launched the Maryland Society for the Abolition of Slavery and the Relief of Free Negroes, and Others, Unlawfully Held in Bondage. In 1796, the Methodist General Conference condemned slaveholding and agreed to exclude members who engaged in the slave trade. It also required those in its leadership who owned slaves to begin emancipation.[16] But these early flirtations with antislavery were a far cry from what would take root in Boston four decades later. Advocates never promoted universal, immediate emancipation. Instead, they supported modest proposals to gradually transition enslaved people into freedom. By 1798, the Maryland Society for the Abolition of Slavery was largely defunct, and although antislavery efforts would resurface from time to time, Maryland never developed a cohesive white abolitionist movement.[17]

Instead, most planters transitioning from tobacco to cereal production elected to modify the institution rather than dispense with slavery altogether. Some diversified the duties they assigned to enslaved laborers. In consequence, bondsmen and bondswomen received more training in blacksmithing, spinning, and other crafts.[18] But even with these alterations, planters still found that the cost of slaves' year-round maintenance outweighed the benefits of their labor. In response, many began to hire out their enslaved workers, often to households and craftspeople in Baltimore. Those sent to work in town often had some input in their choice of master and some, like Frederick Douglass, were allowed to live on their own upon surrender of satisfactory wages.[19]

Enslaved blacks from the countryside entered Baltimore to work in an array of industries, for example, making rope, caulking ships, and molding bricks. As of 1813, two of every five craftspeople in the seaport held slaves.[20] Shipbuilding was by far the largest employer of enslaved labor. Dominated by a small cadre of affluent craftsmen, the maritime trades generated the wealth necessary to pay for slaves' maintenance throughout the year. Shipyard owners were also among the first to use bondsmen to undermine journeymen's control over production. This decision would contribute to the fractious relations between black and white workers in Baltimore's shipyards in the ensuing decades.[21] Enslaved women commonly worked inside white homes, scrubbing, sewing, and laundering clothes, freeing their employers from many of the time-consuming and physically exhausting drudgeries of domestic labor. Although many white householders opted to employ free servants, several favored hiring a bondswoman for a term. As one family in search of a "woman to do the cooking, washing and ironing of a family" made plain, "a slave would be preferred."[22]

While hiring out allowed slaveholders to siphon off cash from their property, the arrangement offered risk and reward.[23] By sending enslaved blacks to Baltimore, masters gambled their investment would not slip away. Many bondsmen and bondswomen hired out to Baltimore may have contemplated escape; some like Frederick Douglass chose to flee. In 1829, Robert Alcock offered twenty-five dollars for the return of Harriet, a thirty-year-old bondswoman he had hired out for a six-month term. Harriet, he believed, would "try to pass for a white woman" in Baltimore.[24] To Alcock's dismay and Harriet's delight, a fugitive might vanish easily inside the city. Baltimore's harbor bustled with ships dropping anchor and setting sail, and Pennsylvania's border loomed less than fifty miles away. Matilda, enslaved by D. H. White, lived and labored in Baltimore for nine months without detection. And even after White located her, she "absconded" again.[25] Harriet Jacobs' brother Benjamin escaped from North Carolina via the Maryland seaport, or, as she put it, he rode "over the blue billows, bound for Baltimore."[26]

As the nineteenth century advanced, the sheer number of black people who lived and labored in Baltimore made it increasingly difficult for slaveholders to detect and recover fugitives. Slaveholders, in turn, responded to the insecurity inherent in hiring out with a promise to free their slaves after they labored for a term, typically between five and fifteen years. By enticing enslaved blacks to remain faithful and work hard, masters attempted to lessen their own responsibility. Term slaves cost a fraction of workers who were enslaved for life and could be purchased for only a person's most productive years. Hiring out released slaveholders from the cost of caring for slaves in early childhood and providing for them into old age. For those held in bondage, delayed manumission agreements enabled them to set their sights on a specific freedom day. In this way, manumission, hiring out, and term slavery each became essential components of slaveholding in post-Revolutionary Baltimore.[27] Under such a system, slavery continued, at least for a time. In 1790, 5,877 slaves resided in Baltimore County and 1,255 lived in Baltimore Town. Ten years later, Baltimore Town's enslaved population had more than doubled to 2,843 (Figure 4).

Delayed manumission would play itself out eventually, however, for at one point or another term slaves would be free. As this technicality became a demographic reality, the city's free African American population ballooned. As of 1820, Baltimore's free black community topped 10,000. Two decades later, nearly 18,000 free African Americans resided in the seaport. But while its free black community was increasing, Baltimore's enslaved population was not keeping pace; in fact, it was shrinking. By the third decade of the nineteenth century, Baltimore housed both the nation's largest free black community (14,790) and a relatively small enslaved black population (4,120). As of 1840, census takers counted 3,212

A.

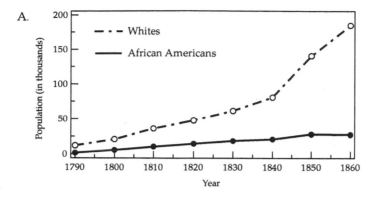

B.

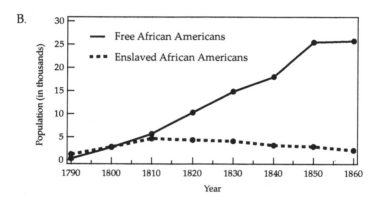

FIGURE 4. Population growth in Baltimore, 1790–1860. (A) Total number of whites and African Americans. (B) Total number of free African Americans and enslaved African Americans. Source: Charles Varle, *A Complete View of Baltimore* (Baltimore: Samuel Young, 1833), 11; Christopher Phillips, *Freedom's Port: The African American Community of Baltimore, 1790–1860* (Urbana and Chicago: University of Illinois Press, 1997), 15.

enslaved blacks in the city. And by 1850, while more than 25,000 free black people lived and labored in the city, fewer than 3,000 African Americans remained enslaved (Figure 4).[28]

In demography alone, Baltimore did not resemble cities above or below the Mason Dixon Line. As of 1840, one in five of its residents was African American. But while this percentage dwarfed that of Philadelphia (11 percent), New York (5 percent), and Boston (less than 3 percent), it also paled in comparison with New Orleans (40 percent) and Charleston (55 percent), as did Baltimore's enslaved population. At 3,199 in 1840, it did not come close to that in either New Orleans (18,208) or Charleston (14,673), capitals of the domestic slave trade. Moreover, where more than 20 percent of New Orleans' total population and one-half of Charleston's was enslaved in 1840, only 3 percent of all Baltimoreans were enslaved at that time.[29]

These numbers do a great deal to account for free black Baltimoreans' educational opportunity relative to their counterparts in other slaveholding communities. The word relative is important here, for while free blacks' access to schooling surpassed that of their counterparts in other slaveholding cities, it also paled in comparison with that which was available to African Americans living in most northern communities. Unlike Baltimore, for example, Boston and New Haven provided public schooling to black children from the turn of the nineteenth century.

Nor should white tolerance for black education in Baltimore be read as evidence that white people in this slaveholding seaport were more liberal in their racial attitudes than those in other slaveholding communities. Many white working people resented black laborers, while white elites with greater influence and authority appreciated literate free blacks as a cheap source of skilled labor. Baltimore's particular relationship to slavery enabled white employers to capitalize on an educated black labor force without worrying it would endanger the city's racial order. The boundaries that divided enslaved from free in Baltimore were porous, if not fleeting. Slavery's ongoing existence gave rise to a network of restrictions that effectively checked free blacks' literal and socioeconomic mobility. In particular, the racial structure of Baltimore's labor market—shaped by the contours of slavery—made possible free African Americans' educational opportunity.

Visitors to the slaveholding seaport were frequently surprised to find black schooling so prevalent. In 1839, a free black New Yorker remarked that "even Baltimore, in the slave State of Maryland, has schools superior to ours: surrounded as the colored people there are by all the influence of Slavery, they support several very respectable private schools."[30] Two decades later, a former Virginia bondsman evinced similar astonishment: "When I came among the colored people of Baltimore, I found, to my surprise, that they were advanced in education, quite beyond what I had conceived of."[31] In no other slaveholding city did black schools operate as openly, free from legislative fiat and mob assault. Chapter 3 seeks to understand why, for the most part, white resistance to African American education did not materialize in Baltimore through an examination of the relationship among race, labor, and literacy. To do so, it mines three distinct kinds of sources—apprenticeship contracts, help-wanted advertisements, and census schedules—that individually and collectively illustrate the ways in which white dependence on free black labor within the context of slavery fostered a climate conducive to African American literacy. By extension, African Americans in Baltimore valued vocational and literary instruction both for the social status they signified and for the economic benefit they might provide to themselves and their children.

Chapter 4 explores how black parents, teachers, and activists succeeded in schooling black children beneath the shadow of slavery. All three contingents exploited African Americans' socioeconomic position in the city carefully, sustaining white lenience by framing their educational objectives in terms that complemented whites' economic self-interest. While black schools offered lessons in a variety of subjects, publicly, black educators stressed their intention to prepare students to serve their station. Moreover, black activists chose their moments deliberately, discerning, for example, when the political climate was sufficiently calm to petition the city for school funds and when these efforts were not worth the cost. As members of the nation's largest free African American community, black Baltimoreans created a network of educational institutions that did not, at least overtly, challenge the racial order. While not always agreeable, compromise coupled with protest enabled African Americans to make Baltimore an enclave of educational opportunity in the slaveholding South.

CHAPTER THREE

Race, Labor, and Literacy in a Slaveholding City

O n October 8, 1831, weeks after the movement to build an African college collapsed in New Haven, a small notice appeared in the *Baltimore American*. The "Prospectus of a School for Colored Girls" advertised a boarding school for black girls operating out of a three-story house in the northwestern corner of the city. In addition to religion, students at St. Frances Academy for Colored Girls received lessons in "English, French, Cyphering and Writing" along with "Sewing in all its branches, Embroidery, Washing and Ironing."[1] The school welcomed black girls from the local area for a two-dollar per quarter fee, but for four dollars, African American families who lived outside Baltimore could board their daughters if they chose.

Given the turmoil surrounding African American higher education concurrently breaking out in Connecticut, one would think the Catholic managers of the Baltimore boarding school could have chosen a better moment to advertise. Less than a month after white townspeople in New Haven assembled against the proposed African college, trustees of St. Frances Academy for Colored Girls publicized their activities, and in a white paper with little sympathy for free blacks, no less. While the two institutions differed dramatically in scope and intent—one was a college for black men, the other an academy for adolescent black girls—their common timing provides a useful window into understanding why Baltimore's black schools escaped white violence during the antebellum period.

In contrast to the proposal for the African college, which coupled higher education with abolition, St. Frances' advertisement emphasized how black education could complement the city's existing racial order. Teachers at St. Frances stressed an appreciation for hard work and thrift, crucial lessons for any young woman who might one day run her own household or toil in someone else's. "These girls will either become mothers of families or household servants," St. Frances' prospectus pronounced. "In the first case, the solid virtues, the religious and moral principles, which they may have acquired, when in this school, will be carefully transferred as a legacy to their children." As for those who "are to be employed as servants, they will be instructed with domestic concerns and the care of young children. . . . How important then . . . that these girls should have imbibed religious principles, and have been trained up in habits of modesty, honesty, and integrity!"[2]

From timing alone, one would anticipate this advertisement to have incited white animosity, particularly as it, like the proposed African college, appeared in the wake of Nat Turner's rebellion. As in New Haven, events in Southampton dominated Chesapeake papers throughout the fall, and many white Baltimoreans feared violence would soon strike closer to home. On September 21, 1831, an anonymous individual alerted Baltimore's mayor William Stewart that a "number of Blacks" were "Assembling in Military Uniform—toward the west of Saratoga Street." He cautioned "Citizens of Baltimore [to] be on your guard."[3] Another asserted that he "herd the colerd peple intend risin" in Baltimore the following weekend.[4] Yet despite such concerns, days passed, the advertisement repeated, and for all the publicity, St. Frances Academy for Colored Girls remained undisturbed.

In fact, some white Baltimoreans did not just tolerate St. Frances Academy, they rallied behind it. Upon learning of the institution, an otherwise unidentified white editorialist, "Scipio," penned in a fervent response to the *American*. Unlike Aristides who argued that any advantage African Americans obtained would come at whites' expense, Scipio asserted that black education could benefit the entire community by improving African Americans' vocational abilities. A student "might receive that degree of instruction which would consist with his avocations and render him more useful," he affirmed. In so doing, "His condition might be ameliorated with advantage to society at large." The school's desire to improve black women's domestic skills pleased him especially: "Parents cannot but felicitate themselves on the prospect which is thus opened to obtain a permanent supply of candidates for employment, who have been educated with a view to services indispensable to society in its present organization."[5]

In his support for the academy, Scipio tapped into a popular rationale for white women's education that emphasized civic duty and then connected it to all women's economic capabilities.[6] In the post-Revolutionary period, a proper literary education had marked a young woman as virtuous, capable of conversing in civil society herself and of raising upright and honorable sons to guard the republic.[7] As the "cult of true womanhood" replaced "republican motherhood" later in the nineteenth century, education continued to connote morality and respectability, virtues many whites sought to withhold from African Americans. Black women's instruction, Scipio suggested, could be understood similarly. While skin color prevented their sons from becoming citizens, the labor black women performed inside white households made their own education also a matter of civic interest. In Scipio's formulation, as nurses, or the "medium between the parent and child," black women aided the moral development of white citizens. "The great purpose of education being to form the man and the citizen, that he may be virtuous, happy in himself and useful to society," Scipio argued, "to attain this end his education should commence in the nursery."[8]

But not all black institutions in Baltimore would be as fortunate as St. Frances Academy for Colored Girls. The city's sobriquet was "Mobtown" after all.[9] As one resident groused in 1838, "our city has become the scene of the most disgraceful outrages, perpetuated by desperate fellows who hang upon society some how or other, and who, when the fit seizes them, give loose to their devilishness, and raise what they are pleased to call a row."[10] Seven months after this complaint, a "terrible scene of fright and confusion" erupted during evening services at Sharp Street African Methodist Church.[11] In response to rumors that "disorderly negroes" had attacked a night watchman, whites ransacked the black church, pelting it with stones and bricks. Such was the terror inside the building, one witness reported, that congregants leapt "out of the windows" and were "considerably injured."[12] In the aftermath of the attack, some white Methodists petitioned Mayor Samuel Smith to dispatch police to guard "Coloured Congregations" not just at Sharp Street but also at Asbury Church and Wesleyan Chapel.[13]

But as Scipio's support for St. Frances Academy for Colored Girls suggests, despite some whites' proclivity for racism and riots, a number of black schools operated openly in this slaveholding community. In fact, in

1833 Charles Varle's *Complete View of Baltimore* publicized the locations of four different "Public African Schools," including the one at Bethel African Methodist Church, which Frederick Douglass had attended.[14] Advertisements for black day, night, and Sabbath schools also appeared regularly in local papers, as did notices for fairs, public exhibitions, and calls for donations to sustain these educational institutions. By 1830, white elites—shopkeepers, manufacturers, and craftspeople—depended upon free blacks to sweep their streets, wash their clothes, and deliver their loads. Yet they also sought African Americans to labor in workplaces that revolved around literacy: printing presses, bookstores, and newspapers. As employers, in consequence, elite whites prized free blacks' literacy and vocational abilities.

White elites' eagerness for literate African American workers should not be read as evidence of a larger atmosphere of racial progressiveness in Baltimore. To the contrary, white elites could capitalize on free blacks' literacy precisely because slavery's existence circumscribed free blacks' liberty. First, working-class white Baltimoreans harassed and feared free African Americans, but the presence of slavery helped to allay their fears that literate free blacks might challenge their own place in the city's socioeconomic order. Second, slavery fundamentally disconnected African Americans, enslaved and free, from the rights and privileges of citizenship. While propertied African Americans voted with some regularity in the eighteenth century, in 1810, Maryland amended its constitution to eliminate black suffrage. Free blacks may have retained the right to petition, but they could not testify in court except in cases involving other African Americans. There is no telling how often whites took advantage of this vulnerability, but at least a few likely enjoyed black craftsmen's inability to use the courts to recover payment for their services. Similarly, falling into debt or a criminal conviction carried the threat of sale, even for African Americans born into freedom. And for the many black people who toiled in jobs with irregular or nighttime hours, curfew laws made earning a living wage even more challenging.[15]

Thus the very notion of freedom for black people in antebellum Baltimore must itself be carefully qualified. As a gathering of free people of color at Bethel Church observed in 1826, "Though we are not slaves, we are not free. . . . [S]urrounded by the freest people and the most republican institutions in the world," we still enjoy "none of the immunities of freedom."[16] While the limited nature of black liberty did help to assuage white fears about black literacy, white tolerance for African American education should not be confused with an enthusiasm for racial equality. To the contrary, white support for black schooling existed only in so far as whites stood to benefit from it. In the end, regardless of free blacks' educational opportunities, Baltimore remained a society with slavery.

*   *   *

To query the relationship among race, labor, and literacy in Baltimore, the institution of apprenticeship is an ideal place to begin. A labor source and a means of obtaining literacy, apprenticeship, like slavery, evolved around the turn of the nineteenth century as whites sought more flexibility from their workforces and African Americans looked for ways to sustain their families in freedom. In the eighteenth century, most apprentices were white boys who entered into these arrangements on their own or, more often, on their parents' accord. For families hoping to provide their sons with the means to become autonomous, apprenticeship offered literacy and vocational instruction in exchange for a term of service. At the same time, masters retained control over their charges' daily lives. Like slaves, apprentices lacked basic civil rights. They could not travel without their masters' permission and were forbidden from marrying or visiting taverns. They also agreed to forgo certain vices including "cards, dice, or any other unlawful game," "swear[ing]," and "fornication" and promised to "faithfully" execute their master's command.[17]

In 1793, Maryland's legislature remade the institution of apprenticeship, and in so doing, its racial composition transformed. That year, Maryland empowered the courts to involuntarily apprentice black children who could not provide proof of employment or ongoing vocational training, no matter their age. As the courts ordered more African American children into these arrangements, the gap between instruction and servitude widened. In 1817, Maryland's legislature formally released masters of apprentices from the responsibility of providing literacy to their black charges. If they so desired, they could substitute a small sum of money in exchange. Thereafter, black girls customarily received twenty dollars in lieu of literacy; African American boys collected thirty.[18]

For black families, the consequences of the 1793 law and its 1817 revision could be devastating. Parents in dire financial circumstances, many recently free themselves, faced the choice of apprenticing their children or waiting for the Trustees of the Poor, the body that supervised the public almshouses, to take action. In 1826, for example, free black Baltimoreans

Sarah and Samuel Ogle bound their son Samuel to Charles Green for seven years, seven months, and four days, for just thirty dollars.[19] And while the Ogles appeared to have entered into this arrangement willingly, not all African American families had such liberty. In 1829, Baltimore County's Orphans' Court declared Catharine Jones "unemployed and without means sufficient for her maintenance," despite being just seven years of age. Using the guidelines of the 1793 legislation, it bound her to Charles McCann until she turned eighteen. In exchange for eleven years of service, McCann agreed to instruct Catharine in "plain sewing and house-work" and to teach her to read, although if he so desired, McCann could substitute her literacy for an additional twenty dollars of freedom dues.[20]

In spite of the 1817 legislation, however, masters continued to promise literacy to African American apprentices. A survey of surviving contracts filed at the Maryland Hall of Records confirms this assertion. Between 1826 and 1830, 130 black children were apprenticed in Baltimore, forty girls and ninety boys. Of these agreements, over 60 percent included a stipulation for literary education. Some contracts worded this expectation in terms of competency—reading and writing, for example—while others phrased it in terms of time—six months of night school, for instance. The most common provision entailed achieving a certain level of proficiency. Over 50 percent of these agreements included such a clause. When the Baltimore City Orphans' Court apprenticed fifteen-year-old Charles Barnes to William Hutson, for example, Hutson agreed to provide Barnes with "reasonable education in reading, writing, and arithmetic" and to teach him the "the art and mystery of caulking vessels."[21] Similarly, when Samuel P. Jones apprenticed himself to house carpenter Patrick Hamilton, Hamilton promised to teach Jones to "read write and cypher as far as the Rule of three."[22] In fact, more than 25 percent of contracts filed during this time period included provisions that pledged to teach black apprentices to read; 10 percent promised to teach both reading and writing; and 15 percent agreed to provide instruction in reading, writing, and mathematics.[23] While there is no telling how often masters honored these agreements, the prevalence of such passages suggests that most employers did not oppose giving their black apprentices rudimentary instruction and that some like Hamilton and Hutson were willing to provide that and more. After all, under the 1817 provision they had no legal obligation to supply literacy to African American apprentices.

Clauses specifying the period of time a master would make schooling available appeared less frequently in these agreements, however, suggesting that white employers' commitment to their black apprentices' education did not stray much beyond basic literacy. Just over 10 percent of contracts included a specific stipulation for schooling, and time allotments varied greatly.[24] Robert Barney, for example, obtained a comparatively generous commitment from Elisha Barnett in 1829. With his mother's consent, the Orphans' Court apprenticed Barney to Barnett at age five. Barnett agreed to teach Barney to farm and to pay for a year of "regular school."[25] The same year, seventeen-year-old free black Alexander Gibbs accepted a similar provision. His master, John Durham, consented to teach him the art of oak coopering and to provide him with three months of night schooling a year until he turned twenty-one.[26] In comparison with the vast majority of black apprentices, Robert Barney and Alexander Gibbs entered into arrangements with liberal educational provisions.

While Gibbs's and Barnett's masters promised them at least one year of schooling, most black apprentices received assurances for less. A provision for one term of night school that an apprentice could attend after he or she completed work for the day appeared most commonly in agreements filed during this period. In 1827, for example, the Orphans' Court bound sixteen-year-old William Goulding to William Yearly for five years in response to rumors that his father was "living idle and running about." Yearly agreed to teach Goulding the "art or trade of a Cooper" and to give him two quarters' night schooling. Goulding must have been displeased with the situation, however, for less than a year later, Yearly signed Goulding over to another white master, Bristol Brown, along with the authority to apprehend him if he ran away.[27] By the 1820s, it was unusual for slave owners to apprentice their bondsmen and bondswomen—only one did so between 1826 and 1830—but even this single agreement highlighted the connection between apprenticeship and literacy. When Rebecca Everett bound Milly Mills to Henry Trump in 1831, she requested that he have her "taught to read the Holy Scriptures."[28]

While it is impossible to know how many masters entering into such arrangements kept their word, apprenticeship provided at least some black people with vocational instruction they might not have otherwise obtained. In 1828, for instance, Trustees of the Poor bound fifteen-year-old African American Edgar Butler to William Mills to learn the "art and mystery of Biscuit Baking." Assuming Mills honored the agreement, Butler benefited from his term of service. Both "deaf and dumb," it is unlikely he would otherwise have been so trained.[29] In fact, of the ninety black boys apprenticed between 1826 and 1830, over 40 percent entered into agreements that included instruction in a skilled or semiskilled trade.[30]

For African American parents, the opportunity for their children to obtain a trade, one of the primary avenues to economic independence, was a likely incentive for them to enter into such arrangements. Between 1794 and 1830, nearly two-thirds of black boys apprenticed at their parents' behest were promised craft instruction; in comparison, just half of those the Orphans' Court apprenticed received a similar assurance.[31] Such figures suggest that African American parents either specifically sought out masters willing to train their children or pressed for vocational and literacy instruction to be included in apprenticeship contracts. In 1826, free black Archibald Thompson apprenticed his seven-year-old son William to James Goth until May 22, 1840, William's twenty-first birthday. In light of the provisions in this agreement, it is possible that Archibald Thompson, himself illiterate, pushed Goth to provide his son with literacy, or as the contract specified, to teach him to "read, writ[e], and so forth."[32] In 1829, George Jones, Sr., apprenticed his fifteen-year-old son William Jones to David Polk. While father, son, and master were all illiterate—each signed the contract with their mark not their name—Polk consented to teach William "the trade or mystery of a Cordwainer" and to "read and write."[33] On occasion, free black adults apprenticed themselves in exchange for both vocational and literacy training. In 1828, twenty-one-year-old Thomas Elliott bound himself out to David Lomax, an illiterate Baltimore caulker, to learn his trade. Lomax agreed to pay the presently illiterate Elliott six dollars a year and to provide him with three months of night schooling.[34]

In spite of the small number of black people apprenticed in Baltimore during this time, that such a high proportion either requested or were promised literacy and vocational education highlights the value all parties involved placed on such instruction. Employers agreeing to provide apprentices with literacy or vocational training stood to benefit if their workers' skills improved. Often personally familiar with slavery, black parents who apprenticed their children understood just what it meant to surrender one's liberty, particularly to a white person. For mothers and fathers hoping to save their children from a life of exhausting work for a pitiful wage, a trade could be more valuable than property. Should their children wish to leave Baltimore, they could carry that knowledge with them. Should they choose to remain, vocational training could bring independence: the ability to provide for one's family, to fund a friend's freedom, and to educate one's children similarly.

To understand the value of occupational training in this context, consider that a preponderance of African Americans "lived poor" in antebellum Baltimore: a "hand to mouth existence characterized by minimal control over their own labor, periodic spells of material privation, precarious living situations easily jeopardized by external forces, and the high likelihood of needing public welfare or private charity in the aftermath of an illness," according to historian Seth Rockman.[35] Baltimore's volatile economy exacted a heavy toll on those with little savings and job security, often, although not always African Americans. A few statistics help to illustrate the vulnerability endemic to Baltimore's black community. In 1830, for example, African Americans represented nearly 20 percent of the city's almshouse residents but less than 15 percent of Baltimore's total population.[36] Housing conditions made poverty especially pernicious. Black Baltimoreans lived in houses that fronted on alleys on a scale ten times that of whites in the 1830s, spaces notorious for poor light and terrible ventilation. Often overlooked by street scrapers and trash collectors, alleyways were highly vulnerable to outbreaks of typhus, cholera, and other contagions.[37] As was typical of urban areas throughout the antebellum period, the annual number of African American deaths in Baltimore far exceeded their percentage of the city's total population.[38]

It is also worth noting that, as in other urban areas, Baltimore's free black population clustered in jobs that provided the least security, status, and compensation. In 1835 *Matchett's City Directory* recorded the name, address, and occupation of 1,255 workers that it described as "colored." Of the African Americans it listed, nearly one-quarter were included with no occupation at all. Such an omission suggests these individuals accepted what work they could find and labored without steady employment. As carters, draymen, and porters, another 14 percent of black entrants spent their days lifting and carrying loads. Similarly, *Matchett's* described another 20 percent of black entrants as laborers.[39] Unskilled workers in Baltimore often earned no more than a dollar a day, and those days might last between fourteen and sixteen hours.[40] In light of Baltimore's erratic economy, these men could also expect unpredictable and irregular periods without an income. Vocational training in crafts like carpentry, caulking, shoemaking, and blacksmithing could spare a child from a lifetime of digging ditches, scraping streets, or hauling loads. As of 1850, a tradesman such as a carpenter earned $1.40 a day on average.[41]

While African Americans in Baltimore often worked as unskilled laborers and domestics, a sizable minority did perform semiskilled and skilled crafts, a testament to the importance of free black workers to the city's labor market. Seventeen percent of African Americans *Matchett's* listed in 1835, for example, held jobs that required significant vocational training including caulking, brick making, and hairdressing.[42] City directories like *Matchett's* are less useful at documenting the working lives of Baltimore's black women. Because directories did not list those who resided within white homes, it is difficult to obtain a clear picture of the sheer number of black women who "lived in." In 1830, census takers recorded 2,328 free black women residing within white households, nearly a third of the free black women in Baltimore.[43] The numerous notices from white families looking for a "colored woman" to "do the washing, cooking, and ironing" highlight the frequency with which black women were channeled into domestic service and, by extension, into white homes. Such an arrangement commonly meant separation from family and friends and unyielding surveillance from white employers. As with women's work in general during the antebellum period, in any given day a household servant might complete a wide range of duties: emptying chamber pots, tending to children, scouring floors, or preparing meals. Servants' wages were so low in Baltimore they made even day labor seem promising. In 1850, the average *weekly* wage for a domestic in the city was $1.40.[44]

For black women in search of autonomy, taking in laundry was preferable to living in. Washing clothes enabled a woman to set her own schedule, work from home, and be available to care for her children. It was, however, grueling work. First, the laundry had to be picked up from its owner and transported home. Before the washing could begin, a laundress had to procure soap and haul in buckets of water, often from some distance away. She would then place the clothes into boiling water, scrub them against a washboard, wring them out, and hang them to dry. When they were ready, she would iron and fold the clothes and deliver them back to their owner, only to pick up more laundry and begin the process again.[45] In Baltimore, the majority of laundresses were women of color. As of 1835, *Matchett's* recorded seventy-nine black women who worked in this capacity.[46] By 1840, 440 of 526, or more than 80 percent of washerwomen listed in the city directory were African American.[47]

Help-wanted advertisements paint a particularly grim picture of the occupational lives of the city's youngest black workers. As Jonathan Glickstein points out, communities "either through free market processes or through more blatantly coercive means, traditionally relegated their menial and 'dirty' work to their most powerless and desperate elements:

slaves, despised minorities, women and children, the enfeebled."[48] Child labor in Baltimore illustrates that inclination. Employers often advertised for black boys to reset ten pins in saloons and bowling alleys or to work as chimney sweeps, one of the dirtiest, most dangerous jobs any person might perform in an antebellum city.[49] Because early-nineteenth-century flues were typically too small or crooked to clean by brush, a sweep had to physically descend into the chimney and remove the soot by hand. "In order to pass through the smallest openings, a sweep wore no clothing but his underwear and a stocking cap with eye slits to cover his face, however inadequately," write historians Paul Gilje and Howard Rock. Working conditions were so toxic that a sizable number of chimney sweeps became afflicted with scrotal cancer.[50]

As was typical of urban areas in general during the antebellum period, black men, women, and children performed a disproportionate amount of Baltimore's dirty work. However, one aspect of Baltimore's hiring practices did differ dramatically from those of other slaveholding communities. Where many white southerners refused to permit black people to work in professions that exposed them to the printed word, some white employers in Baltimore sought out literate black employees (Figure 5). Unlike Georgia, for instance, which prohibited enslaved and free blacks from working on printing presses, Baltimore's printers often advertised for African American assistance. In 1851, for example, James Lucas, a wealthy "Book and Job" printer, searched for a "Stout Colored Boy to work" in his office. He also requested the assistance of a "roller boy, either white or colored."[51] Given that Betsey Boley, the thirty-seven-year-old black woman he employed in his home, could not read and write, Lucas likely valued literacy in his workers only insofar as it enabled them to perform tasks specific to their position. While some employers preferred to hire whites at a higher wage, with nine children between the ages of twenty-three and two under his care, Lucas no doubt enjoyed the cheap cost of free black labor.[52] Hanzsche and Brothers Book and Job Printing Office similarly advertised for an African American to work as a roller boy.[53] Unlike white employers in other slaveholding cities, Lucas and the owners of Hanzsche and Brothers prioritized profit over presumptive safety.

In addition to publishing, Baltimore's employers hired black people to work in other capacities prohibited in other southern cities. For instance, some whites employed free blacks to sell newspapers. When trader Basil Phillips set out to retrieve his absconded mulatto apprentice, Abraham Bull, he described the boy as a "well known . . . seller of papers"

sale by STICKNEY & NOYES,
Agent for the Manufacturer
F12-tf No. 12 South Cha·t·s·

FOR SALE—A COLORED BOY, 14 years old, to serve till he is twenty-one; is a first rate house servant—would suit a gentleman for a valet de chambre. Apply at the Sun office. F23-1w*

FOR SALE—A COLORED APPRENTICE BOY, 14 years old, to serve till he is 21. He can read, shave, and is an excellent cook. Would prefer disposing of his time to a Quaker. Apply at the office of the Sun. F23-1w*

WANTED TO PURCHASE—A FEMALE HOUSE SERVANT, and a BOY and GIRL, from 10 to 12 years of age—would prefer a woman, and two chil-

need apply. To such constant employment and liberal wages will be given. Apply to STANLEY & McCONKEY, N. E. corner of Light and Lombard streets. se4-3t*

WANTED—A young MAN competent to take charge of a retail Drug Store. References, as to qualification and character, required. Also, a smart, active colored BOY, one that can read would be preferred. Apply to JNO. W. BARRY & Co., apothecaries, corner of Baltimore and Pearl sts. s4-3t*:

WANTED—A GIRL, 10 or 12 years of age. to take care of a child 3 years of age. Inquire at 146 AISQUITH STREET, near Gay. 1t*

gardener, has a perfect knowledge of every thing connected with farming and gardening, and the use of hot beds and forcing frames. His wife is competent and willing to take charge of a dairy. The very best city and country reference given. Please address "GARDENER," Sun office. a20-3t*!

WANTED—Two free COLORED MEN, of genteel appearance and address, of good character, and capable of reading and writing, to act as carriers of Reed's Improved Ethereal Oil. Wanted, also, a WHITE YOUTH, from thirteen to sixteen years old, to assist in our store. Apply at 58½ Sharp street, east side, four doors below Pratt, to a20-9t* READ & CO.

WANTED TO RENT—A two-story BRICK HOUSE, suitable for a small family, in a genteel neighborhood, not over 10 minutes' walk from the

cy Work, can obtain employment, on good terms, by applying at the FRANKLIN WORKS, Gwynn's Falls, or to WETHERED BROTHERS, German street. o23-4t

WANTED—A COLORED MAN, to act as Porter. None need apply unless they can read, write and understand figures, and bring satisfactory references. The highest wages will be given. o22 3t*

WANTED, immediately, five or six BOYS, to learn the Coach Lace and Fringe Weaving business. Apply to JNO. GADE, No. 29 North Gay

FIGURE 5. FOR SALE—A COLORED APPRENTICE BOY, *Baltimore Sun*, February 24, 1838; WANTED, *Baltimore Sun*, April 3, 1850; WANTED, *Baltimore Sun*, August 20, 1852; WANTED, *Baltimore Sun*, October 24, 1839. Courtesy of the American Antiquarian Society.

in the market.[54] Another notice in the *Sun* sought "an intelligent Colored Man . . . to obtain subscriptions to *Illustrated Works*," a local periodical.[55] Some whites hired free blacks as bill posters. *Matchett's* 1835 directory listed two men, John Pridgeon and Abram Williams, employed in that capacity.[56]

Not only did white Baltimoreans not exclude African Americans from occupations that exposed them to the printed word, some made the ability to read or write a prerequisite for their employment. Employers of black porters, in particular, appeared especially eager to hire literate workers. One wished to find a "smart active colored BOY" who "must understand how to read" to work in his "Wholesale House."[57] The owners of Constable and Fisher's advertised for "a smart, active COLORED BOY, to act as Porter," adding, "[o]ne that can read preferred."[58] When a shopkeeper on Pratt Street advertised for a colored boy to work as a porter in his bookstore, he noted that "To read and write is indispensable."[59] Another like-minded bookstore owner advertised simply for "a smart intelligent COLORED BOY, about 16 or 18 years old."[60]

It is not difficult to understand why a bookshop owner might want his workers to read, but Baltimore employers also advertised for educated free blacks in situations in which the need for literacy was less obvious. One grocery store owner advertised for a "smart, intelligent COLORED BOY, about 14 years old, who can read and bring satisfactory recommendations as to character."[61] Another storeowner sought a "smart active COLORED BOY [to] take care of a horse, and do the draying." He stated that "one who can read will be preferred."[62] Similarly, an additional employer took out a notice for a boy, "White or Colored," to drive an express wagon, and again, the only requirement for the position was that the applicant must be able to read.[63] Another boss was a bit more particular in his search for someone to "take charge of a public building." He preferred the applicant be "yellow" and "produce testimony as to his honesty, fidelity and sobriety." In addition, he "must be able to read."[64]

Some employers looked for black workers who could write as well as read. The owner of John W. Barry Apothecaries advertised for a "smart, active colored Boy" to work in his store and preferred one who could read and write.[65] Another hoped to secure several "free COLORED MEN" of "genteel appearance and address" who were "capable of reading and writing" to deliver his "IMPROVED ETHEREAL OIL" throughout the city.[66] Occasionally, employers also demanded numeracy from their black employees. One individual looking to hire an African American porter noted that "the highest wages will be given." But "None need apply unless they can read, write and understand figures."[67]

The notices that masters placed in an effort to hire out their bondsmen similarly attest to the economic value white employers and slaveholders attached to African American literacy. Some masters, for example, included brief descriptions of enslaved blacks' literary abilities in their advertisements. One slave owner sought a seven-year placement for his "COLORED APPRENTICE BOY" who was to be freed at age twenty-one. "He can read, shave, and is an excellent cook," he noted.[68] When looking for work as a "Waiter or Porter," one "COLORED MAN" also boasted about his "tolerable good education."[69] Another white person sought to find work for his "slave for life," whom he described as "an intelligent, active and honest colored man" who would make an "excellent servant or driver." He anticipated he "would also be very serviceable in a store, as he reads well and writes a little."[70] In these instances, slave owners attempted to profit from enslaved blacks' literacy by using that ability to elevate the purchase price. Such advertisements suggest that literacy was a valuable commodity in Baltimore's labor market, particularly when whites stood to reap the rewards.

To appreciate the significance of these notices, consider the divergent experience of another enslaved black man, Henry Bibb, when he was auctioned off in Kentucky. Bibb recalled purchasers frequently inquired about his literacy. But in contrast to Baltimore employers looking to hire an African American man who could read and write, Bibb's abilities prevented his sale. As he observed, "the most rigorous examination of slaves by those slave inspectors, is on mental capacity. If they are found to be very intelligent, this is pronounced the most objectionable of all other qualities connected with the life of a slave."[71] No doubt Bibb's experience was the norm in many slaveholding areas. The majority of slave owners did not publicize bondsmen's literary skills. Nonetheless, these help-wanted and for-hire advertisements suggest that several white employers in Baltimore were willing to pay a premium for literate black workers.

As one auction store owner made plain, he was looking for "the smartest colored boy that can be found."[72] Unlike their counterparts in other parts of the urban South, Baltimore's white entrepreneurs and shopkeepers did not eschew literate black employees. They recruited them. Their decision to publicize such labor needs also suggests they did not fear their customers would object to encountering literate African American employees in stores and on job sites. Despite the prevalence of these notices, however, white Baltimoreans' educational imagination had its limits. White employers sought educated African Americans to perform unskilled labor; they did not advertise for literate blacks to perform skilled trades. In addition, not a single advertisement solicited a literate black woman. It seems that while white employers valued literacy for free black men, for free black women mired in the ranks of servants and domestics, whites generally considered such a skill unnecessary.

Like apprenticeship contracts and help-wanted advertisements, census records tell a similar story of how the racial structure of Baltimore's labor market helped to assuage white concerns about black literacy. Slavery provided white people in the city with specific economic and legal advantages at the same time it undermined African Americans' ability to capitalize on their literacy. First, as mentioned, despite white Baltimoreans' willingness to hire literate black workers, African Americans remained almost universally excluded from "mental" professions that generally conveyed higher status and paid better wages than physical labor. Second, although African Americans were able to find work in the skilled trades, which offered superior job security and salaries relative to unskilled occupations, they were almost universally excluded from a central avenue to citizenship and upward mobility: property ownership. While no formal legal statute precluded black people from holding real estate, as slavery lingered on in Baltimore and its surrounds, few African Americans either inherited property or amassed estates to pass down to their children. Baltimore, in fact, had the lowest rate of free black property ownership of any city in the nation.[73] Finally, for black Baltimoreans, in contrast to whites, literacy also did not correlate with the category of work a person performed. This observation suggests that literacy conveyed a greater occupational advantage to white workers than it did to African Americans. In other words, while the ability to read and write might have made it easier for a black man to *find* a job in Baltimore, it did not change African Americans' overall place in the labor market. Ultimately, slavery and the racist structures to which it gave rise ensured that even when free blacks could take advantage of their educational opportunity, they continued to experience profound challenges to their legal standing and economic stability.

Like apprenticeship agreements and help-wanted advertisements, census schedules provide a wealth of information about the relationship among race, labor, and educational opportunity in the mid-nineteenth century. As they had in previous decades, census takers compiled numerous details about Baltimore and its demography in 1850. For the first time, however, they also inquired about literacy and school attendance. Marshals asked householders to share critical details about their family's educational experiences and abilities. Who in the home had attended school at one point in the year? Which residents twenty years of age and older could not read and write? They then recorded answers to these questions into log books, otherwise known as schedules, which became the raw data for the comprehensive tabulations presented in the census. Because census schedules detailed literacy and school attendance for individuals and households, these documents make it possible to identity which factors— age, occupation, and gender, for example—correlated most with educational opportunity. There are, however, limits to what these documents can reveal. First, while census takers asked individuals to identify illiterate people in the household, they did not define that term precisely. Second, respondents were responsible for assessing their own literacy and for sharing that appraisal with a census taker.[74]

As of 1850, twenty wards radiating out from Baltimore's inner harbor constituted the city (Figure 6). African Americans resided in every ward, although their numbers and proportions varied dramatically.[75] Ward 17, the southernmost district and the focus of this analysis, contained the city's largest absolute number (2,400) and concentration (24.4 percent) of African Americans.[76] Sandwiched between the middle and northwest branches of the Patapsco River, its northern edge skirted the city center and then curved around the outer harbor's southern shore.[77] From there, the ward jutted south to form a prominent peninsula. Because it contained such a large black population, Ward 17 should not be considered representative of Baltimore in its entirety. At the same time, because of the sheer number of African Americans who resided in the area, the district allows for a detailed examination of a large concentration of black households; in fact, African Americans headed nearly one-quarter of all families in the ward.

As of 1850, Ward 17 contained 1,684 households: 1,287 were headed by whites and 397 by African Americans.[78] This demography highlights the extent to which free labor had supplanted slavery by 1850. Just a fraction (2.3 percent) of white households included an enslaved laborer, and of those that did, holdings were small. Thirteen of the ward's slaveholding families owned one slave, while the largest slave owner in the district held five: two females and three males, who ranged in age from eight to twenty-three. In total, just forty-five enslaved blacks resided in Ward 17.[79] With a total population approaching 10,000 (9,774), the majority of its residents

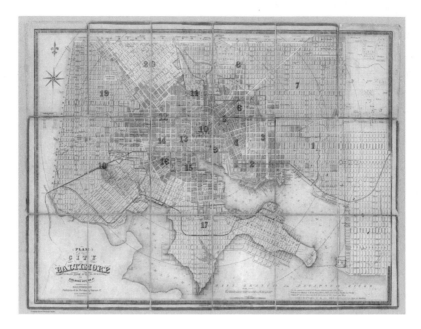

FIGURE 6. Lucas Fielding, Jr. "Plan of the City of Baltimore Compiled from Actual Survey,"
1852. Courtesy of the David Rumsey Map Collection, www.davidrumsey.com.

hailed from Maryland (7,112), but the district also contained a sizable
German population (1,441) and a noticeable number of Irish (399).

Census schedules from Ward 17 provide a portrait of the racial structure of Baltimore's labor market similar to that which *Matchett's City Directory* had detailed fifteen years before (Appendix 1). While few black
people worked in mental professions, a significant number labored in
skilled crafts, even as Baltimore's immigrant population climbed (Table
1). With a reputation for hard work and thrift, Germans typically avoided
the most grueling forms of unskilled labor, becoming craftsmen or shopkeepers instead. In Ward 17, for example, twenty Germans worked as bakers, twenty-four as butchers, and thirteen as grocers. The Irish competed
more directly with African Americans, particularly for jobs on the lowest rungs of the occupational ladder. Irish men predominated in unskilled
positions, while Irish women often toiled as domestics. Census takers
described eighty-eight of Ward 17's Irish residents simply as "laborers."[80]
But even after decades of steady foreign immigration, African Americans
retained a foothold in skilled trades, highlighting the extent to which the
city continued to rely on black labor. In Ward 17 alone, some 200 free

TABLE 1 **Occupation and Color of Household Heads in Baltimore Ward 17, 1850**

	Black, % (n = 365)	Mulatto, % (n = 32)	White, % (n= 1,287)
Nonmanual	1.4	0	9.5
Skilled	42.4	25	46.2
Unskilled/semiskilled	39.7	37.5	30
Service	2.5	12.5	0.002
None	0	0	1.2
Soldier	0	0	0.003
Blank	14.0	25	12.67

Source: Census Schedules, Baltimore, 1850.

blacks molded bricks. African Americans also worked as rope makers, comb makers, blacksmiths, barbers, bakers, carpenters, hatters, shoemakers, wheelwrights, and tanners, although in smaller numbers.[81]

But while many black men in Ward 17 labored in skilled crafts, just a few supported themselves with nonmanual labor, as lawyers, clerks, and merchants for example. Mental professions like these typically necessitated more advanced literary education and connoted higher status than skilled or unskilled physical labor. In Ward 17, just more than 1 percent of black household heads worked in a nonmanual occupation: thirty-two-year-old teacher Benjamin Brown; forty-year-old trader Bassel Owings; and fifty-six-year-old sexton Edward Travers. To put those numbers into context, consider that nearly 10 percent of whites labored in that capacity. All twenty-five clerks in Ward 17 were white, as were the ward's four physicians. Ward 17's division of labor illustrates how ideologies of race, class, and gender informed occupational opportunity in the antebellum period. Nationwide, African Americans repeatedly observed that whites called attention to black people's absence from mental occupations to assert their own intellectual superiority. Recall that proponents of New Haven's proposed African college rallied around the institution precisely because of its potential to create a black professional class whose existence would undermine white justifications for denying higher education to African Americans.

But just as skin color did not prevent Ward 17's free blacks from working in skilled trades, it also did not shield whites from performing physically demanding, poorly compensated, and irregular labor. Forty percent of blacks and 30 percent of whites in the district swept streets, dug ditches, or toiled in other kinds of unskilled occupations. Thirty-year-old African American George Hooper shuttled bricks and stones throughout the city as a hod carrier, as did eight of his black neighbors, none of whom could read and write according to census takers. Henry Briver, a thirty-six-year-old German immigrant, dug graves, an equally exhausting and likely even more depressing way to earn a living. Service occupations, however, did remain highly segregated. Just two whites in the ward, fifty-four-year-old Luke Luman and twenty-eight-year-old Joseph Hart, worked as waiters, an occupation typically performed by black men—twenty-five of whom labored in that capacity in Ward 17.[82]

At the same time, however, while African Americans penetrated the skilled professions, they were almost universally excluded from property ownership, a key means of economic mobility and a signature of citizenship in the antebellum period. Ward 17, in fact, included just one African American property holder: Garriston Cromwell, a thirty-one-year-old waiter, whose estate was valued at $600, the eleventh highest in the district.[83] In contrast, Charles Cornish, a thirty-eight-year-old ship carpenter, William Williams, a forty-two-year-old blacksmith, and Thomas Watts, a thirty-nine-year-old rope maker did not own real estate, despite the fact that they performed skilled occupations.

African Americans' almost universal exclusion from property ownership provides yet another illustration of how slavery's existence and its legacy undercut free blacks' economic independence. Instead of accumulating wealth, many free blacks used their spare funds to procure freedom for others. As few black people earned sufficient wages to pay for a loved one individually, African Americans often considered these purchases a communal responsibility. To this effect, black churches and benevolent societies sponsored an array of fundraising activities. In 1841, for example, the Old Town Baptist Church ran a weeklong fair and sold a "variety of useful and fancy articles" to help bondswoman Mary Heath "purchase her freedom."[84] Two weeks later, Heath's fair was still in operation, now running out of the house of Perry Reeds, a free black man who lived on Elbow Lane.[85] In fact, as of 1850, just 0.4 percent of all free blacks in Baltimore—101 of 25,442—owned property. To put that percentage into context, 6.56 percent of their counterparts in New Orleans and 1.37 percent in Charleston held real estate, according to census records. Black women in Baltimore were even less likely to be homeowners. Census takers noted that just ten out of more than 14,000 free black females in the city owned property in 1850.[86]

Thus despite elite whites' willingness to hire literate black workers, whites of all classes retained significant economic advantages over African

Americans. Consider the extent to which skilled white laborers were able to amass property in comparison with their black coworkers. For Ward 17's white residents, real estate holdings and occupation did, in fact, correlate closely. Whites who performed nonmanual labor owned far more real estate on average ($155.40) than those who worked with their hands. Grocer William H. Abey, for example, owned $6,000 of real estate, while furniture dealer Casper A. Weaver possessed $3,000 worth of real property. Similarly, skilled white workers also owned more property on average ($76.79) than their semi- and unskilled counterparts, although holdings varied considerably. Thirty-two-year-old machinist Charles Reeder owned $30,000 of real estate, making him the ward's largest property holder. More typical of skilled workers in the ward, shoemaker John Dickey held $2,000 of property, while baker John G. Frank's estate was assessed at $1,500. In contrast, whites who worked in unskilled or semiskilled vocations owned holdings of just $10.44 on average. As with African Americans, the preponderance of Ward 17's unskilled white workers owned no real estate whatsoever.

Just as white householders were vastly more likely to own property than free blacks, they were also far more likely to be able to read and write, suggesting a persistent connection between race and returns from educational opportunity in the city (Table 2).[87] While 16 percent of whites in Ward 17 twenty years of age and older described themselves as illiterate, 73 percent of African Americans made a similar claim. Most importantly for this analysis, occupation and literacy correlated for white people in ways that that they did not for African Americans. Not surprisingly, whites who performed nonmanual labor were the most likely to be literate. Just 6.5 percent of this subgroup informed the census taker that they could not read and write. By extension, 13.5 percent of skilled white workers described themselves as illiterate. Unskilled and semiskilled white workers taken together, however, possessed a higher illiteracy rate: 32 percent, nearly twice that of skilled white workers alone.

In contrast, among African Americans the ability to read and write had no connection to whether a person performed skilled or semi-/unskilled labor. In fact, of those who worked with their hands, skilled and semi-/unskilled black workers had exactly the same illiteracy rate: 75 percent. This observation is not meant to imply that literacy did not make it easier for a person of color to secure work. After all, as help-wanted advertisements illustrate, several employers sought out black workers who could read and write. But remember, employers advertising for literate black

TABLE 2 **Illiteracy Rates of Household Heads by Occupation in Baltimore Ward 17, 1850**

	Black, % (n)	Mulatto, % (n)	White, % (n)
Nonmanual	20 (5)	—	6.5 (122)
Skilled	74.8 (155)	62.5 (8)	13.5 (595)
Unskilled/semiskilled	74.8 (145)	58.3 (12)	31.6 (386)
Service	55.6 (9)	75 (4)	0 (2)
None	—	—	0.7 (15)
Soldier	—	—	0 (4)
Blank	76.5 (51)	87.5 (8)	26.4 (163)
Total	52.7 (365)	68.8 (32)	19.7 (1,287)

Note: A dash (—) indicates categories for which *n* = 0.
Source: Census Schedules, Baltimore, 1850.

employees were seeking porters, drayers, and carriage drivers; they were not targeting literate African Americans to perform skilled labor.

Among African Americans, gender also correlated with illiteracy in ways that it did not for whites (Table 3). White men and white women had exactly the same illiteracy rate: 17 percent. In contrast, black women were more likely to be illiterate (76 percent) than black men (70 percent). Moreover, for those individuals whom the census taker described as "mulatto," gender correlated with skin color more tightly, suggesting that lighter skin, or the status it conveyed, entailed more access to literacy for men than for women. Seventy-three percent of women identified as mulatto affirmed they could not read and write, in contrast to 54 percent of their male counterparts. These findings are in line with anecdotal evidence in help-wanted advertisements. Recall that no employer sought a literate black woman, and one employer in search of a literate African American man to care for a public building specifically requested the applicant have light skin.

At the same time, white tolerance for black literacy was predicated on the existence of other forms of racial control, many of which were a direct outgrowth of slavery. Because free blacks often held jobs with irregular or nighttime hours, curfew laws made it even more difficult to earn a living wage and represented another reminder of how blurry the boundary between slavery and freedom could be in Baltimore. In 1827, the city's mayor Jacob Small ordered the night watch to arrest African Americans out past eleven o'clock at night who could not provide a pass from a white person.[88] Three years later, Small was still complaining about the "hords [*sic*] of colored persons . . . swarming" in the city. In response, he ordered watchmen to deliver free blacks home one hour earlier, at ten o'clock instead.[89] Like

TABLE 3 **Illiteracy Rate, Color, and Gender in Baltimore Ward 17, 1850**

	Female, %	Male, %	Total, %
Black	75.8	70.7	73.3
Mulatto	73.2	53.8	66.0
White	16.9	16.9	16.9
Native born	19.3	17.0	18.2
Foreign born	13.1	13.3	13.2

Source: Census Schedules, Baltimore, 1850.

many others hoping to avoid poverty, David Roberts worked two jobs, one as a porter during the day and another as an oyster opener at night. After completing his second shift, he was frequently "molested by the watch" on his way home.[90] Perry Boadley's job at the Assembly Trading Rooms kept him occupied between "ten and two o'clock some nights." In hopes of holding on to this position, Boadley petitioned the mayor to exempt him from the curfew. But in order to secure this leeway, Boadley needed a white person to vouch for him.[91] This requirement fostered an informal system of patronage, binding blacks to whites and serving as another form of racial control. Even for those with no desire to travel during late-night hours, the very existence of a curfew signaled the precarious nature of freedom in a slaveholding city. One free black man described the constant stress these statutes inflicted: "A colored man might live in Baltimore fifty years without actually experiencing any of the many disabilities under which we labor. On the other hand," he observed, "he is never safe, he is liable to false imprisonment at any moment."[92]

Not only did curfews circumscribe free blacks' economic independence, they also impinged upon African Americans' social lives. Free blacks who wished to entertain guests after ten o'clock were expected to petition the city for permission. Before Abraham Williams could host a ball for "a select number of coloured ladies and gentlemen" that would continue past midnight, he had to submit references attesting to his "high character for order and respectability."[93] Hoping to hold a similar affair, Daniel Kobourn had to ask two white men, William Solomon and John Stansbury, to testify to his "orderly behavior."[94] Impositions like these led Kobourn to conclude that even pigs had more freedom than free blacks in Baltimore. While "hogs" were permitted to "run about" Kobourn complained, "colored people" could be "taken up at any time."[95]

In addition to curfew laws, other measures enacted to protect slaveholders' interests circumscribed free black liberty in Baltimore. As in most slaveholding states, enslaved and free black people in Maryland could not possess firearms or gunpowder without permission, nor could they purchase munitions or alcohol. The state legislature also prohibited enslaved and free African Americans from attending religious meetings led by black preachers. And although it exempted free blacks in Baltimore and Annapolis from this provision, it ordered them to end their activities by ten o'clock at night. In 1842, the Maryland legislature forbade black people from meeting in "secret societies."[96] White Baltimoreans did release free blacks from some of these statewide restrictions, however, particularly when it was in their interest to do so. Preferring to avoid providing black people with poor relief, the city allowed African Americans to form benevolent associations, but they were still required to have a white police officer at every meeting. Similarly, Baltimore did not outlaw blacks' literary gatherings, provided that attendants respected curfew laws. In 1849, for example, Sharp Street Church publicized a lecture series where for fifty cents one could hear five different talks including G. C. M. Roberts' discussion of "Scripture and Astronomy by the use of the Magic Lantern."[97] In 1853, black Baltimoreans sponsored a Colored Literary Festival.[98]

Such exemptions should not be read as evidence that white Baltimoreans were any less hostile toward free black workers than their counterparts in other northern and southern cities. To the contrary, as early as 1812, in response to rumors of African Americans making pro-British remarks, whites attacked two free black men and demolished the house of another.[99] As the nineteenth century advanced, working-class whites repeatedly and often violently attempted to expel free blacks from job sites.[100] In 1836, while working on William Gardiner's shipyard, Frederick Douglass received a beating from white mechanics so severe that "for a time [it] seemed to have burst [his] eye-ball." His attackers charged that black workers like Douglass were "eating the bread which should be eaten by American freemen."[101] In Douglass's estimation, white employers wittingly stoked feelings of insecurity and competition to prevent white and black laborers from banding together to demand better wages and working conditions.

Not only did working-class whites express hostility toward those black people who worked alongside them, they also denounced those who labored independently. In 1827, a contingent of white men lobbied the state to stop giving African Americans licenses to operate carts and drays. In an effort to undercut free blacks' financial independence, whites sought to cast these self-employed, independent black workers as disorderly, dishonorable, and disobedient, or "more easily influenced by temptations to steal, less influenced by the desire of maintaining an honest reputation, and have[ing] far less fear of the operations of the law, than the white people."[102] In 1831, Maryland's General Assembly forbade whites from buying certain agricultural staples from African American hucksters who lacked written authorization. Sixteen years later in 1847, white Baltimoreans requested the state to ban blacks from selling straw or hay.[103] The irony inherent in these efforts was likely not lost on some African Americans, who understood that by undermining their self-sufficiency, these proposed regulations threatened to transform them into the very dependent, impoverished, and propertyless people petitioners had accused them of being.

After 1850, as Baltimore's economy withstood frequent booms and busts, white laborers' hostility toward their black coworkers spiked. A handful of white employers followed the lead of D. Dorsey, who fired all his black employees from the Exchange Hotel in 1850 and replaced them with "industrious, sober, and intelligent white men."[104] Job site tensions only worsened in the wake of the panic of 1857. In May 1858, seventy-seven whites requested an ordinance to "Prohibit the Colored Population from Renting and Licensing Stalls in the different parts of the city."[105] The same month, some thirty white men tried to drive African American workers from Tomas and Donnely's brickyard. At the end of the day, one black man was shot dead, and several others fled the premises. Racial antipathy intensified the following year at a Fell's Point shipyard, when white workers attacked free blacks who refused to abandon their jobs.[106] In 1860, whites lobbied to prohibit African Americans from working in any mechanical trade whatsoever.[107]

But when one examines the results of the above efforts, it becomes clear that although white working people chafed at free blacks as occupational competition, white elites prized the freedom to hire from a large labor pool far more than racial segregation.[108] Of the petitions described above, only one was ever realized. The 1827 memorial, for example, which sought to prevent black people from laboring as carters and draymen, never succeeded. Moreover, immediately after the memorial was submitted, one hundred whites counterpetitioned against the proposal, recasting carters and drayers as "persons of color of the most decent, orderly, and respectable character."[109] Only the 1832 request to curtail African Americans' ability to sell certain agricultural products was ever enacted, and that legislation came at the behest of rural whites hoping to eradicate their competition. Furthermore, while this measure checked free blacks' right to vend on their own behalf, it did not limit their ability to labor for whites. Antebellum white Baltimoreans ultimately excluded African Americans from just a handful of professions whose pitfalls were obvious: ship captain, government representative, and policeman.[110] As one visitor to the city observed, "It is said that the free blacks in Maryland are not by law excluded from any trade or employment which may be practised by the whites, except from the vending of spirituous liquors, and from the command of vessels; and both of these restraints have a reference to the slaves, lest they should be allured to intemperate habits, or should be secretly conveyed to distant ports."[111]

Baltimore's enthusiasm for free black labor was little secret outside the seaport. Several legislative conflicts between urban and rural whites arose specifically from this reliance. Baltimore employers, for example, often rejected state efforts to deport free blacks or to restrict the kind of work they might perform. In 1842, whites in the city opposed a proposal to tighten Maryland's manumission policy, fearing the new guidelines would increase labor costs.[112] In 1859, urban whites again found themselves at odds with rural planters hoping to pass legislation to make it easier to remove free blacks from the state. In their opposition, white Baltimoreans contended the proposal "would deduct nearly fifty per cent from the household and agricultural labor furnished by people of this color . . . [and] would produce great discomfort and inconvenience to the great body of households."[113]

In sum, the particular structure of Baltimore's labor market, reliant upon free black workers kept in check by slavery, inadvertently created an atmosphere conducive to African American literacy. The sheer size of Baltimore's free black community made its vocational and literary ability a matter of white self-interest. And even when working-class whites objected to working alongside African Americans, they lacked sufficient social or economic power to alter the arrangement. In contrast to New Haven—dependent on white workers and without slavery to limit free blacks' advancement—Baltimore relied on free blacks' labor and maintained an array of regulations, appendages from slavery, to check their socioeconomic mobility.

African American Educational Activism under the Shadow of Slavery

Sometime in the late 1820s, Frederick Douglass's master, Hugh Auld, uttered a few phrases that would come to epitomize white opposition to black education in the antebellum South. Upon discovering that his wife Sophia had been instructing the young Douglass to read and to spell, he forbade her to continue: "It was unlawful, as well as unsafe, to teach a slave to read." A literate bondsman, he prophesized, "would at once become unmanageable, and of no value to his master." As for Douglass, "it could do him no good, but a great deal of harm. It would make him discontented and unhappy."[1] Reading, Auld appreciated, promised spiritual, intellectual, and political empowerment. Writing offered Douglass the means both to escape slavery and to challenge the ideology that perpetuated it.

Auld likely did not appreciate, however, that his admonition would push Douglass to continue his studies. "In learning to read, I owe almost as much to the bitter opposition of my master, as to the kindly aid of my mistress," Douglass recalled. "That which to him was a great evil, to be carefully shunned, was to me a great good, to be diligently sought; and the argument which he so warmly urged, against my learning to read, only served to inspire me with a desire and determination to learn."[2] After Sophia discontinued their lessons, Douglass exploited every means available to become literate. He fished "scattered pages of the Bible" out of "filthy street-gutters."[3] He befriended white boys, trading bread for lessons. He lingered in Baltimore's shipyards, tracing carpenters' letters in his own hand.[4] After years of "tedious effort" he mastered the art of reading and writing. And just as Hugh Auld predicted, that knowledge intensified his determination to escape. Literacy, Douglass affirmed famously, pointed him on "the direct pathway from slavery to freedom."[5]

While Douglass documented the many obstacles impeding his access to literacy, he also revealed the many educational opportunities available to Baltimore's free black community. Free African Americans and the institutions they sustained made it possible for Douglass to advance in his studies. He attended religious services at Bethel African Methodist Church, one of five black churches in the city, slipping into a "Sabbath school amongst the free children" to receive "lessons with the rest."[6] He acquainted himself with free black caulkers able to "read, write, and cipher" and willing to instruct him. They encouraged him to join their East Baltimore Mental Improvement Society, a space for Douglass to sharpen his oratory skills.[7] Despite his own difficulties, Douglass equated Baltimore with educational opportunity. Upon opening a "little Sabbath school" for black children in St. Michael's, Maryland, he remarked that if he "could not go to Baltimore" he could "make a little Baltimore" there.[8]

Baltimore's white children also enjoyed greater access to schooling than boys and girls who came of age in other southern communities. While individual southerners lobbied for public education in the antebellum period, in comparison with New Englanders, southern whites generally showed less interest in common schools and were more hostile to interference from state legislators and northern reformers.[9] Baltimore, in contrast, sustained more than eighty public schools by 1860 that enrolled some 12,000 students collectively.[10] But unlike their counterparts in Boston, New Haven, and other northern cities, white Baltimoreans excluded black children from common schools and refused to fund separate black schools, all the while taxing African Americans for public education.[11]

Sustaining black schools in Baltimore posed particular challenges to black parents, educators, and activists. Because the majority of African American adults in the city could neither read nor write, many black parents looked to educators to assume this responsibility. But few could afford to pay tuition *and* forgo their children's contributions to the household. Yet even in the face of difficult choices, many families provided all of their children with at least some time in the classroom.[12]

Slavery's existence also compelled African American teachers, who often held positions of prominence within Baltimore's free community, to choose between competing priorities. Many worried that agitating for emancipation would stoke white fears that they were encouraging their students to resist similarly. In consequence, some black educators eschewed abolitionist agitation in a preemptory attempt to protect their schools from white violence. That decision, however, did not come without a cost. In so doing, others charged, they cast aside their enslaved brethren to the South and their free compatriots to the North and aligned themselves with Baltimore's white majority.

To dismantle the injustice inherent in Baltimore's tax code and to secure the economic well-being of their own institutions, African Americans also petitioned the city three times between 1839 and 1850. That they could protest publicly attests to both their relative educational opportunity and to the shrewd manner in which they used a language of deference to lodge radical appeals. Baltimore's black parents, teachers, and activists understood that for all their educational freedom, they lived within a society that sanctioned chattel slavery. With protest and with compromise, they made Baltimore one of the few slaveholding communities in which black schools survived.

* * *

To appreciate free black Baltimoreans' success at self-education, it is useful to glance briefly at African Americans' educational opportunities in other slaveholding cities. Laws outlawing slave literacy, like the one Hugh Auld had once invoked with Sophia, existed in a handful of southern colonies beginning in the mid–eighteenth century.[13] But in the aftermath of David Walker's *Appeal* (1829), which linked literacy with resistance, white southerners began to police African American education more aggressively. In the decade to follow, Louisiana, Georgia, North Carolina, South Carolina, and Virginia each passed legislation to limit black literacy. Georgia prohibited African Americans, enslaved and free, from working on printing presses and levied fines of $500, whipping, or prison on those who taught enslaved people to read.[14] In Louisiana, individuals like Sophia Auld who tutored slaves in reading or writing could be imprisoned for a year.[15] North Carolina forbade giving written material to enslaved blacks; free blacks found guilty of this offense might be lashed thirty-nine times.[16] Those who followed in the tradition of David Walker, writing or distributing literature to "excite insurrection, conspiracy, or resistance in the slaves or free Negroes," could be whipped or jailed. If convicted a second time,

they faced "death without benefit of clergy."[17] Likewise, Virginia prohibited free and enslaved blacks from assembling for instruction in reading
and writing in an act slated to go into effect in June 1831, just two months
before Nat Turner's rebellion.[18]

After the Southampton massacre, southern white opposition to black
education climbed. Virginia banned free and enslaved African Americans
from attending religious services led by black preachers—no doubt a
nod to Nat—and required bondsmen and bondswomen to obtain written
permission from their master to attend a religious meeting after sunset. In
1838, free blacks who left the state for instruction were prohibited from
returning.[19] A decade later, in 1848, Virginia earned the dubious distinction of being one of just two states to criminalize the schooling of both
enslaved and free African Americans. Five years later in 1853, Norfolk
prosecuted and convicted a white woman, Margaret Douglass, for operating a school for free blacks; in so doing, Norfolk became the first community in the nation to imprison a teacher for the crime of teaching.[20]

Baltimore's tolerance of black schooling was exceptional even in
Maryland. Contrary to Hugh Auld's assertion, Maryland never legislated against African American education, enslaved or free. But not all
whites, particularly those residing outside Baltimore, agreed with this
decision. When Douglass left Baltimore for St. Michael's, Maryland, the
dramatic contrast in white attitudes toward African American education
struck him immediately. In Baltimore, Douglass had attended a Sabbath
school alongside free black children. On the eastern shore, he was neither "allowed to teach or to be taught. . . . The whole community among
the whites, with but one single exception, frowned upon everything like
imparting instruction, either to slaves or to free colored persons," Douglass recalled. Determined to provide black children in St. Michael's with
an education akin to that which he had received in Baltimore, he agreed
to teach a "little Sabbath-school" out of the home of a free black man,
James Mitchell. With little more than a "dozen old spelling-books and a
few Testaments," Douglass instructed some twenty students. One week
after their first meeting, however, whites attacked the class with "sticks"
and "missiles." "[S]urely enough," Douglass recalled, "we had scarcely
got to work—*good work,* simply teaching a few colored children how to
read the gospel of the Son of God—when in rushed a mob," and with it,
Douglass's school met its demise.[21]

While whites in St. Michael's managed to break up this institution,
their efforts only made Douglass more determined to share literacy with

other African Americans. With the long light of summer to aid him, Douglass found "some twenty or thirty young men" eager to attend a Sabbath school he operated "under the shade of an old oak tree." Equipped with a desire to learn and the cast-off books of their "young masters or mistresses," Douglass's students understood the need to keep their activities "as private as possible." Yet despite their discretion, the school would not stay secret for long. Once again, white men descended "ferociously" upon Douglass and his students, "armed with mob-like missiles" and forbade them from meeting "on pain of having our backs subjected to the bloody lash." Should slaves become literate, Douglass's attackers informed him, they might be inspired to oppose the system that bound them. After whites in St. Michael's shut down his Sabbath school a second time, Douglass persuaded another free black man to open his home to a clandestine classroom. Despite the threats, more than forty students came, many of whom "succeeded in learning to read" with Douglass's help.[22]

Perhaps the most infamous episode of white Marylanders' opposition to African American education involved Samuel Green, a former Dorchester County bondsman and Methodist preacher. In 1857, a court sentenced Green to a ten-year jail term after he was caught with a copy of Harriet Beecher Stowe's antislavery novel, *Uncle Tom's Cabin.* According to Green's persecutors, he had violated an 1841 law prohibiting possession of "incendiary" or "abolitionist" texts. Green served five years, until the middle of the Civil War, when Maryland's governor pardoned him provided he leave the state and never return.[23] In 1858, thirty-two Frederick County residents petitioned the state legislature to ban free African Americans from operating schools.[24] Two years later, legislators considered a bill that provided that "no person shall keep a school or other place of resort for negroes, under a penalty of not over $100."[25] While Maryland's legislature honored neither request, these petitions attest to white uneasiness with black schooling, particularly in the countryside.

None of this is to suggest, however, that Baltimore was an educational haven for African Americans. A quick comparison of literacy rates in Baltimore, Boston, and New Haven supports this contention. As of 1850, in New Haven County and Suffolk County, which contained the cities of New Haven and Boston, respectively, around 15 percent of African Americans aged twenty and older reported to the census marshal that they could not read. In contrast, nearly 60 percent of Baltimore County's free blacks aged twenty and older described themselves as illiterate.[26] No doubt, free black Baltimoreans guarded their literacy more closely than their northern counterparts, and such statistics by themselves do not chart educational opportunity exactly, but they do suggest that African Americans in communities that provided public schooling to black children generally had better access to education on the whole. Still, for free black children growing up in a region that often legislated against their literacy, they could not do much better, educationally speaking, than Baltimore. As Douglass affirmed, the slaveholding seaport was "the very place of all others, short of a free State" where he "most desired to live."[27]

White children in Baltimore also had superior access to schooling than boys and girls in other southern communities. In the eighteenth- and early-nineteenth-century South, class had generally determined educational opportunity. Private tutors instructed the children of white elites, while the middling classes sent their children to subscription schools and academies. If they attended school, children of more modest means typically enrolled in charity schools for elementary instruction, often subsidized with public funds.[28] But in 1825, inspired by the success of Philadelphia, New York, and Boston, white Baltimoreans petitioned Maryland's legislature to fund a common school system. As one Baltimorean remembered when reflecting on the city's decision to create common schools, "the true idea of education by the State was the making of good citizens."[29] Akin to northern proponents of public education, petitioners anticipated that these institutions would provide children with common values and a collective experience at a cost far less than that of private academies. They also predicted that common schools would soften divisions between rich and poor by teaching the "youth of the higher as well as the lower classes" to "fear God and love one another."[30] In so doing, public education could foster social equality and socioeconomic mobility simultaneously.[31]

Maryland's General Assembly responded to this appeal with an "Act for the Establishment and Support of the Public Schools in the City of Baltimore" that proposed to create a system of tax-supported schools supervised by elected commissioners.[32] Opponents of the measure, usually older and wealthier than its supporters, labeled the scheme "monstrous" and "alarming" and denounced being taxed for a service from which they received no benefit.[33] "Is it right," queried an editorialist dubbing himself an old bachelor to take furniture from poor widows to pay for the education of other people's children?[34] Given that the old bachelor supported other institutions he did not patronize personally—alms houses and canals, for example—his comments expose a particular discomfort with a central premise of the common school movement, specifically, the idea that schools existed to benefit the individual *and* the community. His hostility also exemplifies historian Robin Einhorn's more general observation that slaveholding areas like Baltimore were less willing to tax private property to fund the public good than free communities.[35] In light of the hostility it engendered, the bill lost by a narrow margin. But despite this setback, the General Assembly passed a measure the following year that empowered Baltimore to create schools and to assess property holders for their services. While a series of intracity squabbles stalled implementation for another three years, in 1829 Baltimore opened two boys' schools and one girls' school, enrolling 235 and thirty-four pupils, respectively.[36]

Black children's exclusion from Baltimore's common schools must have been a foregone conclusion, for neither white petitioners nor state legislators raised the issue of race during their discussions. That they did not consider creating separate schools for black children attests to how slavery worked to exclude all people of color, enslaved and free, from the body politic in the white imagination. In this respect, public education in Baltimore differed dramatically from Boston and New Haven, which both sustained separate schools for African Americans. School attendance rates illustrate the long-term consequences of this distinction. While 79 percent of black children in Suffolk County, which included Boston, reported attending school in 1850, just 22 percent of their counterparts in Baltimore County made the same assertion.[37]

Baltimore's earliest public primary schools emphasized reading, writing, and arithmetic, while some pupils also learned history, geography, and grammar. At Jones' Falls Boys School, teacher Randolph Fossmall used the monitorial system made popular by Joseph Lancaster. This arrangement relied on older children to supervise the learning of younger students and appeared particularly well suited to crowded or poorly funded schools.[38] In 1829, Fossmall reported that of his 123 pupils, sixty studied grammar and arithmetic, twenty-four could "write on paper, read and spell, . . . 16 [could] write occasionally on slates read and spell . . . 13 [could] spell in two or more syllables," and ten were "in the alphabet and beginning to spell."[39] Harriet Randolph conducted similar lessons at the girls' school.[40] At the "Public School West of Jones' Falls," however, William Coffin furnished "explanations to the whole school at once," a method he dubbed "simultaneous instruction." Like Fossmall, Coffin asked older children to look in on younger students, but he opposed requiring them "to teach what they themselves do not understand."[41] This pedagogical style eventually became the preferred teaching method in Baltimore's public schools.[42]

Despite initial resistance, demand for public schooling quickly exceeded the space available, forcing teachers to turn away students eager
to attend. Coffin reported that more than one hundred "unsuccessful ap-
plications had been made" to his school in just the first three months after
it had opened.[43] As this statement suggests, even after Baltimore sponsored
primary schools, many white children did not have access to education, for
just as the city's common schools were not really common, they were also
not truly public, at least not in the contemporary conception of the term.
While taxes helped to offset tuition, students still paid a small sum, typically
one dollar per quarter. Many children could neither afford the modest fee
nor the lost wages necessary to study. As one editorialist observed, while
"it is true that we have our public schools . . . their advantages do not reach
all classes."[44] In 1837, petitioners even failed to persuade the city council
to exempt orphans from tuition. In rejecting this request, council members
asserted that "Any act to reduce the price or make it a Gratuity to any class
of citizens would have a tendency to lessen Said Schools in the Estimation
of the Publick."[45] Whether or not their prediction would have proved true,
their logic underscores the fact that for Baltimore's black *and* white children, the right to an education was neither guaranteed nor universal.[46]

While public schools served white children from Baltimore's middling
classes, black Baltimoreans received the majority of their literary education in religious institutions. Fortunately for black students, Baltimore's
network of black churches was among the strongest in the nation. As the
nexus of social and spiritual life in the city, these institutions supplied the
clergy, who doubled as teachers, the space for assembly and the social networks to raise funds for students who could not afford tuition. If possible,
most utilized tuition and rent from their pay schools to offset the costs of
free Sabbath instruction. While white Sunday schools drifted away from
teaching basic literacy after 1830 as public schools assumed that responsibility, black Sabbath schools continued to teach children to read and
write throughout the antebellum period.[47] By 1838, the *Baltimore Literary
and Religious Magazine* reported that "Hundreds of colored youth, and
some of advanced years" were receiving "Sabbath school instruction . . .
and a respectable number of persons have devoted their attention on the
Sabbath day, to instruct the coloured population."[48] At the time of this
observation, Baltimore housed at least nine black Sunday schools, whose
curriculum did not differ much from that of the city's primary schools.[49]

Most black churches in Baltimore provided congregants with religious
and literary instruction from the time of their founding. As early as 1802,

Sharp Street Methodist Church defined its mission, in part, to provide "for the education of black children of every persuasion."[50] Sharp Street's first instructor, Daniel Coker, supervised a day school and offered free Sabbath classes. Born around 1780, purportedly to an enslaved African father and an indentured white mother, Coker spent his childhood in slavery on Maryland's eastern shore. His earliest education came from his master's son, whom he accompanied to school. Sometime before his twentieth birthday, Coker fled Maryland for New York City, where he continued his studies. In 1802, Bishop Francis Asbury ordained Coker as a deacon in the Methodist Episcopal Church. Upon his return to Maryland, Coker led classes at Sharp Street for African American adults and children. While he emphasized religion, he also taught English, French, mathematics, philosophy, and history. When a contingent of black Methodists joined with Richard Allen in 1816 and split from Sharp Street to open an independent congregation, Coker transferred his school to the new institution, Bethel. By 1820, he instructed more than 150 students, some of whom had traveled from as far away as Washington, D.C., to attend.[51]

After Coker left for Bethel, another black educator, William Lively, relocated his private school to the classroom in Sharp Street. His institution, Union Seminary, offered lessons in "Ancient and modern History, Geometry, Composition, Natural Philosophy [and] also, the Latin, French & Greek Languages."[52] In contrast to white classrooms, boys and girls studied side by side, as was customary in many black schools in the region.[53] Although Union Seminary charged tuition, the rent Lively paid Sharp Street helped it to finance free instruction. As of 1835, its Sunday school enrolled more than four hundred students, enslaved and free, although only a quarter attended regularly. Pupils read from the Bible, the *Methodist Union Sunday School Hymn Book*, and *John Comley's Speller*. Lively also donated four hours a week to lead "gratuitous" classes for black women.[54]

Sharp Street experienced challenges similar to any school serving a predominately poor population. Throughout its history, for example, it struggled to maintain a suitable space for students to study. In 1835, one visitor described its school as "clean" and "well-fitted up" but lamented the "two swine . . . dozing" underneath its steps and the "narrow and dirty lane" he had to pass through to enter.[55] Conditions only deteriorated in the years to come. While the church launched renovation campaigns in 1846 and 1852, in July 1854, a fire broke out in its classroom that displaced students for some time.[56] As Sharp Street's history suggests, black teachers could ill afford to be choosy about their meeting places. In fact, because Sharp Street owned its own building, the church had it better than most. Pupils at the Old Town Colored Presbyterian Church, in contrast, assembled in the second story of a rented warehouse.[57] "Their room, which is a small one, is entirely full," one observer noted in 1835, "and they are now greatly in want of more extended accommodations." One can only imagine what classes were like there during the heat of a Baltimore summer.[58]

In 1828, for reasons that are unclear, another black instructor, John Thompson, lost his schoolhouse altogether. While someone donated a parcel of property to him on which he could build a new school, Thompson, a bootblack by trade, lacked the funds to finance construction. Appealing to the community for assistance, he invoked the rhetoric of common school reformers, who equated education with a prepared and principled citizenry. "Every thinking person knows how important it is to have an educated and virtuous population," he affirmed. This salesmanship must have succeeded, for one year later the *Genius of Universal Emancipation* reported that "some spirited philanthropists, in this city, have recently established an African Free School, in which are taught, every Sabbath, from 150 to 170 scholars."[59] Thompson's contemporary, Jacob C. Greener, similarly advertised for donations to sustain his "African Orphaline School," which provided "indigent colored children" of "both sexes" the "rudiments of a common English education," most likely instruction in reading and writing. In 1828, the *Baltimore Patriot and Mercantile Advertiser* informed its readers that Greener had "exhausted his individual resources." It prayed "the benevolent citizens of Baltimore" would assist him.[60]

While many black teachers offered lessons in a range of literary, historical, and scientific subjects, publicly they stressed their efforts to prepare their students to become excellent employees. Like Thompson and Greener, schoolmaster Mary F. Hollon also doubled as teacher and fundraiser. In 1841, she advertised a fair for her charity school in the *Baltimore Sun*, hoping to reach a broad audience of potential donors. With just a few lines at her disposal, Hollon succinctly described her "chief" objectives: to instruct "children of color, in those branches necessary to enable them to fill properly the different situations in which they may afterwards be employed" and to teach "the principles of virtue and religion, which alone can preserve [students] from the dangers of vice." "Should she meet with encouragement from the benevolent," Hollon predicted, "many a poor, destitute child, and friendless orphan, will thus be enabled to receive that moral and Christian education, without which they cannot be good and useful members of society."[61] Here Hollon took care to point out her desire to instill students with virtues that would appeal to whites seeking deferential workers and to black parents aspiring to raise independent sons and daughters.

Black women's educational activities in Baltimore extended beyond fundraising. The most extensive example of their contributions was St. Frances Academy for Colored Girls, the boarding school advertised so prominently in the *Baltimore Advertiser* in 1831. The school opened in 1828, a collaboration between James Hector Nicholas Joubert de la Muraille, a white Sulpician priest and immigrant from San Domingo, and an order of black Catholic women known as the Oblate Sisters of Providence. Led by Marie Magdelaine Balas and Elizabeth Lange, St. Frances Academy enrolled predominately middle-class pupils, but it did admit some children who could not pay tuition. In a similarly inclusive spirit, while the school had a Catholic affiliation, it served students from several denominations. Pupils studied English, French, and cyphering and received vocational instruction to prepare them to secure positions as nurses and domestics.[62]

While St. Frances Academy enrolled women exclusively, in the 1850s, it also established a male academy on the same property. By 1854, more than fifty boys attended this institution annually.[63] Three years later, in 1857, the Oblates moved to open a fourth school, but progress stalled after some whites destroyed their school door, reportedly "leaving a place large enough for a person to enter."[64] Because the Catholic school was located in a neighborhood known for its hostility to Irish immigrants and the attack occurred in the midst of election riots, they probably targeted the school for its racial and religious affiliations. Despite the delay, the new academy opened without incident the following year. By 1858, the Oblates operated four schools for African Americans in Baltimore: St. Frances' boys' and girls' schools, St. Joseph's, and now St. Benedict's, which instructed boys and girls together.[65]

Like Mary Hollon and the Oblate Sisters of Providence, African American women also coordinated the majority of fundraisers for black schools in Baltimore. To amass money for textbooks, teacher salaries, and room renovations, black women sponsored parties, fairs, and teas, typically held around Christmas, Easter, and other holidays.[66] In 1838, Mary Wells, Lydia Bowser, Mary Ridgly, Hester Hughes, and Mary Ann Chubs collaborated to raise money for the Colored People's Public School. As their advertisement pronounced, "The managers have spared neither pains nor expense to make this Fair comfortable, brilliant, and interesting, to all who may favor it with their presence."[67] Their fair ran from ten in the morning until nine at night during the week between Christmas and New Year's Eve. In addition to charging a modest admission, the women also sold items "tastefully prepared by a number of colored children."[68]

The frequency of these festivities suggests they provided a steady source of funding for African Americans' religious and literary instruction. In 1846, black women affiliated with Sharp Street Church held a Christmas fair for two weeks to raise money to renovate their schoolroom.[69] This festivity seems to have become an annual tradition, for in 1852, "the Ladies of Sharp Street church" again advertised a holiday "SALE OF USEFUL AND FANCY ARTICLES"—no doubt many of which they also made— to raise money to repair their classroom.[70] While it is difficult to ascertain precisely how much money these events brought in, in 1842 the women of Strawberry Alley Methodist Church reported that after expenses, their fair had raised $147.43.[71] In 1859, women affiliated with St. James' Protestant Episcopal Church reported their Easter fair had amassed $344.43.[72]

While African Americans patronized these events with enthusiasm, organizers also sought out white attendants. In 1838, the "Colored Young Ladies" of the "Methodist Protestant Church of Color" sponsored a Christmas fair to which they charged twelve and one-half cents admission. In their notice they remarked that "white ladies and gentlemen are respectfully invited to attend."[73] The publicity surrounding these events provides even more evidence of the care African Americans took to construct an image of their educational activities that would be palatable to their white neighbors. In all likelihood, these women would not have spent scarce resources on advertisements that triggered animosity. In 1850, such festivities even received an endorsement from the Democratic *Baltimore Sun*. Editors publicized two black school fairs, one located in the Sharp Street schoolroom and the other at St. James.[74]

Like Sharp Street, St. James' Protestant Episcopal Church also relied on public donations to sustain its educational activities. By the late 1820s, its minister William Levington instructed seventy students, free and enslaved, and held public exhibitions to celebrate their progress. At one such gathering, pupils performed "moral and religious pieces" they had authored after the death of two female classmates. Levington also presented fifteen silver medals to honor his "most studious pupils." To raise money for his school, he charged twelve and one-half cents to attend exhibitions.[75] He also boarded students in his home and offered private lessons. One pupil agreed to travel from Albany to study with Levington and to pay him $100 annually for that instruction. But in 1831, when Maryland forbade people of color from outside the state to remain longer than ten days, such an arrangement became impossible. Levington lost many students and could no longer personally supplement St. James' school. To make matters worse, the church had also amassed a sizable debt, which Levington feared might force it to close down.[76]

In 1833, determined to save his church and school, Levington left Baltimore for "the middle and Eastern States" in search of assistance.[77] Armed with a letter of introduction from white Protestant ministers attesting to his "prudent, pious" character and "respectable intelligence," Levington secured audiences with congregations in cities including Albany, New York, Boston, and New Haven. Reminiscent of John Brown Russwurm's "tour to the Eastward" to raise funds for *Freedom's Journal* and Alexander Crummell, Henry Highland Garnet, and Thomas Sidney's journey to Canaan, New Hampshire, northern segregation made Levington's journey even more draining. At Christ Church in Boston, he looked up from his lecture to see African Americans looking back at him from separate seats "in the galleries."[78] And just as Russwurm had experienced six years before on his voyage to New Haven, Levington was also refused permission to go below deck while traveling from New York to Albany. According to one of his associates, Levington "had to pass the whole night on deck, with nothing to lie upon but the bare boards," despite the "extremely cold" weather.[79] Ironically, some white residents of Connecticut welcomed the black teacher from Baltimore warmly, despite the hostility to African American education erupting in their own community. The *Connecticut Courant* reported being "favorably impressed" with Levington and his objective: "to sustain [the] Church and School under his care."[80] He preached at the North Church without incident.

Sixth months after his departure, Levington returned to Baltimore with $600, enough to clear half the debt of St. James. While he raised $35 at Christ Church in Boston, congregants at St. Philips' African Episcopal Church in New York donated $65.[81] Two years later, Levington's school enrolled approximately eighty pupils who each paid from $1.50 to $1.75 per quarter. Upon his death in 1837 from "a short and painful sickness," another African American instructor, H. H. Webb, assumed responsibility for St. James.[82]

Like Baltimore's black educators, African American parents also sacrificed to school their children. Because of the precarious financial state

TABLE 4 **Children's School Attendance in Baltimore Ward 17, 1850**

Attended School	Black, % (n = 740)	Mulatto, % (n = 56)	White, % (n = 2320)
Total	16.9	21.4	42.7
Male	17.0	32	45.3
Female	16.8	12.9	40.1

Source: Census Schedules, Baltimore, 1850.
Note: The children included are age 4–16.

of many black households in Baltimore, children's labor, both inside and outside of the home, could make the difference between poverty and stability. To school their sons and daughters, parents not only needed to cover tuition, they also had to compensate for their children's contributions in terms of wages and household labor. Because public schools excluded African American children, it is not surprising that white children's school attendance rates surpassed those of African Americans, an assertion that held true across gender lines (Table 4). Yet when one looks at the individual choices parents made for their sons and daughters, African Americans' commitment to providing their children with some schooling is evident.

To explore the educational choices parents made for their children, a close analysis of Ward 17 is again instructive. Recall that beginning in 1850, census takers asked householders who in their family had attended school during the year. As with the information that can be obtained about literacy, there are limits to the conclusions about school attendance one can draw from census records alone. First, as with literacy, many African American parents may have been reluctant to report their children's schooling to a white official. Second, census takers asked only if a child had attended school at least once during the year. They did not ask about the kind of institution—religious or literary, for example—the child had attended, nor did they inquire about the length of time he or she had spent in school. Census marshals, in other words, did not distinguish between those boys and girls who attended school on occasion and those who attended regularly, nor did the surveys speak to the content or level of education children received inside the classroom. With these limitations in mind, however, census records do reveal some fundamental details about school attendance.

First and foremost, attendance rates highlight the consequences of Baltimore's decision to deny public education to black children. Of the 2,329 school-aged boys and girls (ages four through sixteen) who lived in Ward 17, 43 percent of white children attended school, in contrast to 17 percent of their African American counterparts (Table 4). However, when one looks at the percentage of parents who sent at least one child to school, black Baltimoreans' commitment to schooling their children privately is apparent (Table 5). Of the 309 black households with one or more school-aged children in Ward 17, 26.5 percent sent at least one child to school, a higher proportion than individual attendance rates imply. Household school attendance rates further suggest that black parents who schooled their children made some compromises to achieve that objective. Some, for example, opted to school just one child at a time, while others limited the length of time their sons and daughters spent in the classroom.

So which children in Ward 17 were most likely to attend school? As with literacy, for boys more than for girls, lighter skin correlated with educational opportunity to some degree. Thirty-two percent of boys whom census takers referred to as "mulatto" attended school, in contrast to 17 percent of their "black" counterparts. For African American girls, however, light skin and school attendance showed little to no connection. Seventeen percent of "black" girls attended school as did 13 percent of those labeled "mulatto." However, if one pushes the data just a bit further, it becomes clear that while gender in and of itself did not correlate with black parents' decision to school their children, it did make a difference in the number of years a child might spend in the classroom. Specifically, African American boys attended school earlier and left later than their female counterparts (Figure 7). Among African American children, not a single girl enrolled before her sixth birthday. In contrast, some four- and five-year-old boys attended school at one point in the year. Rates of school attendance for African American boys and girls remained even from ages six through nine. But after age ten, boys' school attendance began to outpace girls'. While 40 percent of eleven-year-old African American boys attended school, for example, just 18 percent of girls had that opportunity. At age thirteen, girls' school attendance (27.8 percent) surpassed boys by a modest percentage (21.42 percent), but from that point on, what had once been an education gap was now a chasm. Although 30 percent of fifteen-year-old African American boys attended school at age fifteen, just 8 percent of girls had an equivalent experience. On the whole, these figures suggest that while black parents sought some schooling for all of their children, they faced difficult choices. In general, they gave their sons longer and thus probably more advanced instruction than their daughters.

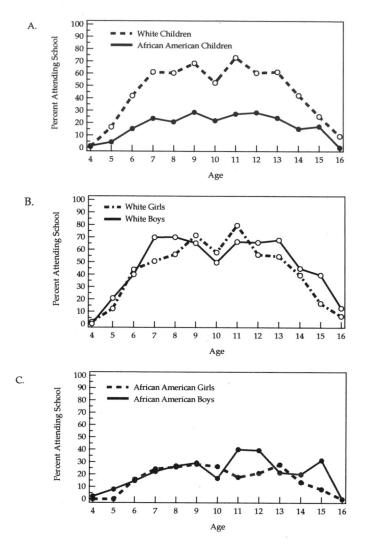

FIGURE 7. Children's school attendance by race, gender, and age in Baltimore Ward 17, 1850. (A) Percentages of white or African American children attending school, ages four to sixteen. (B) Percentages of white boys or girls attending school, ages four to sixteen. (C) Percentages of African American boys or girls attending school, ages four to sixteen. Source: Census Schedules, Baltimore, 1850.

Parental occupation also appeared to make some difference in children's school attendance rates. Not surprisingly, children from families in which the household head performed nonmanual labor were more likely to spend time in school than children from families whose household head performed physical labor, a distinction that held constant across racial lines. Given that literacy sustained these families financially, it is not surprising they would put a premium on schooling. On the other hand, whether a household head performed skilled or unskilled labor did not appear to correlate with children's school attendance (Table 5). In fact, a slightly larger percentage of semi- and unskilled black household heads (33.3 percent) sent at least one of their children to school compared with those who performed skilled manual labor (23.2 percent). It is conceivable that black parents with a trade to pass on to their sons felt somewhat less compelled to school their children than those who could not pass on any form of economic security, yet in light of the limits to what this data can reveal, it is impossible to know their motivations for certain. Such an explanation also does not account for why household heads with a skilled trade would have opted not to school their daughters.

A more useful, while by no means complete, means of assessing which black Baltimoreans decided to school their children is to peer inside those families who educated all of their children. Of Ward 17's black households with more than one school-aged child, just nine families (13.64 percent) sent all of their children to school. Among these families, it is possible to point to some commonalities, but in light of the small sample size it is

TABLE 5 **Race and Occupation of Household Heads and Children's School Attendance in Baltimore Ward 17, 1850**

	Percentage of Household Heads that Schooled Their Children	
	Black	White
Nonmanual	83.3	71.9
Skilled	23.2	58.7
Unskilled/semiskilled	33.3	42.6
Service	20	100
None	—	54.5
Soldier	—	33.3
Blank	24.5	44.3

Source: Census Schedules, Baltimore, 1850.

difficult to make definitive conclusions. In seven of the nine families, two parents resided in the household, which makes sense given that children with one parent inevitably assumed greater responsibility to provide income and care for their siblings. Thirty-eight-year-old Charles Cornish—the ward's only single black father to school all his children—worked as a ship carpenter, a skilled profession that likely provided a comfortable living for him and his three children, ten-year-old John; twelve-year-old Julia; and eight-year-old Margaret.[83] On the other hand, Sarah Chrison, a thirty-five-year-old single mother who could neither read nor write herself, also reported sending all of her children to school: Henry, Margaret, and Sarah, aged eleven, nine, and seven, respectively. As Chrison's eldest daughter, twenty-year-old Mary, resided with the family, the child care and domestic labor she contributed possibly helped to give her siblings the time necessary to study.[84]

The only characteristic common among black parents who schooled all their children is that with the exception of thirty-four-year-old porter Benjamin Smith and sixty-year-old brick maker Thomas Boon, none of these mothers and fathers could read and write themselves.[85] It is conceivable that their own illiteracy influenced their decision to send their children outside the home for instruction, as they did not possess the skills to teach their sons and daughters independently. In general, however, literate parents were more likely to school at least one of their children than parents who could not read and write, a trend that held constant across racial lines (Table 6). Sophia and Thomas Boon, for example, had five children between the ages of six and twenty-three living in their home. While Thomas could read, Sophia could not. Thomas had clearly made an effort to pass down his trade to his three eldest sons, Richard, Jacob, and John Henry, who all worked as brick makers in 1850. Their two daughters, Rebecca

TABLE 6 **Race and Literacy of Household Heads Who Schooled Their Children in Baltimore Ward 17, 1850**

	African American, %	White, %
Percent of household heads with school-age children who sent at least one child to school	26.5	40.2
Percent of literate household heads who sent at least one child to school	31.4	41.3
Percent of illiterate household heads who sent at least one child to school	24.7	36.2

Source: Census Schedules, Baltimore, 1850.

and Mary F., aged fifteen and six, respectively, attended school. Given that the three oldest boys remained within the home, it is possible that their contributions helped Sophia and Thomas to educate their daughters. At fifteen, Rebecca Boon would likely have been one of the oldest, if not the oldest, girl in school.[86]

For Sophia and Thomas Boon, as for many black Baltimoreans, schooling often represented the only inheritance they could bequeath to their sons and daughters. African Americans' school attendance rates suggest that many black parents did what they could to provide their children with at least some time in school. Some chose not to school all their children simultaneously, and more opted to school their sons than their daughters. These were unsavory choices, but with literacy a crime less than one hundred miles away, free black Baltimoreans' success at self-education was no small achievement. Unfortunately, while census records reveal whether or not a family schooled its children, they are silent about the hopes that parents held for their sons and daughters after they left the classroom. Given the extent to which black Baltimoreans were excluded from mental professions, few parents likely expected their children to make a living from their literacy.

When reflecting upon the meaning that free black Baltimoreans attached to schooling, Frederick Douglass's conception of education as a means of liberation is again instructive. Given the many ways that slavery worked to withhold freedom from all African Americans, the power of schooling to undermine racial oppression must have been seductive. But while Baltimore's black community commonly joined together to school its children, black teachers split over whether to prioritize resistance to slavery or access to instruction. As educators, they understood the importance of schooling for children's individual intellectual, spiritual, and economic development, but as leaders of a black community living beneath the shadow of slavery, they appreciated that sustaining white tolerance for their educational activities did not come without sacrifice. Prioritizing education above other forms of activism, teacher William Levington took great pains to reassure whites that he did not seek to use schooling to alter the city's racial order. Schoolmaster William Watkins, in contrast, considered Levington's logic foolish if not fanciful. Without resistance, he argued, slavery and racism—the very circumstances that had circumscribed African Americans' educational opportunity in the first place—would continue indefinitely. In 1835, tension over precisely this question erupted between Watkins and three other black teachers in the city: William

Levington, John Fortie, and Nathaniel Peck, who ministered to congregations at St. James, Sharp Street, and Bethel, respectively.

Sometime in the summer of 1835 for reasons that are unclear, Levington, Fortie, and Peck delivered a signed letter to a white newspaper distancing themselves and other free black Baltimoreans from abolitionism. In this correspondence, they denounced "any views or movements which tend to disturb the peace, to alienate the feelings, to provoke the jealousies, or to jeopardize the safety of the citizens of the said community" and condemned those "commotions that have taken place in different parts of the country." In so doing, they affirmed their desire to act "as good and conscientious citizens."[87] Although their decision to invoke citizenship in such a fashion might appear radical, in actuality, the identity they described was more akin to a good subject than a good citizen, for while they stressed their efforts to execute the responsibilities of citizenship, they demanded none of its privileges.[88]

The conception of citizenship they articulated emphasized loyalty and deference. "Whatever may be the excitement in the community in which we live, or elsewhere," they affirmed, "we deem it our paramount but humble duty, to pledge our fidelity." As evidence of such "good citizenship," Levington, Peck, and Fortie pointed to four spaces in which African Americans had displayed upright behavior: the workplace, the church, the benevolent society, and the schoolhouse. In their day and Sabbath schools, black teachers like themselves had encouraged students to "keep the good order and appreciate the peace of the community in which they live as good citizens." "We, and our brethren," they asserted, "have always been a docile people, and have endeavored to conduct ourselves in a peaceable and orderly manner, . . . carefully and scrupulously avoiding all interference, and attempts to interfere with the peculiar interest, concerns and laws of the community in which we live." They closed their letter by asking rhetorically, "Can the thinking, wise and humane part of the white citizens of this great community be led to believe that we or our brethren . . . be so perfidious as to become the abettors or destroyers of the public order and tranquility in any way whatsoever?"[89] Such comments suggest that Levington, Fortie, and Peck believed that because they lived inside the peculiar institution they lacked the freedom to fight for abolition.

Their preemptory declaration appalled William Watkins, who operated one of the largest black schools in the city. Born to free black parents, Watkins had attended Daniel Coker's school at Sharp Street. In 1820, at the age of nineteen, he assumed responsibility for Coker's classes when his former teacher departed to Sierra Leone. For two dollars per quarter, his school offered lessons in reading, writing, arithmetic, history, philosophy, and music.[90] With help from his son William J. Watkins and his niece, the poet Francis Ellen Watkins Harper, William Watkins' Academy enrolled approximately fifty black boys and girls annually and remained open for more than two decades.[91] As of 1850, his other sons, Richard, George, John, and Henry, worked as teachers in Baltimore, while his remaining three children, fourteen-year-old Henrietta, nine-year-old-Robert, and five-year-old Lloyd, attended school.[92]

In addition to supervising his academy, Watkins worked as an agent for the *Liberator* and authored several editorials in other periodicals including *Freedom's Journal*. Under the pseudonym "A Colored Baltimorean," Watkins repeatedly attacked the American Colonization Society and its underlying ideology of removal, rejecting its claims about black intelligence as confused and contradictory. In 1828, he rhetorically asked readers in *Freedom's Journal*, "If we are found in Africa, 'capable of everything praise worthy,' does not this prove that the barrier to our moral elevation here is not of our own creating?"[93] Three years later, he informed subscribers to the *Liberator* that he and other black people in Baltimore would "rather die in Maryland under the pressure of unrighteous and cruel laws than be driven, like cattle, to the pestilential clime of Liberia."[94] African Americans, Watkins insisted, should demand nothing less than the immediate death of slavery.

Upon reading Levington, Fortie, and Peck's disavowal of abolition in 1835, Watkins penned an angry letter to William Lloyd Garrison, railing against their decision to acquiesce and the callow language of their appeal:

> In their eagerness to figure before the public, these brethren (who according to their repeated avowals intended to "pursue a middle course") have overshot the mark. They have told the public that neither themselves nor those whom they assume to represent will "be so perfidious as to become the *abettors* or destroyers of the public order and tranquility in any way whatsoever." Verily, then, they are bad citizens!

In his comments to Garrison, Watkins turned Levington, Fortie, and Peck's definition of good citizenship on its head by asserting that resistance and not deference defined the good citizen. He feared, however, that other members of Baltimore's black community did not share this opinion. On the outside of the envelope, Watkins informed Garrison that because of his comments, "I am threatened with a coat of tar and feathers."[95]

Historical hindsight allows for the conclusion that Levington, Fortie, and Peck's decision to distance free black Baltimoreans from the abolition movement may have paid off, for Baltimore's black schools did escape the mob violence that erupted in most northern cities during the 1830s. But as Watkins noted correctly, African Americans could not acquiesce indefinitely, for without protest, emancipation would continue to elude them. In reality, despite the animosity the dispute triggered, Watkins and Levington were less far apart than they seemed. Recall that just two years earlier, Levington had embarked on a one-man pilgrimage to save St. James. It is hard to consider someone who undertook such a journey as docile or compliant. Rather, his actions, more than his words, suggest he understood education itself as a powerful act of resistance, and on this point, he and Watkins concurred.

One year later, Watkins addressed the Moral Reform Society in Philadelphia:

> I most firmly believe that a good education is the great *sine qua non* as it regards the elevation of our people. Give them this and they cease to grovel;—give them this and they emerge from their degradation, though crushed beneath a mountain weight of prejudice;—give them this and they will command respect and consideration from all who respect themselves and whose good opinions are worth having;—give them this and they acquire a moral power that will enable them to storm and batter down that great citadel of pride and prejudice—that great Babel of oppression that impiously lifts itself to the clouds, vainly hoping to thwart the designs of Him who is thundering in the heavens.[96]

Had Levington been in the audience, he would probably have agreed.

While tensions over agitation and acquiescence divided some free blacks in Baltimore, most African Americans eschewed either extreme. Instead, as in their fundraising advertisements, black educational activists more often utilized the language of deference to launch radical appeals. As historian Linda Kerber notes in her discussion of white women's political participation in the early nineteenth century, "Deference represent[ed] not the negation of citizenship, but an approach to full participation in the civic culture."[97] Black Baltimoreans' educational activism can be understood similarly.

Perhaps the best example of how black Baltimoreans used the language of deference to make radical appeals occurred in their protest against the school tax. Free blacks petitioned the city in opposition to the city's decision to tax them for public education on three occasions prior to 1850. As was typical of petitions authored during this period, black Baltimoreans' appeals underscored their own subordinate status and the superior standing of those they addressed. As a form of political protest, petitioning was ideally suited to individuals like themselves, looking to exercise their voice and to affirm their citizenship in the face of exclusion from suffrage and other forms of civic expression.[98] At the same time, however, in requesting to be released from the school tax specifically, petitioners also displayed their willingness to abstain from two activities that personified good citizenship: paying taxes and attending public schools.[99] In that respect, their appeals also acknowledged, at least tacitly, the signers' appreciation for how slavery's existence precluded them, and all other black people in Baltimore, from securing citizenship. In so doing, they exposed a willingness to prioritize education above demanding full and equal civic privileges.

As many African Americans petitioning against the school tax were probably aware, the decision to assess them in such a way was not the regional norm. When the nominally slave state of Delaware created its public education system in 1831, it both denied black people access to the classroom and exempted them from the school tax.[100] Along similar lines, Maryland's Kent, Montgomery, and Anne Arundel counties also opted to not tax blacks for institutions that excluded them.[101] As in 1847, black Baltimoreans paid taxes on more than $150,000 of property to sustain schools for white children.[102] By 1860, African American property holders in the city paid nearly $500 a year to support these institutions.[103]

In 1838, after city council members failed to pass a proposal to release people of color from the school tax, black Baltimoreans filed their first appeal. In February of that year, the council had debated an ordinance to exempt the property of persons of color from the payment of the public school tax.[104] In April, the first branch of the city council approved the measure, but the second did not.[105] In the aftermath of this defeat, James Corner and fifty-five other free black Baltimoreans appealed to the city council to reconsider. They reassured council members that they had no intention of expanding the parameters of their educational activism. Specifically, they were not, nor would they ever be, seeking to integrate the city's common schools. As they explained, "The Coloured people are not at all interested in the public schools directly or indirectly." They sought only to be released from this "unjust" burden.[106]

Upon receipt of their request, the city council directed the Committee on Ways and Means to study the issue. But after just one week's consideration, it rejected the proposal as "inexpedient."[107] Despite swift defeat, that free blacks were able to agitate so publicly in Baltimore, especially during the tumultuous 1830s, attests both to their educational freedom and to the style of rhetoric they utilized in their appeal. They explicitly highlighted the moderation of their request and included assurances of their limited objectives. And while the measure failed, it did not appear to trigger white reprisals. In fact, coverage of the petition and subsequent city council deliberations ran openly in local papers. And even with such publicity, their actions did not attract much attention, violent or otherwise, within the white community.

Five years later, in 1844, some forty black Baltimoreans petitioned the city for similar relief. This time, however, instead of requesting to be released from the school tax, they asked for a share of its proceeds, a radical request given that slavery still existed in the city.[108] After "considerable expense," they informed the city council, they had "succeeded in establishing two schools in different sections of the city for the benefit of coloured children." But as students' financial circumstances prevented them from "paying a high rate of tuition," they observed that "the small amount thus received is barely sufficient with the strictest economy to meet the current expenses of the schools." Because they could no longer continue to support both public and separate institutions, they "humbly" requested "that so much of the nett [sic] proceeds of the School Tax as may become due or be collected hereafter from coloured property holders be appropriated to the use of the two aforementioned schools."[109]

Of twenty-three identifiable petitioners who endorsed this appeal, some commonalities appear. All were men; fourteen could read and write; and most worked in the skilled trades, as carpenters, butchers, shoemakers, and brick makers, for example. A smaller number performed unskilled work as laborers or draymen, and just two signers, Lee Levin, a Methodist preacher, and John Fortie, a teacher, worked in nonmanual occupations. Recall that nine years earlier Fortie had joined with Peck and Levington to denounce abolition and to affirm black Baltimoreans' orderly behavior. Not surprisingly, several signers owned property and, as such, paid the school tax personally. As of 1850, at least seven petitioners held real estate, which ranged in value from $700 to $40,000. Samuel Hiner, the wealthiest individual to sign the appeal, worked as a butcher, although it is unclear how he amassed such a large estate. Born in Maryland in 1791, he could read and write, although his wife Frances could not. The remaining property-owning petitioners held estates valued at around $1,000. All were married, five of the seven were literate, and with one exception, all had at least one school-age child at the time they signed the appeal.[110]

Black Baltimoreans were not the first African Americans to make such a request. Fifteen years earlier, free blacks in Hartford, Connecticut, had successfully undertaken a similar campaign. In 1830, African Americans including Joseph Cook, Aaron Jacobs, Thomas Sheen, John Blackston, and Primus Babcock petitioned the Connecticut legislature to allocate African Americans' contributions to the school fund specifically to black institutions. Like Baltimore petitioners a decade later, Cook and his associates pointed legislators to the inherent injustice of requiring African Americans to support both public and private schools. "Unable to bear the burden . . . any longer" Connecticut's black petitioners prayed the "the Hon. Legislature [would] grant said colored children, such proportion of the school fund money as is just and reasonable to be appropriated for their education." It seems that the legislature assented, for by 1833 the city of Hartford supported at least one school for "colored children."[111]

A decade later, a sympathetic member of Baltimore's city council, Representative Farquharson, drafted an ordinance to release African Americans in that city from the school tax as well. As it had five years before, the city council referred the request to the Committee on Ways and Means. This time, however, in contrast to 1839, the committee endorsed the plea. While they did not advocate giving African Americans a portion of the school fund as legislators had done in Hartford, they did conclude that as free blacks "derive no benefit from the application of that tax it is unreasonable to require from them any contribution towards it." Still, despite "strenuous" advocacy from Farquharson and another representative, D. Grieves, the measure failed by a vote of twenty-two to six.[112]

As in 1838, signers of the 1844 petition did not appear to endure any reprisals from whites for making such an appeal. In fact, they even received the endorsement of one white editorialist who coincidentally dubbed himself "Aristides" and also invoked justice. "As regards the equity of the proposed tax," this Aristides observed, "there can be but one opinion. It must, by every reflecting, considerate man, be pronounced unjust." He also defended black Baltimoreans' efforts by pointing to their "orderly" and "industrious" behavior and praising them for eschewing "any act of insubordination."[113] His comments again highlight how free blacks' public displays of deference could work to advance their educational opportunity. While the city chose not to release black Baltimoreans from this "unjust" burden, the city council did entertain a dialogue. It is unlikely similar conversations would have occurred as openly in other slaveholding communities.

Six years later, in 1850, black Baltimoreans again petitioned the city council to free them from the school tax, and, as they had in their last appeal, they ratcheted up their request. This time, they asked the city to establish "public schools for colored children."[114] Presently, they noted, African Americans independently financed a school for some eighty black children located between East and Douglas streets, but the burden was growing too heavy to sustain. They hoped the city council would aid them in their educational endeavor by returning the taxes they paid to school white children.[115]

Soon after the city council received this appeal, over one hundred white men, including some of the city's wealthiest residents, submitted a petition endorsing "the establishment of schools for the instruction of the free colored children of the city, in the elementary branches of English Education." They pointed to Baltimore's decision to create a common school system as evidence of community-wide enthusiasm for public education. Next, as others had done before, they highlighted the injustice inherent in taxing black parents for schools that refused to serve their children. "[J]ustice would seem to require," they noted, "that the colored people should not be taxed for the education of the children of others, while their own children are excluded from all opportunities of instruction." Finally, they emphasized the importance of capable black workers to the entire community. "[T]he true interest of the white population, as well as of the colored," they observed, "will be promoted by the instruction of the children of the latter, in such elements of learning as may prepare them to fill, with usefulness and respectability, those humble stations in the community to which they are confined by the necessities of their condition."[116] According to Frank Towers, of identifiable signers, 68 percent were "Professionals," 16 percent were "Store Owners," and just 5 percent were "Workers."[117] These numbers provide further evidence that the most enthusiastic white supporters of African American education were those who, as employers, stood to benefit directly from black people's literacy and vocational abilities.

While the city council entertained these requests, the proposal to create public schools for African American children nonetheless generated little enthusiasm among the white community. The Joint Committee on Education to which the petition was referred reported that the General Assembly did not envision black schools when it created the city's school system. Should Baltimore take such action, they believed the state legislature would "immediately withdraw the city's proportion of the fund," effectively destroying public education in the city. With those words, African Americans' campaign against the school tax came to a close again.[118]

But just two years later, African Americans' efforts to release themselves from the school tax seemed poised to succeed. In 1852, white Baltimorean Martin J. Kerney, the Democratic chairman of the Maryland Assembly's Committee on Education, introduced a series of sweeping educational reforms, including a proposal to eliminate taxing African Americans for common schools. Section 16 of his bill, "Establishing a Uniform System of Instruction in the Public Schools of this State," held that the city could no longer assess "the property of persons of color" to fund public education.[119] The city council, in response, examined Kerney's proposal and endorsed it. It also considered a separate provision to establish public schools for black children. As part of its deliberations, the city council set out to determine African Americans' precise financial contributions to Baltimore's public schools. It had not undertaken such an inquiry before.[120]

Kerney's proposal generated praise from other whites as well. The *Baltimore Sun,* the city's largest Democratic press, declared that while it did not endorse publicly funding "African" schools, it also did not believe the city should continue to tax blacks for white schools. As it made clear, "there is nothing very agreeable in the fact that we are taxing a proscribed class for the support of an institution for the education of our children, while we compel them to do the best they can for the education of their own."[121] Not one of the three previous attempts had sparked so much enthusiasm. African Americans who had lobbied without success just two years before must have rejoiced upon learning that a Democratic state representative—the chairman of the Committee on Education, no less—had endorsed their campaign. But this time, black Baltimoreans remained silent. They did not author a broadside or editorial, nor did they file another appeal. Given their previous record of agitation, this silence is striking. Why would African Americans not enter the discussion when success was so close at hand?

When one subjects the Kerney Bill to closer inspection, a possible explanation for their reticence comes into view. Catholics, chary of the Protestant underpinnings of public education, often preferred to patronize parochial schools. In consequence, Catholic church leaders who opposed democratic control of common schools rejected what they deemed double taxation—requiring Catholic parents to finance private *and* public institutions.[122] A devout Catholic and Irish native, Kerney's concern, then, was not what he claimed. Rather, he sought to manipulate recognition of one injustice—taxing black property holders for schools that excluded their children—to create support for what he believed to be an equivalent, if not more egregious inequity: taxing Catholics for what they contended were Protestant schools. Consider how Kerney constructed his argument in the local press. "I ask you, do you approve of a system that is supported from a fund that is in part raised by taxes levied on the property of the colored property holder, who receives not one cent from that fund?"[123] After acknowledging the absurdity of that principle, he leaped to his primary agenda.[124] Just as blacks should not be taxed for schools they could not attend, Kerney argued, Catholics should not be forced to support schools they chose not to attend. To remedy this injustice, he proposed to Baltimoreans "that a small pittance of your taxes be set apart to pay for the education of your children in the schools of your choice."[125] Section 27 of his bill laid out the specifics of his proposal: "Whenever any white child . . . shall be taught gratuitously or at the same rates as pupils in the Public Schools, in any Orphan Asylum, School, Academy, or other place of learning in this state, it shall be the duty of the Board of School Commissioners of the City of Baltimore, and the Trustees of the School Districts of the Several Counties to pay . . . for the education of each child taught, as aforesaid, in said institutions. . . . "[126] Kerney, in other words, sought to divert funds directly from public schools to private schools and in so doing, some charged, aspired to eradicate the entire foundation of public education in the city.

Once Kerney's motivations became apparent, support for releasing African Americans from the school tax vanished and tensions between Protestants and Catholics erupted. Some 3,800 "citizens of Baltimore" petitioned the state legislature in opposition to Kerney's proposal.[127] Other members of Kerney's Joint Standing Committee on Education wrote public letters of protest, accusing him of seeking to destroy "a system of education which the citizens of Baltimore have adopted, fostered and supported."[128] One parent whose children were making "handsome progress" in the city's public schools predicted that Kerney's proposal would "awaken and promote the 'wicked spirit of Sectarianism', alike detrimental to the peace and happiness of our citizens." As such, he considered it "anti-republican, anti-democratic, and anti-American."[129]

For the next year and a half, Protestants and Catholics debated school taxation on street corners, in public assemblies, and on the pages of the local press.[130] Protestants assembled in mass meetings devoted to the "Threatened Destruction of the Public Schools," and Catholics fired back with equally vitriolic rhetoric.[131] Editors at the *Baltimore Sun* agreed with Kerney about the injustice inherent in taxing African Americans for public schools, but they rejected any connection between that inequity and complaints against the school tax lodged by some Catholics. Unlike those Catholics who opted out of the common schools voluntarily, black children could not attend if they wanted to, even with their parents' contributions. "There is no force in the objection that those who chose to send their children to other schools have an equal right to exemption with the colored population," they observed, because "the colored people have no right of access to a public school at all."[132]

When one considers the uproar Kerney's proposal unleashed, one rationale for black Baltimoreans' public silence comes into view. While it is impossible to recover their precise motivations, it is conceivable that African Americans recognized the inherent danger of Kerney's proposal and elected to remain silent in an effort to shield their schools from white retribution. While black Baltimoreans had petitioned three times for a similar measure, by showing whites that they were orderly and did not engage in acts of subordination, particularly during a time of crisis, they sought to convey their respect for peace and stability in the city. As their silence during the Kerney affair suggests, Baltimore's black educational activists chose their moments carefully. They understood that resistance and acquiescence each had a time and place in the struggle for educational opportunity.

PART III

Education's Divide:
Boston, Massachusetts

The very terms, *Public School,* and *Common School,* bear upon their face, that they are schools which the children of the entire community may attend.[1] —Horace Mann, 1848

From the time Boston's Puritan progenitors set foot on the banks of the Charles River in 1630, religious and political elites aspired to make literacy widespread.[2] Many in the community believed that every individual, regardless of race, gender, or social station, should be able to read the Scriptures, both for their individual salvation and for the greater good of the colony.[3] Boston's economic and commercial vitality, they further understood, relied upon a literate merchant class, capable of keeping accounts and communicating with trading partners throughout the Atlantic world. And because access to citizenship was generally diffuse, at least along class lines, they also considered free schooling essential to prepare boys for this looming responsibility.

In the early national period, Bostonians channeled that enthusiasm for universal literacy into the construction of common schools, which would provide a shared, or uniform, education to the students of the commonwealth. As Joel Spring has argued, in addition to lessons in reading, writing, and arithmetic, these institutions delivered a standardized "political and social ideology" to the pupils they served. The children attending common schools came from a variety of socioeconomic backgrounds, and so the shared values they were to be taught would, it was expected, unite all classes by fostering a collective understanding of the rights and responsibilities of citizenship.[4] As the nineteenth century advanced, white school reformers extended this idea to include not just class but also ethnicity. The schoolhouse, they asserted, was an agent of Americanization, an institution whose central purpose was to create a loyal and homogeneous citizenry. As Irish Catholic immigrants flooded the new nation's ports of entry, schooling for citizenship assumed an even greater urgency.

Nowhere was this crisis more acute than in Boston. In 1845, even before immigration's strongest swells, nearly 40,000 foreigners and their children lived in Boston, amounting to almost a third of the city's population. Five years later, more than 60,000 immigrants and their offspring resided in the city proper; almost one in two Bostonians, in other words, was foreign born.[5] Boston's native white Protestants, who often associated these new arrivals with the forces of urban disorder and social decay, looked uneasily toward the day when the children of Irish Catholic immigrants would become citizens. School reformers, in turn, capitalized on this xenophobia to gain broader support for public education. Maintaining that common schools would encourage these future citizens to transfer their loyalties from the pope to the Constitution, reformers envisioned public schooling as a potent means by which immigrants' ethnic and religious identities might be erased.[6] Still, one significant obstruction to that vision stubbornly persisted: the stigma of slavery.

The first people of African descent had reportedly entered Boston harbor in 1638, less than a decade after whites had settled on the Shawmut Peninsula. After victory in the 1637 Pequot War, colonists in Massachusetts had attempted to enslave native women and children in Massachusetts and to sell native men to slaveholders in the West Indies.[7] Five years later, the Bay Colony codified Native American and African slavery with ambiguous, if not irrelevant, limitations. Its optimistically entitled *Body of Liberties* asserted that "There shall never be any bond slaverie, villinage or Captivitie amongst us, unless it be lawfull Captives taken in just warres, and such strangers as willingly sell themselves or are sold to us."[8] As the language of the *Body of Liberties* suggests, Massachusetts's early forays into slaveholding were fraught with ambivalence. Torn between slavery's economic potential and the threat it posed to their spiritual mission, many colonists were uneasy with the presence of all people of color in the region—Native American and African. As the number of enslaved blacks increased in the late seventeenth century, whites attempted to temper the impact of their presence. Legislators began to stitch a loose patchwork of restrictions around people of color, targeting those activities—drinking, gambling, and assembling, for example—that they associated with disorder.[9] This collage of race-based regulations belies any mythology that slavery in Massachusetts was benevolent or benign.

But while white Bostonians enacted several measures to mark black people as dangerous and dependent, they did not limit their access to literacy. To the contrary, many agreed with Boston slaveholder and minister Cotton Mather's assertion that "If the Negroes might Learn to Read the Sacred Scriptures, which make Wise unto Salvation, Vast would be the Advantage thereof unto them."[10] For first-generation Africans, unacquainted with English language or custom, slaveholders like Mather concentrated their educational efforts on acculturation. For individuals born into slavery, masters focused on instructing them to serve their owners on earth and to secure salvation in the hereafter. In either formulation, they envisioned education not as a means of liberation, but rather as a way to strengthen the institution of slavery. In contrast to proslavery ideologues who would later decry that literacy would make enslaved blacks defiant, Mather argued that reading could make them compliant, if supervised properly.[11]

America's first published poet of African descent, Phillis Wheatley, took full advantage of white Bostonians' willingness to educate those they enslaved. Captured in Africa around eight years of age, Wheatley's journey to America mirrored that of many Africans ensnared in the transAtlantic slave trade. Upon her arrival into Boston harbor in 1761 on a slave ship called *The Phillis*, the young girl was sold to John and Susanna Wheatley. Phillis mastered written and spoken English quickly, according to John Wheatley. Some years later, she began to experiment with various forms of verse. In 1773, Phillis Wheatley released her *Poems on Various Subjects, Religious and Moral*, which included thirty-nine entries and embodied the spiritual and classical emphasis of her early education. From her prescribed place at the bottom of Boston's socioeconomic order, she elegized luminaries including George Whitfield and George Washington. Once printed, her writings became literary images of the contradictions inherent in her situation. Recall the iconic picture of her which has survived: a young woman euphemistically described as "a Negro Servant," perched midsentence at her writing desk, book to her left and paper, quill, and ink in hand (Figure 8). Attracting comment within Boston and across the pond, Phillis Wheatley and her poetry belied the essentialist doctrine of black people's purported ignorance that suffused white rationalizations for slavery. While *Poems on Various Subjects* would be her first and last published volume, it did allow Phillis Wheatley to see freedom, providing her with sufficient notoriety to entice John Wheatley to manumit her in 1774.[12]

FIGURE 8. Frontispiece from *Poems on Various Subjects, Religious and Moral by Phillis Wheatley.* 1773. Courtesy of the American Antiquarian Society.

By the mid–eighteenth century, Boston's black population edged near 1,500, highlighting the extent to which slavery had contributed to the city's commercial and economic development. On any given afternoon, a person strolling through the streets of Boston might spy people of African descent sweeping streets, caulking ships, and hauling loads. Enslaved blacks worked in an array of service occupations, as waiters, carriage drivers, and domestics, and in a range of trades including carpentry, shipbuilding, shoemaking, and leather tanning. Alongside Newport, Rhode Island, the seaport also served as the hub of New England's lucrative slave trade. Those eager to procure slaves need travel no farther than to the taverns on King Street, which transformed into temporary slave markets, or to the slavers that sailed into Boston Harbor, docking briefly to sell their cargoes and then departing to restock their loads.[13]

If human bondage unnerved some Bostonians before their break from England, after independence, calls to eliminate chattel slavery increased in frequency and intensity.[14] Then, in 1783, Supreme Court Chief Justice William Cushing ruled in favor of Quock Walker's freedom suit against his master, Nathaniel Jennison. Cushing invoked a clause in the freshly minted Massachusetts Constitution that held that "all men are born free and equal." Those words, he contended, defined slavery as inherently and indefinitely incompatible with the egalitarian spirit of the new nation.[15] While Massachusetts's legislature never formally decreed slavery's demise, in the wake of the Cushing decision, the state shifted from a labor system accepting of slavery to one supposedly premised on citizenship. Although some black people remained enslaved into the 1780s and 1790s, by 1800, census takers described all of Boston's 1,174 African American residents as free.[16]

Although Boston extricated itself from slaveholding several decades before Baltimore and New Haven did, the city was no sanctuary for free blacks in the early national and antebellum periods. While black Bostonians departed from the city's public schools ostensibly on their own accord around the turn of the nineteenth century, about the same time that slavery in Massachusetts drew to a close, by the 1830s, such separation was no longer voluntary. Black Bostonians repeatedly requested to reenter the public schools, and each time the school committee denied their pleas. African Americans' failed appeals give the lie to white Bostonians' professed enthusiasm for educational opportunity in the antebellum period. While city boosters lauded Boston with laurels like the "Athens of America" and the "Headquarters of American Learning," such characterizations wholeheartedly ignored the divergent experiences of black children, who resided outside the rationale for common school reform.[17]

Although Boston's contemporaneous crusades for public education and school desegregation have received considerable attention in their own right, more often than not, the two stories are plotted on parallel paths, sharing the same space and time, yet rarely intersecting. But it is impossible to appreciate the expansion of educational opportunity in all its complexity without taking ideas about race into consideration; at the same time, one also cannot fully understand the meaning of race in the antebellum period without examining formal educational institutions. Chapter 5 examines two episodes in which whites' desire for racial segregation collided with their enthusiasm for universal public education in the antebellum period. The first occurred in 1834, when white residents of Beacon Hill blocked the city from building a school for black children in the neighborhood. Their resistance stemmed less from a wish to restrict black access to education—although certainly that impulse was present—than from their desire to literally and figuratively lay claim to space and in the process to mark people of color as outsiders and noncitizens. The second traces Horace Mann's decision to disregard the budding movement for school desegregation while serving as secretary of the Massachusetts Board of Education and crusading for the expansion of common schools. Chapter 6 opens in the aftermath of the 1850 Fugitive Slave Law, when many black Bostonians were coming to believe that their liberty depended upon an ability to assert American identity. They understood that to realize their basic rights—to life, to liberty, and now to education—they must be recognized as full and equal members of society, with all the "privileges and immunities" guaranteed to their white counterparts.[18]

In their push to integrate Boston's public schools, African Americans including Benjamin Roberts and William J. Watkins expressed an understanding of the common school as an Americanizing agent, an institution whose central purpose was to fuse children from all religions and ethnicities into a single American citizenry. As Roberts asserted in 1849, "It is with feelings of amazement that we witness Englishmen, Frenchmen, Irishmen, Germans, Scotchmen, and others, in our community, who enjoy all the local privileges, and are not ignorant of the fact that we are shut out from the institutions of learning *in the land of our nativity*." That exclusion, he contended, was especially galling given African Americans' participation in and many sacrifices during the Revolution.[19] As Patrick Rael has demonstrated, "black elites" like Roberts frequently "crafted challenges to racial inequality that appealed to cherished American values rather than stepped outside the bounds of the American ideological landscape" during the antebellum period.[20] In other words, African Americans divided over desegregation did not invent their conceptions of schooling in a vacuum. To the contrary, they drew heavily on the prevailing interpretation of education available at the time: common school reform.

CHAPTER FIVE

Race, Space, and Educational Opportunity

In contrast to Baltimore and New Haven, whose "free" schools charged a modest fee, Boston's schools lived up to their name. First in the nation to craft a common school system open to boys *and* girls, the New England seaport allocated more of its resources to public education than any other American city in the antebellum period.[1] In many respects, African Americans benefited from this educational commitment. Compared with their counterparts in Baltimore, black Bostonians stood a greater chance of receiving some schooling, as the New England seaport ostensibly provided public education to African Americans free of charge—aside, of course, from their tax contributions.[2] And unlike their counterparts in New Haven, white Bostonians did not resort to violence to suppress black access to education. But such reticence should not be read as evidence of an allegiance to equal education for African Americans. Rather, white Bostonians' loyalty to the promise of public schooling broke down in the face of their discomfort with racial integration.

In the seventeenth century, Massachusetts's religious and political elites embraced the idea that access to basic education should be widespread. As early as 1642, legislators obliged all household heads to provide dependents—black and white, boys and girls, free and enslaved—with "so much learning as may enable them to read the English tongue" and to understand the "capital laws" of the colony. The Massachusetts General Court advised selectmen to keep a "vigilant eye" on families to ensure they instructed their children and apprentices appropriately.[3] Five years later in 1647 the court expanded this directive to include formal schooling, commanding every village of fifty or more families to maintain at least one institution that provided instruction in reading and writing. It also ordered towns of one hundred households and larger to operate a grammar school, which could prepare boys to attend a university.[4] Boston surpassed these educational expectations with ease. By 1635, when the town contained no more than twenty or thirty coarse homes, settlers opened a Latin school modeled on an English predecessor. By 1682, a community of around 4,000 people sustained two writing schools at a cost of fifty pounds annually. Unlike the Latin school, these institutions instructed boys who did not aspire to attend a university.[5]

But while early Bostonians supported public schooling generously, they defined that concept more narrowly than their antebellum counterparts. While elites believed that access to basic education should be diffuse, they considered advanced instruction necessary for just a few. Prior to the Revolution, Boston's common schools enrolled boys exclusively; no provision existed for schooling girls. If young women attained any formal education, they received it from tutors or in private schools at their parents' expense. As a result, for Boston's colonial daughters more than for its sons, class dictated educational opportunity. Family finances did, however, delineate boys' educational prospects to some extent. Boston's first town-supported schools required students to be literate prior to entrance. Pupils generally attended private "dame" schools before they enrolled in town-sponsored institutions. And again, parents were responsible for funding this preparatory education. For boys born into families without sufficient means, Boston's free schools remained inaccessible. While the town's educational provisions were ample, especially in comparison with other communities in the colony, their benefits trickled down to just a fraction of the community.[6]

In the midst of the Revolution and the chaos of its aftermath, Massachusetts's residents forsook common schools for more urgent demands. Communities hard-pressed for cash allocated resources to alternate ends; rebuilding infrastructure, reestablishing trade, and revitalizing the economy all trumped the colonial commitment to public education. As a result, public support for the commonwealth's schools—elementary, grammar, and Latin—declined; most institutions in consequence fell into disrepair or closed altogether.[7] But in 1789, Massachusetts ratified the nation's first systematic provisions for public education, requiring every town to sustain one school for six months a year that offered instruction in orthography, reading, writing, arithmetic, and "decent behaviour."[8] The state instructed communities of one hundred households or larger to keep a school open throughout the year. It also expected those with greater than two hundred households to maintain a grammar school, which would provide instruction in "Latin, Greek and English Languages."[9]

In this conception of public education, schools were viewed not as egalitarian instruments of socioeconomic mobility for all, but rather as a merit-based opportunity for an exceptional few. Just as Bostonians exceeded stipulations for public education during the colonial period, they easily surpassed state mandates in the early national era. Shortly after Massachusetts enacted its school law, Boston ratified its Education Act of 1789. This landmark legislation set in place a formal system of instruction ostensibly to serve the entire community. Under its aegis, three pairs of writing and reading schools situated in the northern, southern, and central sections of town would offer instruction in reading, writing, and arithmetic to children from seven to fourteen years of age. Pupils ten years and older who mastered these fundamentals could apply to the Latin School for college preparation. The act also created a school committee to oversee these institutions that was composed of twelve men, one from each ward, elected annually.[10] By 1800, Boston supported seven separate common schools that enrolled some nine hundred students collectively.[11]

The most momentous consequence of Boston's 1789 Education Act came from its stipulations pertaining to girls. For the first time in its history, Boston opened its common schools to both sexes. Girls' provisions were still inferior—boys were expected to be present year round while their sisters could attend from just April through October—but the city made no distinctions in curriculum.[12] While legislators did not overtly reference citizenship when expanding educational opportunities for girls, the rising ethos of republicanism contributed to this new access. Early national Bostonians still expected women to be the keepers of hearth and home, but the political significance of that duty increased demonstrably after the Revolution. Although they were not explicit political actors, casting votes or holding office, women enjoyed a profound political purpose. They were citizenship's keepers, responsible for raising dutiful, virtuous sons who were willing and able to sacrifice themselves for the greater good of family, community, and country. In anticipation of women's political duty, Bostonians determined to prepare their girls appropriately.[13]

Boston's 1789 legislation also tapped into capitalism's many demands. Eager to restore the commerce and industry the Revolution had decimated, Bostonians rallied around common schools to disseminate the literacy, numeracy, and work ethic necessary for economic recovery. Equally anxious about the future of the republic they helped bring into fruition, Bostonians embraced these institutions as bulwarks against social and cultural decline. Advocates of public education imagined that behind the schoolhouse doors, students from society's sundry strata might learn the skills necessary to protect and promote their new nation, namely, wisdom, deference, and virtue. In this conception of public schooling, the student body's composition was as critical as the curriculum. As one early champion of public education in Boston expounded, "The principle upon which our free schools are established, is in itself, a stern leveler of factious distinctions."[14] As he understood it, schools could unite students from diverse if not divergent backgrounds. That shared experience, in turn, would inspire young people to trade in their individual loyalties for a national identity; social discord would decline as a result. Here, public schooling was not primarily intended as a progressive means to enable ambitious students to rise up through society or as an avenue of socioeconomic equality, but rather as a way to shield the new nation from the fractiousness that had derailed previous adventures in republicanism. He further described this educational philosophy:

> We do not, indeed, expect all men to be philosophers, or statesmen; but we confidently trust, and our expectation of the duration of our system of government rests on that trust, that by the diffusion of general knowledge, and by good and virtuous sentiments, the political fabrick may be secure, as well against open violence and overthrow, and against the slow but sure undermining of licentiousness.[15]

In post-Revolutionary Boston, public schools were thus imagined as palliatives for an assortment of social and democratic ills.[16] While in the colonial period, Bostonians had generally endorsed mass education as a means to create a godly community, in the early national period, the rationale for public schooling became more explicitly political and secular. As Revolutionary republicanism collided with revivalist Protestantism later in the nineteenth century, these ideas would energize the antebellum crusade for common school expansion and reform.

While Boston's 1789 school laws extended educational access along gender lines, the city made less progress in terms of racial equality. In the wake of the Revolution and in the midst of emancipation, black and white people in Boston seemingly had equivalent access to public schools. However, in 1787, just two years before the passage of Boston's groundbreaking educational legislation, a group of free blacks led by Prince Hall, the founder of the first black freemasonry society in America, petitioned Boston Town to fund a separate "African" school. Hall and fellow self-described "freemen of this Commonwealth" charged that their children "receive no benefit from the free schools in the town of Boston" under the present arrangement.[17] Advancing an argument that would later become customary against school segregation, petitioners framed their request for "exclusive" schools in terms amenable to the republican and capitalist spirit of the age. They stressed their contributions as independent, productive citizens. "We have never been backward in paying our proportionate part of the burdens," they asserted. Still, despite fulfilling all the responsibilities of citizenship, African Americans had yet to reap its rewards. Fearing for the future of their "rising offspring," Hall and his associates prayed to the town for a separate institution.[18]

When the town rejected their appeal, black Bostonians opened a private school in Hall's residence the following year. The school remained there for three months, until an outbreak of yellow fever forced it to close.[19] Two years later, in 1800, sixty-six African Americans again appealed to the city for a public school for black children. While the subcommittee charged with evaluating the petition endorsed it, town administrators reiterated their refusal to fund a school for "people of colour" with public money.[20] If black people desired a separate school, Boston officials suggested, they should maintain one independently.

And so they did. When, in 1803, the schoolroom in Hall's home no longer proved adequate, black Bostonians transferred the institution to a small carpenter's shop on Belknap Street in the Beacon Hill section of town. The school remained there until 1808, when community members relocated it to the new Belknap Street Church.[21] Organized in 1805, church founders included Primus Hall, who along with his father Prince had led the African American exodus out of the public schools, and Thomas Paul, whose son of the same name would later divide the black community when, in the midst of the school desegregation controversy, he assumed control of the city's separate black institution.[22] Belknap Street soon became the locus of African Americans' spiritual, political, cultural, and educational activities. In July 1831, for example, black Bostonians including Primus Hall, John Hilton, and Thomas Cole gathered there to drum up support for the proposed African college in New Haven.[23] Over the ensuing decades, black Bostonians would meet at Belknap Street to protest colonization, extol abolition, demand desegregation, and celebrate emancipation.

Akin to black churches in Baltimore, Belknap Street soon became the educational center of Boston's African American community. By the middle of the 1820s, it maintained two Sabbath Schools "open to all who desire[d] SELF-IMPROVEMENT."[24] In 1835, Charles V. Caples opened an evening school there for adults. From February through October, men and women gathered at the church three nights a week to study "Reading, Writing, Arithmetic, English, Grammar, Geography, Chemistry, History, &c. &c."[25] Together these schools served some of Boston's neediest students: children who could not attend day schools, obliged to work instead, and adults, often slavery's survivors, who had little, if any, opportunity to become literate. In a similar spirit, Belknap Street also sponsored an African infant school for pupils too young to qualify for public education. There young children learned "Spelling, Reading, Arithmetic, Geography, [and] Singing, together with various recitations of scripture."[26] Because Boston required that students be literate before they enrolled in public school, many poor children, white and black, could not take advantage of these institutions. By providing literacy at little cost, Belknap Street Church allowed African American children to meet this prerequisite.[27]

From the time Belknap Street opened, it took black Bostonians two years to construct a schoolroom in its basement; individuals including Primus Hall, Abel Barbadoes, and Cyrus Vassell plastered and lathed the classroom in their spare hours. Thereafter, black Bostonians sustained the school for a decade, a burden that carried the benefit of autonomy. African American men served as the school's earliest instructors. In fact, one of the first teachers was none other than John Brown Russwurm, a founder of *Freedom's Journal,* who taught there for a time before leaving Boston for Brunswick, Maine, to study at Bowdoin College.[28] In 1812, for reasons that are uncertain, the school committee began to subsidize the Belknap Street School. In 1815, Abiel Smith, a white benefactor, granted the institution a sizable endowment, after which point it became known as the Smith School in honor of his bequest. Probably enticed by the school's ability to finance itself, the school committee assumed control of the institution in 1816.[29]

When the private black institution entered the public school system, African American control over the school diminished and complaints from black parents increased in frequency and intensity. The school committee was now appointing white teachers instead of African Americans.

In 1818, for example, the school committee fired a black instructor, Peter Tracy, and replaced him with a white man, James Waldack.[30] Some African American parents believed white instructors would inevitably be indifferent to their children. In December 1833, African American parents and community leaders pleaded with the city to replace the white instructor, William Bascom, with "one of our own Choir [color]," accusing Bascom of being "inattentive and unfaithful" and "frequent[ing] a house of ill fame" during school hours. Bascom, they complained, was just one of multiple "Evils Devising from the Existing neglect of our Grammar School," which had "greatly declined from its former flourishing state."[31]

Moreover, while white children were free to enroll in their neighborhood school, black children had no such luxury. The school committee mandated that they attend the Smith School no matter their address. And while white children could advance as far as high school if they so desired, Boston's secondary schools refused to admit black students.[32] In 1824, for example, Thomas Paul, Belknap Street's black minister, petitioned the school committee to allow his son Thomas to attend the Latin School, Boston's preeminent educational institution. Although the committee assented, Mayor Josiah Quincy personally compelled Paul to withdraw.[33] As Thomas Paul's experience suggests, the limitations white Bostonians levied on African Americans' educational advancement were purposeful. Just four years after opening the first high school in the nation, for example, Boston's school committee maneuvered to keep advanced education accessible to white students only. In March 1825, it extended the age that black pupils could attend the Belknap Street School beyond the age it required white students to exit grammar schools. It then authorized Belknap Street's white schoolmaster William Bascom to teach black students any subject offered to white students in schools for white children.[34]

Given that Bascom supervised between forty and sixty students of varying ages and abilities for a fraction of what Boston paid other schoolmasters, it is doubtful he would have had the energy or inclination to revamp his curriculum.[35] Instead, the school committee probably intended the measure as a way to preempt requests from African American parents seeking to provide their children with equivalent access to advanced instruction. In the same year that the school committee extended the age limit and curriculum of the black grammar school, it also requested $2,000 from the city council to open a high school for girls. When Barney Smith, brother to benefactor Abiel, petitioned the city a few months later to open a high school for the "coloured children of the city" as well, the school committee shot down his request. They deemed a high school for black children "inexpedient."[36]

Black Bostonians further asserted that the educational facilities the city afforded to African American children suffered in comparison with those it provided to white boys and girls. By 1833, Belknap Street's schoolroom had, in fact, deteriorated beyond repair. The "Committee on the structures of the several school houses" reported that "Nothing short of removal to another situation and another building can remedy the great evils of its construction and location."[37] According to another subcommittee, the classroom, now three decades old, was "low and confined . . . hot and stifled in Summer [and] cold in winter." "The obvious contrast between the accommodations of the coloured and other children, both as to convenience and healthfulness seems to your committee to be the principal cause of this School being thinly attended," it concluded—a "distinction" it deemed "invidious and unjust." When "it is considered that during all the time that the coloured inhabitants have been paying their proportion of taxes towards the education of all the white children and youths in the city," it added, "the wonder will be that they did so much, not that they did not do more for themselves." To remedy this injustice, the committee advised the city to locate a site for a new school "forthwith."[38]

As news of the search trickled through the city, whites lobbied the mayor and city council to locate the new black schoolhouse in any neighborhood but their own. Homeowners on Southack Street, which already housed one "Evening School for People of Color," moved first, arguing that their property values could not withstand another.[39] On July 28, 1834, approximately fifty-six whites pleaded with Boston's aldermen and its mayor, Theodore Lyman, to halt plans "to locate a school house for coloured children" in their neighborhood. With reasoning eerily prescient of twentieth-century arguments levied against integration, petitioners predicted that the introduction of such an institution would trigger a downward spiral of decay. First, it would stymie their efforts to revitalize the district. It had taken years, they asserted, to rid this section of the city of the "Ruffians & Prostitutes" which had once been "great in number." A black school would attract such undesirables back into the community, and white families would "be continually harassed and annoyed with insults and violence" as a result. Next, the "respectable part of the community" would abandon it.[40] As these antebellum pioneers of gentrification dispersed, the neighborhood would descend into disaster. As Boston's former mayor Harrison Gray Otis envisioned the process, "The respectable

citizens who are now building and improving that part of the city will be . . .
forced to desert it and you will have two quarters of the city for the colored
population instead of one."[41] In the end, housing prices would plummet.
Petitioners estimated their losses to be "at least, twenty per cent."[42]

On August 18, 1834, twenty-four whites who lived in the area surrounding Garden Street filed a similar appeal.[43] The remonstrance also included
signatures from white residents of neighboring streets including Cambridge, Myrtle, and Butolph. In addition, twenty-five whites signed a third
petition that they appended to the Garden Street appeal. While shorter,
the second and third documents advanced arguments that echoed the
Southack Street petition. These petitioners also stressed their past efforts
to make the area a place of "quietude, good order, and morals." They too
feared that the introduction of a black school would bring social and economic disaster. "The taxable value of all the estates in the vicinity" would
plunge, they predicted. Petitioners' hostility to the proposed schoolhouse
clearly stemmed from more than just a desire to avoid living alongside
black people. Well before the city's proposal for a new schoolhouse, African Americans "thickly inhabited" this community. In total, nearly one
hundred black people lived in the area immediately surrounding the proposed site. At least eighteen resided on Southack Street, near what was to
be the new schoolhouse, while twenty-four lived on Belknap Street in the
vicinity of the Belknap Street Church.[44]

Because petitioners stressed their standing as property owners, it is
helpful to explore their socioeconomic backgrounds to make sense of
their claims. In so doing, some key details emerge (see Appendix 2). First,
despite their preference for residential segregation, at least three petitioners currently rented property to African American tenants. Thomas Darling, for example, leased five properties to black laborers: three located
on West Center Street and two on Southack Street. John Low and Elias
Kingsley, who co-owned a home on Butolph Street, also let property to
an African American laborer, Aaron Gall. Likewise, white business partners Mitchel and Dunbar rented a home on Southack Street to seaman
Thomas Robbins.[45] Such practices suggest that, in the past, some petitioners' resistance to residential integration had broken down in the face of
their ability to profit from it.

Moreover, petitioners' black neighbors bore no resemblance to the
fictive paragons of sloth and disorder that white signers predicted would
flood the neighborhood should a black schoolhouse be erected. Petitioner
Benjamin Bayley, for example, scribbled beside his signature that he lived

in the "*next house* to Barbadoes." In all likelihood, Bayley was referring to James G. Barbadoes, abolitionist, proponent of the proposed New Haven college, and used-clothing dealer.[46] Co-petitioner Loring Dunbar made no distinction between Barbadoes and his own black neighbor, a man he charged had "been in [a] house of correction and *lives in a brothel.*"[47] This glaring juxtaposition suggests just how overtly petitioners tried to link all black people with crime and disorder, irrespective of their social or economic standing in the community.

Contrary to petitioners' claims, most African Americans who lived in the Southack Street neighborhood were neither idle nor unemployed; many worked in semiskilled or service positions, as sailors, waiters, or hairdressers, for example.[48] Further, at least eleven black people owned their own homes, while eight of those eleven owned multiple properties. Joseph Sprague, the largest black property owner in the area, held the deed to eight different residences.[49] Most of these homeowners performed skilled trades or worked in nonmanual occupations. Jonas W. Clarke, William Riley, and John Robinson, for example, purveyed used clothes; Primus Hall and Joseph Woodson worked as a soap maker and a blacking maker, respectively; George Putnam and Oliver Nash styled hair; while the remaining men labored in positions of service or performed unskilled labor.[50] To appreciate the extent of African American property ownership in this area, recall that as of 1850, Baltimore's Ward 17 included just one black real estate holder. While few African Americans living on the north slope of Beacon Hill amassed vast financial fortunes, most embodied the good citizen: they paid taxes, owned property, went to work, and schooled their children.

Even more, despite their decision to refer to themselves as the "owners of Estates on Southack St," many of the signers did not actually own their own homes. Landlord Stephen Titcomb and his five tenants who all signed the appeal illustrate the range of individuals who united against the proposed school. As the owner of seven residences in the area, it makes sense that Titcomb saw his financial fortunes as rising or falling with property values. His tenants' claim to be at the mercy of local real estate prices, however, seems more specious. Warren Boles, a housewright, Stephen B. Franklin, a furniture maker, and Reuben Frost, a drain digger, resided together in one of Titcomb's properties located at 60 Myrtle Street. All signed the appeal. They held no real estate and little personal property, especially when compared with their landlord. All three paid just a modest amount of tax each year.[51]

So what is one to make of the Southack Street petitioners, who on the one hand, associated African Americans' presence with an assortment of social and economic ills, and on the other, like Thomas Darling, John Low, and Elias Kingsley, made a living renting property to white and black tenants? It is not enough to simply dismiss petitioners as disingenuous in their appeals. After all, three separate contingents authored documents that advanced a similar narrative about neighborhood revitalization and decay. At the same time, the arguments petitioners levied against the school were fraught with contradictions. With all their talk of deteriorating real estate prices and moral values, for example, one would think the city planned to erect a penitentiary or poorhouse, not an educational institution. And Bostonians generally understood schools as palliatives for crime and destitution, not magnets for decay. Moreover, while petitioners decried black people for their degradation, they were, in fact, resisting an institution with the potential to elevate them. Finally, while they charged African Americans with perpetual vice, they predicted black people would flood the neighborhood to "uplift" their children. How should one account for this multiplicity of inconsistencies?

It is possible that Southack Street residents resisted the proposed school because of its potential to elevate African Americans' socioeconomic circumstances, as opponents of the proposed African college had done three years earlier in New Haven. But the occupational composition of the petitioners suggests that fear of black people's socioeconomic mobility was not their primary consideration. The vast majority of signers hailed from the middling and upper classes. Like many antiabolitionists of the era, they were predominately, although not entirely, "gentlemen of property and standing"[52] (see Appendix 2). They included several housewrights, shopkeepers, mechanics, and merchants, like Samuel French, a mason, Benjamin Judkins, a grocer, Asa Bird, a cabinetmaker, and William Crombie, a tavern keeper. Just one manual laborer, drain digger Reuben Frost, signed the appeal. At the other end of the socioeconomic spectrum, Harrison Gray Otis, Boston's former mayor, who resided in a mansion on Beacon Street, also signed the remonstrance and appended a personal letter of protest.[53]

In contrast, black Bostonians dominated just a few professions, namely, hairdressing and clothing sales.[54] And comparatively few African Americans in the city labored in a skilled trade. *Stimpson's 1830 City Directory* listed one black confectioner and one soap maker, for example, and not a single African American blacksmith, baker, or carpenter. To contextualize those numbers, consider that the directory recorded thirty black mariners, fifteen black waiters, ten black laundresses, nine black bootblacks, and six black laborers.[55] As one visitor to Boston reported in 1827, "very few [blacks] are mechanics; and they who are, almost universally relinquish their trades for other employments."[56] Black women's occupational opportunities in Boston were equally circumscribed. As of 1830, over one thousand African American women lived and labored in the New England seaport. But as of 1834, the *Liberator* reported that Boston contained not a single black milliner, mantua maker, or female tailor; and, what was worse, not "one girl of color in Boston" was studying "any of these useful trades!"[57]

Instead, black women more often toiled as laundresses or domestics, jobs that demanded arduous effort and offered little reward. Such positions often required servants to live within white homes, away from their families and under their employers' watchful eyes.[58] For women who were the sole breadwinners of the family, the arrangement was undesirable, but few alternatives existed. In 1845, for example, "A Colored Woman" pleaded for work in the *Boston Evening Transcript*. Recently widowed and "entirely destitute with four children under seven years of age" in her care, she wished to "support herself and her family by washing" but could find no one desiring such a service. She hoped someone might take pity on her with their patronage.[59]

While it is impossible to identify the exact plot of land the city selected for the new schoolhouse, because protest radiated from two groups, the self-described residents of Southack Street and Garden Street, the site was most likely located near the intersection between the two (Figure 9). Given that the existing Belknap Street School was just three streets from this corner, the specific geography of the immediate area helps to elucidate petitioners' concerns. Running east to west across the north side of Beacon Hill, Southack Street traveled through the epicenter of Boston's black community. Perpendicular to Garden and West Center streets, it bisected Ward 6, which, as of 1830, encompassed more than six hundred African Americans, nearly a third of Boston's African American community.[60] Cambridge Street, which ran east to west on the bottom of Beacon Hill, demarcated the northern edge of the neighborhood. Poor whites and African Americans usually resided in smaller, lower lying properties located on the slope between Cambridge and May streets, which included the cross streets of Garden, Butolph, Russell, and Belknap. Whites with more wealth and social standing lived in larger estates further up the hill,

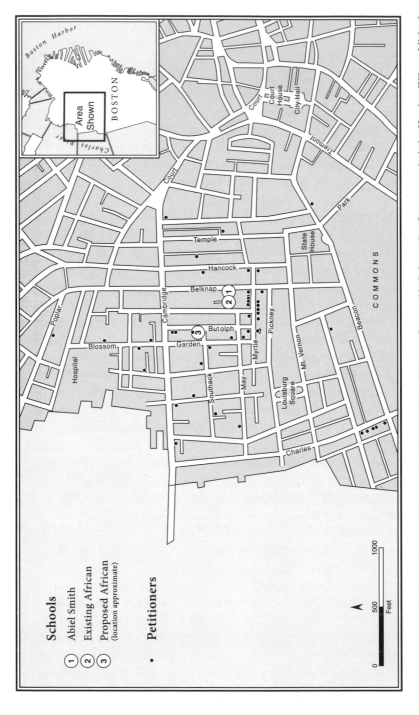

FIGURE 9. Map of Southack Street petitioners, 1834. Map by Harry Johnson; Geographic Information Systems analysis by Heather Wilson; Michael Horwich and Andy Anderson, contributors. Sources: Plan of the City of Boston, 1844, Boynton, G. Special Collections and University Archives, W.E.B. Du Bois Library, University of Massachusetts, Amherst; Map of Boston, 1842. http://www.lib.utexas.edu.

on Mount Vernon and Chestnut streets, and in the posh Louisburg Square. From that point the land sloped south until it leveled off at Beacon Street, which bordered Boston Common.

This geography suggests that petitioners' resistance to the proposed location did not stem just from the school's proximity to their own homes. The largest cluster of petitioners, in fact, did not live in the area surrounding the suggested site but rather on Myrtle Street, two blocks to the north. This location is significant for a few reasons. First, because Southack Street terminated at Garden Street, black students who lived on Russell and Belknap Streets would have to use Myrtle Street to reach the new school.[61] In addition, the proposed site was also higher up on the hill than the existing Belknap Street School. It is possible that some petitioners associated the school's literal movement up the slope as part of a symbolic effort on the part of African Americans to elevate their own social standing, perhaps at the expense of whites in the middling and working classes.

To support this point, it is useful to remember that while petitioners opposed the construction of a schoolhouse for black children, they did not ask the city to exclude African Americans from public schools altogether. Remember, a black schoolhouse already existed just a few blocks from the proposed location. Petitioners' concern then was probably not the existence of a black school in and of itself, but rather the structure's potential to undercut their efforts to claim the neighborhood as their own. In Boston, as in many rapidly expanding cities in the antebellum period, schools represented the nucleus of a community; for practical reasons, they often functioned as magnets for families with children. At the same time, the specific affiliations of local institutions like churches and schools also did a great deal to define the racial, ethnic, and religious character of a neighborhood. In this context, some petitioners likely understood the proposed school as part of a much larger—and longer—struggle over the identity of the area.[62]

Recall the specific narrative of the neighborhood's history that petitioners constructed in their appeal. Unlike those African Americans they claimed to have driven out as part of their effort to revitalize the area, a schoolhouse—a metaphorical and literal locus of Boston's black community—could not be as easily displaced. It represented in petitioners' words, "a permanent injury, an injury that cannot be removed."[63] And unlike the classroom in the Belknap Street Church, the new institution was to be located in a specifically public—albeit segregated—facility. Despite the fact that signers lived in the epicenter of Boston's African American community, they emphasized their efforts to regenerate, and thus to remake, the neighborhood as their own. In so doing, petitioners asserted their own rights of citizenship, which stemmed from their standing as property owners, and simultaneously constructed African Americans as outsiders and noncitizens or, more crudely, as temporary tenants, even while both these assertions flew in the face of reality.

To tease out petitioners' rhetorical strategy, it is helpful to look briefly to the literature on race and homeownership in the twentieth century, as historians have mined struggles over race, city space, and property with more frequency during this period. In his discussion of real estate covenants in Kansas City at the turn of the twentieth century, for example, Kevin Fox Gotham asserts that white actors, including real estate agents and social workers, eager to lay claim to certain neighborhoods, "helped nurture and promulgate a segregationist ideology and negative image of the emerging black ghetto as a pathological, dangerous and nefarious place, to be avoided by whites and other ethnic groups." In so doing, they "helped nurture and reinforce emerging racial stereotypes that identified black living space and culture with deteriorating neighborhoods and dilapidated housing."[64] The Southack Street episode suggests that some antebellum whites similarly attempted to lay claim to space by exploiting racist ideas about black people. In their effort to defeat the proposed schoolhouse, petitioners linked their faulty arguments about race with their equally faulty claim to place, in this case the Southack Street neighborhood.

First, petitioners pandered to existing white fears about African Americans' disorderly and dangerous behavior. Recall, for example, petitioners' prediction that "families will be continually harassed and annoyed with insults and violence from those children, with whom ours, will not wish to fellowship." They then mapped those fictive concerns onto tangible economic considerations, in this case, property values in the area. As they put it, the introduction of a black school would "prevent the increase of building and population by the respectable part of the community, and we believe that on examination you would be fully convinced that estates adjourning or opposite would immediately lose in value."[65] Finally, by asserting that the introduction of a black school would, in effect, cause real estate prices to plummet, they sought to illustrate how the city's actions effectively stripped them of their rights as property holders or, more broadly, as citizens. In the absence of another means to oppose the proposal, they utilized a language of fear to strengthen their claim to an area they believed they were entitled to, not because they owned it, but rather because they believed they had revitalized it for themselves and their families.

Ironically, for African Americans who desired to attend school at all, this interpretation had its benefits. Neither the Southack nor the Garden Street petitions, for example, asked the city to refrain from building a school for black children with public money. Instead, petitioners asked only "that the said School House may be erected elsewhere."[66] In the end, their pleas succeeded. The city scrapped plans for the Southack Street location. Yet construction on a new schoolhouse proceeded. On March 3, 1835, the new facility opened on Belknap Street, just steps from the school's original location (Figure 10).[67]

Although African Americans received a new school building in 1835, the quality of their education appeared to improve little, if at all. The Smith School's organization changed somewhat in 1838, although the extent to which the alterations benefited black students is unclear. That year, as the city opened intermediate schools to serve older children who had not yet learned to read, the Smith School added a separate division to serve the same function. The change came at the behest of its instructor, Abner Forbes, who complained about boys being sent to him from the primary school "whose only claim for admission was their notoriously vicious and refractory character."[68] Primus Hall and other black Bostonians asked the city to add another story onto the Smith School to accommodate the new institution, but the city rejected the expenditure as superfluous.[69] Boston's only intermediate school for African American children opened in a small room adjacent to Forbes's grammar school later that year.

Even with the addition of the intermediate school, white visitors charged with inspecting the Smith School continued to report that it performed "considerably below the standard of the other Grammar schools in the city."[70] For that underperformance, however, Forbes and school committee members did not blame poor teaching or African Americans' inferior facilities, but rather black parents' immorality and the "idleness" of their children.[71] White educators in Boston approached the Smith School and its students with the expectation that black children could not learn as well as whites. As one school visitor commented in his report on the Smith School, "This is a school for colored children." As such, it "ought not to be judged as to its merits by comparison with the other grammar schools" of the city.[72]

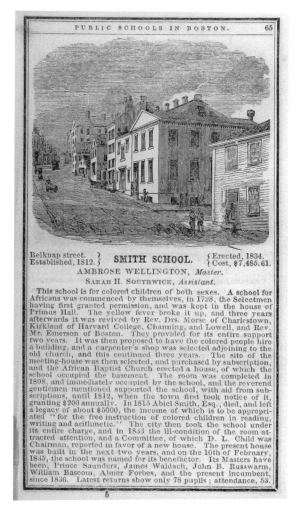

FIGURE 10. The Abiel Smith School for black students, Beacon Hill, Boston, 1849. *Boston Almanac* 1849, 65. Courtesy of the Boston Athenaeum.

School visitor William Minot further suggested that unlike white parents, black parents' "degraded character" led them to discipline their children inadequately. In Minot's estimation, anyone charged with teaching black pupils had a dual responsibility: "the duty of the parent as well as his own to perform."[73] A similar paternalism infiltrated Boston's white public schools, particularly those that serviced children of immigrants as historians like Michael Katz and Stanley Schultz have shown.[74] However, while white educators believed that with sufficient instruction foreigners could become dutiful citizens and productive industrial workers, they displayed a profound ambivalence toward the future of African American children. They doubted whether they could—or should—be molded into workers or citizens at all.

By the early 1840s, African Americans' displeasure with Boston's two-tiered educational system was readily apparent. Throughout 1840 and 1841, black parents entangled themselves in a messy dispute with the school committee over an African American teacher, Nancy Woodson, who was dismissed from the Smith School's primary department with neither notice nor cause—that Woodson was then replaced with a white woman did little to lessen their ire.[75] While black Bostonians had yet to formally petition for school desegregation, the school committee anticipated this action would be forthcoming. In 1843, a white school visitor went as far as to accuse Smith School students of intentionally underperforming during an annual examination at the behest of certain "influences . . . at work to make the scholars discontented with their situation and to discourage the school."[76] Thus it likely came as no surprise to anyone on the school committee when, one year later, they received word: black Bostonians were rallying for desegregation.[77]

* * *

Striving to convince the public to relinquish their children and tax dollars into their care, white school reformers were often chary of entangling themselves with this budding movement for school integration and its proponents, politically spirited free blacks and their abolitionist allies. No individual better exemplifies such reluctance than Horace Mann.[78] As secretary of the Massachusetts Board of Education from its inception in 1837 through 1848, Mann introduced a series of measures to increase enrollment and enhance the quality of public education statewide. His tenure also overlapped with waves of local protest over school segregation. But while Mann stood at the helm of the State Board of Education, he eschewed public involvement with the desegregation movement. Mann himself favored integration, as he acknowledged some years later, but the terms with which he defended public education, most notably citizenship and industrial labor, worked to strengthen the argument that black people existed outside of the mandate for common schools. In so doing, the ideology of common school reform that he articulated provided an implicit yet potent rationalization for segregated schooling.

Given his extensive efforts to expand educational opportunity, Mann's refusal to combat a practice so contradictory to that impulse is worthy of inquiry. His evasion becomes even more striking when one considers that Mann's sympathies fell on the side of the integrationists. As one proponent of school desegregation charged in 1847, a year before Mann resigned his position as secretary, "Horace Mann represents quite a large class who think they worship Truth, but honestly deem it best to sacrifice one half of their deity to secure the rest."[79] In other words, he suggested, Mann had surrendered integration to the greater good of school expansion and reform.

By Mann's own account in 1853, he had supported racially integrated schools long before his instillation as Board of Education secretary. In 1833, for example, while serving as a representative in the Massachusetts State Legislature, he had argued in favor of admitting black children into Samuel Gridley Howe's institute for the blind.[80] Mann expressed the same sentiment in his private correspondence. Arguing against the discriminatory admissions policies of the Perkins Institution, in 1833 he had confided to Elizabeth Peabody that "I should still contend, that as the blacks had been so long and so incessantly sacrificed to the whites, it would be no departure from even handed justice for once to adjust the balance between them."[81] In 1853, Mann recalled that he had expressed the same views years earlier to an assistant teacher at the Bridgewater Normal School. When asked to proffer his opinion on educational integration, Mann recalled that he had replied that "my eyesight was tolerably good, but never would be sharp enough to discern any difference of color between applicants qualified for admission to the school."[82] His avid support for abolition while serving in the United States House of Representatives (1848–53) further suggests that his sympathies probably did fall on the side of school integrationists.[83]

Despite endorsing desegregation privately, Mann sidestepped the issue in public and official pronouncements. His reticence was not lost on integrationists. In 1853, white abolitionist and desegregationist Wendell Phillips penned a diatribe spanning several issues of the *Liberator* that pointedly attacked Mann for his apparent indifference to desegregation. As Phillips charged, while Mann agreed with integrationists in private, he withheld even "one word of recognition, countenance or aid." And for that "systematic and designed silence" he predicted, Mann would "live to repent yet of the wrong he did the colored children of this State."[84]

Mann vigorously disputed Phillips's accusations in the *Liberator*'s next edition, rejecting them as "flagrantly untrue." He affirmed,

> In my Reports, I uniformly stated the law to be such as would confer upon colored children equal school privileges, in all respects, with white ones, which I believed it did. Where the practice did not conform to the theory, I labored to make it do so . . . So anxiously scrupulous, so sensitively punctilious have I always been in regard to this unjustly-treated class of our fellow-beings, that I never went to inspect schools in any town or city, where a separation existed, without making it a point to visit the colored school, so that no group should ever be afforded for a suspicion of neglect by me . . . Under my solemn responsibility to the country, to posterity, and to God, I did the best I knew how.[85]

Regardless of Mann's intentions or the equanimity of his school visitation policy, when one considers the many moments when he could have directly aided the integration movement in his capacity as secretary of the Massachusetts Board of Education, it is clear Phillips's assessment does hold some weight. In 1841, for example, as Mann entered his fourth year as secretary, African Americans on Nantucket launched one of the first school desegregation campaigns in the state. And at no time during the island's five-year conflict did Mann intervene.

As was common throughout New England, Nantucket had initiated its policy of separate schooling in 1825 while in the process of fashioning its public schools. That year, while creating a town school system, the school committee opened the island's first "African" school. It intended this single institution to be primary, grammar, and high school combined and made no additional provisions for African American students who desired advanced education. In an effort to topple the island's two-tiered educational system, Eunice Ross, a black teenager, requested entrance into Nantucket's high school in 1840. Her application provoked a flurry of controversy over integration that subsumed local politics for several years. In a series of annual elections, white supporters and detractors of integration exchanged seats on Nantucket's school board, each time overruling the decisions of the group that had preceded them.

Rather than sanction segregation, African American parents and children opted to boycott the island's black school, York Street, instead. Then, in 1845, over one hundred black residents of Nantucket petitioned the Massachusetts State Legislature for equal school rights. In response—or retribution—for the appeal, more than three hundred white residents of Nantucket lobbied the Massachusetts House of Representatives to uphold racial segregation in their common schools. Some weeks later, Eunice Ross, the young woman whose application to the high school had sparked Nantucket's desegregation debate, submitted an individual appeal. Responding to these petitions, the Massachusetts House of Representatives passed House Bill No. 25 on March 25, 1845, which proscribed discrimination in places of public education. Nantucket resident Phebe Ann Boston and Benjamin Roberts's daughter, Sarah, would later utilize this statute while suing their respective communities in an effort to overturn school segregation.[86]

As whites and African Americans struggled over school desegregation in Nantucket, the coastal community of Salem, Massachusetts, became embroiled in much the same dispute. And yet again, Mann avoided the issue. Salem's tradition of separate schooling traced back to 1807, when a young black minister, Joshua Spaulding, collaborated with the school committee to separate black children into a "School for Young Negro Children."[87] Prior to that point, Salem's black children had attended town schools where they often endured the opprobrium and neglect of white teachers who preferred to focus on white students. Then, in 1823, after the death of African school instructor Chloe Minns, the Salem School Committee agreed to allow black children to enter a single public school located near Roast Meat Hill. But even this undesirable arrangement proved short-lived.

Three years later, in 1826, the city reinstituted segregation, opening an African writing school. The Salem School Committee was reluctant to fund even this institution; it closed one year later. Then, in 1830, a young African American woman applied to enter Salem's East High School after passing the exam for admission. Her request was, at first, denied, although she eventually enrolled months later. Then, following the wave of white opposition to black schooling that rolled through the northeast in the early 1830s, 176 whites petitioned the school committee to reinstate separate schooling in 1834.[88] It relented and opened another African grammar school to serve Salem's entire black community. Thereafter, as many as one hundred children of all ages and abilities crowded into the one-room facility to receive instruction from a single white instructor.[89]

Inspired by the agitation on Nantucket, African Americans in Salem launched a desegregation campaign in 1842. Similar to the arguments advanced by black Baltimoreans, they decried the cycle in which African Americans are "taxed to support a school to educate the whites, and are scornfully . . . excluded from a school supported by themselves," while those "whom they pay their money to educate, fiendishly taunt them for their ignorance!"[90] As in Nantucket, black students in Salem boycotted the African school. In less than one year, average attendance at the institution plummeted, from sixty students to seventeen.[91] And in Salem, as in Nantucket, Mann remained quiet. In his 1853 exchange with Wendell Phillips, he denied that his silence signified any apathy or ambivalence toward African Americans and their educational plight. "An omission to assault and belabor the three or four towns that sustained colored schools, no more proves indifference to the cause of colored children," he contended, "than the omission to name slaves and slavery in the Constitution of the United States proves that a majority of its framers were fond and proud of slavery. Hostility, not favor, caused the omission."[92] It is doubtful that black parents whose children were coming of age in Salem or Nantucket would have agreed.

Finally, under pressure from the boycott, in March 1844 the Salem School Committee relented and allowed black children to reenter the public schools.[93] When explaining the rationale behind its decision to desegregate, Judge Richard Fletcher drew extensively on the republican construction of the schoolhouse that also lay at the heart of Mann's simultaneous movement for common school reform. From the days of the "Pilgrim fathers," Fletcher explained, public education was modeled on a "principle of perfect equality." This notion held that public "schools must be supported at the public expense, and be free and open equally to all classes of the community." It was, he argued, that precise "principle of equality, cherished in the free schools, on which our free government and free institutions rest." Without common schools, the "rich would oppress the poor, and the poor would war against the rich," and the stability of the republic would disappear. Fletcher contended that the decision to admit all classes except African Americans directly contravened that principle of equality that defined the common schools. As he explained, a "colored man is a free citizen, with the same rights, privileges and duties, as any other man, so far as the constitution and laws of this Commonwealth are concerned. He pays his share of expenses, and is entitled to vote and act as any other citizen. . . . The children of colored persons are," he concluded, "entitled to the benefit of the free schools."[94]

Nowhere, however, was Mann's absence more striking than in Boston, the nucleus of both the movements for school desegregation and for common school reform. On the heels of the integrationist victory in Salem, on May 7, 1844, black Bostonians delivered the first of many petitions for desegregation to the school committee. Referencing the ease with which Salem and Nantucket had implemented integration, William C. Nell, Thomas Dalton, Robert Morris, and their colleagues argued that school segregation irreversibly stigmatized their children. "It is very hard to retain self-respect," they explained, "if we see ourselves set apart and avoided as a degraded race by others." They cautioned the school committee, "Do not say to our children that however well-behaved their very presence in a public school, is contamination to your children." Finally, they contended, a separate education by definition could not provide children with an equivalent education. Where white students were allowed to traverse through primary, grammar, Latin, and high schools, their children were combined into a single "colored school." In consequence, "the instruction must be kept down to the average necessities of the scholars, a plan which robs the more intelligent of the benefits of higher education."[95] While the school committee entertained the appeal, it rejected taking action by a vote of seventeen to two.[96] Undeterred, in June 1844, integrationists sponsored a series of public meetings to express their discontent with the decision and to drum up support for desegregation (Figure 11).[97]

As with the Nantucket and Salem cases, Mann again declined to comment. From his private correspondence, however, it is clear that he was well-informed about the controversy in Boston. In the process of calling for integration, local African Americans had simultaneously launched a campaign to remove the Smith School's white instructor, Abner Forbes. Forbes's treatment of their children increasingly troubled black parents. In June 1844, they filed a complaint with the school committee that called for his dismissal. Forbes, they asserted, was frequently absent during school hours, indiscreet in his discipline ("adopting several unusual modes of punishment—in undue severity"), and guilty of "Entertaining opinions of the intellectual character of the colored race of people, that disqualify him to be a teacher of colored children."[98] As it had weeks earlier, the school committee denied black parents' request and reappointed Forbes as Smith School master. This decision to retain Forbes drove some African Americans to boycott the Smith School.

In July 1844, William B. Fowle corresponded with Mann about the desegregation debate in Boston and the controversy surrounding Forbes's reappointment. In Fowle's assessment, African Americans' decision to impugn Forbes and their agitation for integration were directly related. As he informed Mann, "The fact is that the abolitionists are determined to scatter the colored children among the whites and to do this they must

COLORED SCHOLARS EXCLUDED FROM SCHOOLS.

"If the *free* colored people were generally taught to read, it might be an inducement to them to remain in this country. WE WOULD OFFER THEM NO SUCH INDUCEMENT."—*Rev. Mr. Converse, a colonizationist, formerly of N. H. now editor of the Southern Religious Telegraph.*

In those parts of the country where the persecuting spirit of colonization has been colonized, such exclusion has ceased.

in Congress, and in the state legislatures, and fill their places with those who will reverence it. Let liberty be justified of her children! Let churches shut slaveholders out of their pulpits and away from their communion tables. Let ecclesiastical judicatories, instead of electing slaveholding moderators as the Presbyterian church delight to do, silence and excommunicate those who rob the poor,—let religious and benevolent societies no longer employ slaveholders as agents, nor elect them to office, nor invite them to make speeches at their anniversaries, nor insult God in laying on his altar "robbery for burnt offering," by systematically gathering into his treasury the plunder of the poor.

Finally. Let all who buy of the slaveholder what he steals from the slave, and thus make him their agent and proxy to perpetrate robbery, to ply the whip and clutch *for them* the blood-smeared product—cease to be "partakers of other men's sins," and no longer incur the curse of God's indignant charge, "When thou sawest a thief, thou *consentedst* with him."

Can any man in his senses ask what the north has to do with slavery, when a Virginia Senator, at the head of the southern bar, in habits of contact with the leading men of the north for 20 years, could say : "I have never conversed with a single northern gentleman whose sentiments on the subject of slavery gave me *any dissatisfaction?*"

Who does not know that every year our Saratogas, Ballstons, Niagaras, Trentons, Catskills, Nahants, Long Branches, our hotels, public conveyances, promenades, theatres, and *fashionable* churches are thronged with slaveholders, men whose daily business it is to steal the labor of poor men and *women* and children, flogged by a "driver," up to the top of their strength,—men who kidnap babes from their mothers and breed them for the market,—men whose glossy broadcloths and glittering jewelry and burnished equipage were tortured out of the forced, whipped, blood-wet toil of the *unpaid* slave—and yet the wealthy, the fashionable, the literary, the professedly religious of the free states mingle with these plunderers of the poor, lavish on them their complacent smiles, and choicest courtesies, accompany them on pleasure excursions, laugh, sing, dance, attend races and drink toasts with them, make parties for them, regale them on their richest wines and viands, give them public dinners, make them the orators at political meetings, assign to them posts of honor on the platforms of religious anniversaries, and call them to speak and pray in religious assemblies ?

What has the north to do with slavery ? Just what the boon companion of thieves, revelling over their plunder, has to do with stealing,—what the accomplice in crime has to do with the principal—he who harbors traitors, and "gives aid and comfort" to rebels, with the enemies of his country.

FIGURE 11. Colored scholars excluded from schools. *The American Anti-Slavery Almanac,* 1839, 13. Printed text. Courtesy of Manuscripts, Archives and Rare Books Division, Schomburg Center for Research in Black Culture, The New York Public Library, Astor, Lenox and Tilden Foundations.

kill the colored school by killing Forbes."[99] Mann declined to enter the dispute over the white schoolmaster. Privately, however, he recommended another white man, Ambrose Wellington, for Forbes's position. Eight months later, he informed Samuel Gridley Howe, "I think [Wellington] would be a good man" to run the Smith School. "He is an abolitionist, and a sort of non-resistant, and expresses quiet confidence in his power to govern *any* school without asking Solomon how to do it."[100] Shortly after Mann's suggestion to Howe, the school committee, in fact, installed Wellington as the Smith School master.[101]

One year later, in June 1845, black Bostonians again appealed to the primary school committee to end segregation. This time, the school committee called a public meeting to discuss the petition. At the gathering, Boston's citizens, black and white, asserted their views on separate schooling. One committee member, Albert. J. Wright, rose in defense of desegregation, declaring, "We wish [African Americans] to be good citizens! Let us educate them for good citizenship, under the same principles that we do others."[102] Still, despite Wright's vocal support—with its reaffirmation of black citizenship—the committee once more declined to desegregate, this time by a vote of fifty-five to twelve.[103]

Integrationists remained undeterred. One year later, in June 1846, they submitted another appeal for desegregation with the primary school committee. This time, white petitioners including Edmund Jackson and Ellis Gray Loring lent their support by filing an application of their own.[104] George Putnam and eighty-five other black integrationists defended their request by asserting their rights of citizenship. As they informed the school committee, "the establishment of exclusive schools for our children is a great injury to us, and deprives us of those equal privileges and advantages in the public schools to which we are entitled as citizens." Accordingly, they argued, they found the school committee's decision to exclude their children from common schools "unlawful" and "insulting." To defend their position, they appealed directly to school reformers' conception of the common school as an agent of Americanization. But despite generating a lengthy dialogue over integration that included four months of public hearings, integrationists failed to engender enough support. The school committee refused to integrate—this time, by a vote of fifty-nine to sixteen.[105]

As he had twice before, despite black Bostonians' nod to his school reform campaign, Mann declined to make his voice heard. His silence, however, spoke volumes. Although Mann made every attempt to untangle his crusade from the integration controversy, as Boston's black petitioners had suggested, connections between the two movements were unmistakable. Specifically, many of the arguments that he and other reformers were advancing in defense of common schooling were also implicit rationalizations for segregation. Consider two of the key premises underlying common school expansion and reform: the importance of universal education to the survival of the republic and to the vitality of the economy. In the first, common schools were necessary to create virtuous citizens able to subordinate their individual needs for the good of the commonwealth and with the free will and wisdom to make the sacrifice. In the second, common schools were essential for creating an orderly, disciplined workforce to operate the mills and machines necessary to sustain Massachusetts's economic vigor.

In both instances, proponents of public schools including Mann provided inadvertent arguments for African Americans' exclusion. First, as demonstrated, many white Bostonians believed that African Americans were not and would never be citizens; thus, it made little sense to school them for that position. Second, few, if any, antebellum factories employed black operatives; thus there was also no need to prepare them for jobs they would never obtain. In either scenario, the rhetoric of common school reform tacitly suggested that black people did not need the same education as whites. Neither citizens nor industrial workers, African Americans did not need schools to be "common." A separate education would serve their subordinate station.

To elucidate this argument, it is useful to examine the rhetoric of common school reform in some detail. Here the definition of education encompassed far more than reading, writing, and arithmetic. Its greater purpose was to prepare children for the rights and responsibilities of citizenship. According to Mann, the peculiar nature of American democracy made this function of special necessity. As he explained, "the establishment of a republican government, without well-appointed and efficient means for the universal education of the people, is the most rash and fool-hardy experiment ever tried by man."[106] For if America was to avoid the corruption and decay that had beset other forays into republicanism, it must preserve a virtuous citizenry with the tools to subsume private interest to the public good and the wisdom to distinguish the difference. As Mann reasoned, "If we do not prepare children to become good citizens;—if we do not develop their capacities, if we do not enrich their minds with knowledge, imbue their hearts with the love of truth and duty, and a reverence for all things sacred and holy, then our republic must go down to destruction, as others have gone before it."[107]

In light of the spectacular expansion of suffrage that ensued during the early nineteenth century, schooling for citizenship appeared ever more essential. Prior to 1800, less than half of white men could vote, and nearly every state made suffrage contingent on property holdings. But by 1830, most states had eradicated these restrictions; universal suffrage for white men was largely absolute. Democrats, for the most part, did not display much concern that these new voters might be led astray. But Whigs appeared far less comfortable with the emergence of this unbridled but empowered citizenry.[108] As one Whig proponent of school reform predicted, "If the multitude who have the power are not fitted to exercise it, society will be like the herding together of wolves."[109] Only through a proper education in the common schools could citizens prevent such an outcome, he insisted. Accordingly, most Whigs—usually advocates of public schools—argued that if the franchise was to be common, then education must also be. Public schools were thus envisioned as a powerful antidote to Jacksonian democracy.[110] New voters must be instructed to exercise their influence properly. And if every son was now a citizen, mothers needed similar preparation for their responsibility. While many of these arguments in support of public schooling had appeared previously, the expansive nature of Jacksonian democracy gave them a new urgency.

In Boston, increasing foreign immigration also made schooling for citizenship appear even more essential. Beginning in the late 1830s, Boston's foreign population had begun to expand exponentially (Figure 12). As of 1830, just 5 percent of Boston's populace had been born abroad, but with the potato famine's potent push, nearly 45,000 people sailed into Boston Harbor between 1840 and 1845, and over 10,000 entered in 1845 alone. As of 1855, the year the city finally dismantled its segregated schools, a majority of Bostonians were not American-born.[111] To put such numbers into context, consider that as of 1820, African Americans made up less than 4 percent of Boston's total population (Figure 12). And from that time until the Civil War, the proportion of African Americans in the city's total population steadily decreased.

Many native-born Bostonians viewed Irish immigrants uneasily, uncomfortable with their perceived indigence, intemperance, and Catholicism. Even before the number of immigrants in Boston climbed, the Charlestown Convent burning in 1834 and the Broad Street riot three years later were potent indicators of the anti-Irish hostilities to come. Because of

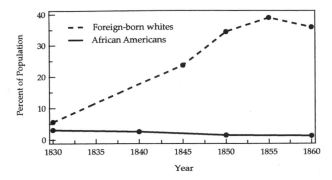

FIGURE 12. Population Trends in Boston, 1830–1860. Source: Peter R. Knights, *The Plain People of Boston, 1830–1860: A Study of City Growth* (New York: Oxford University Press, 1971), 35; Jesse Chickering, *Statistical View of the Population of Massachusetts from 1765 to 1840* (Boston, 1846); Stanley Schultz, *The Culture Factory: Boston Public Schools 1789–1860* (New York: Oxford University Press, 1973), 5, 189, 211.

the poverty endemic in the Irish community, native whites charged these immigrants with causing urban blight and moral decay. The most disturbing offshoot of such poverty, some concluded, was not the suffering that many Irish people endured, but rather the burden they placed on public coffers. As Irish numbers rose, native whites accused them of stealing their jobs and depressing their wages, claims that bore a marked resemblance to those leveled against free blacks in New Haven. Because of Irish immigration, complained one workingman in 1847, "the native laborer is completely forced out of employment." Foreign competitors "underbid his wages at every step" and "[t]he price of labor is reduced to a scale, at which, no man can live."[112] Another concurred, protesting that "While we have been conquering and annexing Texas and Mexico, the Irish have been conquering and annexing us."[113] By 1840, such concerns were so commonplace that help-wanted advertisements regularly noted that no Irish need apply.

Whigs in particular associated foreign immigrants with urban disorder and social decay and looked uneasily to the day when their children would become citizens. Democrats, in contrast, often embraced Irish citizenship, particularly as these new arrivals often lent them their allegiance—as well as their votes.[114] In this respect, Boston's Irish community often lacked the political vulnerability of the city's small African American population who formed no meaningful constituency for either party. One of the Whigs' greatest fears about the ever-increasing Irish Catholic immigration was the impending collision of their political power and their ignorance. City papers described thousands of "foreigners" poised to receive naturalization yet without sufficient knowledge to resist manipulation. The Irish were "ready to be made the tools of any party that will favor them," they charged; in most instances, this referred to the Democrats.[115] Whig reformers like Mann then responded to this xenophobia to amass broader support for public education. "[T]here comes pouring in upon us a new population, not of our own production, not of American parentage, nor the growth of American institutions," he prophesied. "We must provide for them, or we all sink together."[116]

Convinced that most Irish immigrants lacked sufficient morality, temperance, or literacy necessary to prepare children for citizenship, advocates of public education were loath to allow them that liberty. They castigated the Irish for their intemperance and accused them of causing crime rates to skyrocket. As one editorialist remarked, "Our native, stationary population have not deteriorated in morals. But the influx of foreign crime, ignorance and destitution has been increasing as it never was before; statistics of the police show conclusively that nearly nine tenths of the cases of ruffianly outrage, intoxication and riot occur among those, who received their training far away out of the sphere of New England influences."[117] Thus, where the colonial family was once held up as the most important institution to instill children with the virtues necessary to become good citizens and good wives, advocates of public education argued that the schoolhouse should now assume this responsibility.[118] As Mann's Connecticut ally Henry Barnard asserted, "the children of reckless, vicious, and intemperate parents, should not be abandoned to the chance education of the streets, or the demoralizing influence of corrupt parent example." To the contrary, they should be placed under the influence of the public schools.[119]

Mann, Barnard, and their contemporaries further asserted that common schools could encourage these new citizens to transfer their allegiance from their faith to their nation. Here, yet again, their rhetorical defense of public schooling implicitly responded to nativist fears over Irish Catholic immigration. As one local editorialist portended, "any man of common sense must see, that if immigration continues" at its present pace, "Roman Catholics will control the state and the United States in less than ten years."[120] Reformers responded to this concern by conceptualizing common schools as a means to expunge these immigrants' un-Americanness. In other words, public education could be used to dilute ethnic and religious identity. If properly organized and supervised, common schools would take children from disparate backgrounds and give them a common American character with all its republican, capitalist, and Protestant appendages. Still, despite their faith in the power of the schoolhouse to assuage social distinctions, educational advocates like Mann recognized its limitations. While public schools could soften differences in class, national origin, and even religion, they could not erase the stigma of skin color. By making citizenship central to their defense of common schooling, reformers implied that African Americans did not need equivalent preparation. It was not too great a leap to conclude that black people were not part of the public they sought to educate.

Common school reformers did not rest their case for school expansion and reform on political arguments alone. They also contended that Massachusetts's economic vitality depended upon educational opportunity. Once again, educational boosters capitalized on nativists' concerns over foreign immigration to amass support for common schools. In 1842, Mann released his *Fifth Annual Report of the Board of Education* that tapped directly into nativists' worries over immigrants' poverty and economic dependence. Here he suggested that common schools could be used to transform the city's motley crew of new arrivals into a self-sufficient, obedient, and productive workforce.[121] In what he called his "utilitarian view of education," Mann elucidated the financial benefits of common schooling to a manufacturing economy.[122] Building off the premise that "no hungry or houseless people ever were . . . an intelligent or a moral one," Mann listed a series of ways that common schools could yield economic gain.[123] To bolster this assertion, he included testimonials from local manufacturers describing the positive effects of common schooling on their workplaces. First, one industrialist argued, public education elevated his workers' wages, for "very few, who have not enjoyed the advantages of a Common School education, ever rise above the lowest class of operatives."[124] But, more importantly, he asserted, schooling increased productivity. Public schools taught children the self-discipline, obedience, and respect for authority necessary to become model employees. Collectively, the testimonials Mann amassed suggested that the appropriate education would transform unruly, unskilled immigrants into "tractable" laborers, who, in turn, would "acquiesce, and exert a salutary influence upon their associates."[125]

Mann greatly preferred social, political, and moral arguments to such crude monetary ones. His decision to advance this rationale was largely pragmatic, and in many respects, necessary. At the time he released this report, tremors from the panic of 1837 reverberated through Massachusetts's economy, and the state had yet to surface from the depression that ensued. In light of this economic malaise, funding for public education was becoming increasingly uncertain. Further, in 1840, Democratic governor Marcus Morton proposed a measure to terminate the Massachusetts Board of Education and with it Mann's position of influence and authority. While Morton's effort was routed, he did succeed in making educational expenditures increasingly contentious on the local political stage. Given the precarious position of public education within Massachusetts, Mann seized on an easy opportunity to promote common schools as the panacea for the state's economic and demographic ills. At the same time, Mann likely feared that the integration issue would only taint the cause of school reform. No doubt he wished to avoid saddling such a worthy objective with an unpopular distraction.[126]

In light of this rhetorical linkage between education and industrialization, it is no surprise that school reformers like Mann appeared indifferent to integration. As is well documented, few antebellum African Americans were ever employed as machine operatives. At least in Massachusetts, the small size of the black community coupled with intense foreign competition that could capitalize on its whiteness gave the Irish a powerful advantage over African Americans when securing industrial jobs.[127] Thus, African Americans operated directly outside two of common school reformers' central propositions for universal education. First, unlike the Irish, African Americans could not be assimilated into the body politic. There was no need to school them for a status they could not obtain. Second, African Americans also had no reason to be molded into model employees. In light of their absence from industry, there were also no grounds to train them for jobs they could not attain. Thus by promoting public education in terms that necessarily excluded people of color, common school ideology at the very least made segregation acceptable. It makes sense then that African Americans targeted this exact rhetoric in their effort to penetrate Boston's public schools.

In 1848, Horace Mann resigned from his post as secretary of the Massachusetts Board of Education in order to succeed John Quincy Adams in the United States House of Representatives. That same year, as mentioned, Boston's African American community appeared ever more divided over integration in principle and the Smith School in particular. Two men, Benjamin Roberts and Thomas Paul Smith, stood at the center of this dispute. Both understood the painful paradox that defined black education in Boston. While Mann and his reformist associates were toiling to improve white education, black education was languishing at the same time. It was doubtful, however, that either predicted that their differing ideas about integration would bring them to blows in three years' time.

Common Schools, Revolutionary Memory, and the Crisis of Black Citizenship in the Mid-Nineteenth Century

On May 7, 1851, Thomas Paul Smith, a twenty-four-year-old black Bostonian, closed the door of his used-clothing shop and set out for home. His journey took him from the city's center to its western edge, where tightly packed tenements pressed against the banks of the Charles River. As Smith strolled along Second Street, "some half-a-dozen" men grabbed, bound, and gagged him before he could cry out.[1] They "beat" and "bruised" him and covered his mouth with a "[p]laster made of tar and other substances."[2] Before night's end, Smith would be battered so severely that, according to one witness, his attackers must have wanted to kill him. Smith apparently reached the same conclusion. As the hands of the clock neared midnight, he broke free of his captors and sprinted down Second Street shouting, "Murder!"[3]

This dramatic incident is detailed in the case files of the Boston Municipal Court, but it was never reported in the *Liberator* or in other white antislavery publications. The event was not recounted, one can surmise, because it would have failed to further the abolitionists' agenda. Smith's attackers, as he identified them, were all African Americans. Indeed, the intraracial violence did not end on the night of May 7. The next morning, Elijah Smith confronted the leader of his brother's assailants. Armed with a small axe, Elijah seized the man at the corner of Franklin Avenue and Brattle Street, just blocks from Thomas's store.[4] "Flourish[ing]" the hatchet above his rival's head, Elijah declared, "'You are the d[. . .]d villain who attempted to kill my brother!'" According to a city watchman, Thomas's attacker quickly overpowered Elijah, snatched the axe from his hand, and threatened "to blow Smith's brains out."[5]

That evening, presumably in retribution for his brother's act of revenge, a band of black men again accosted Thomas. At 8:45 P.M., men he thought to be acquaintances summoned Thomas from his shop and ushered him into Market Square. They struck him then "felled" him to the ground. As he had the night before, Thomas cried "Murder," scattering his attackers into the night.[6] By the end of this second evening of violence, the Boston Watch had detained six black men, including Elijah, and charged them with criminal assault. The sudden spate of intraracial violence deeply disturbed members of the city's African American community; they organized a vigil at Belknap Street Church the very next night (Figure 13).[7]

The attacks, it soon became clear, were not random. Three years earlier, in 1848, Thomas Paul Smith had gained notoriety for his outspoken opposition to school desegregation. That year, Benjamin F. Roberts had also become the first school desegregation plaintiff in the nation when he sued the Boston School Committee on behalf of his five-year-old daughter Sarah, who had been forced to attend a segregated school. The resulting case, *Roberts v. Boston,* came before Massachusetts's Supreme Judicial Court in December 1849. It concluded unfavorably for Roberts one year later, a year before the attack on Thomas Paul Smith.

Smith's accused attackers included William J. Watkins, one of the city's most vocal advocates of school integration. The son of the Baltimore schoolmaster of the same name, William J. Watkins spent his childhood days studying beneath the shadow of slavery. As he advanced in education and in age, he taught classes alongside his father at Watkins Academy. Sometime around 1849, he left Baltimore for Boston, where he became acquainted with Thomas Paul Smith.[8] Only one building stood between their residences on Second Street.[9] In 1849, Watkins and Smith debated the merits of school desegregation, and by all accounts that public dialogue, as well as their personal relationship, was fraught with tension. Less than six months prior to the May 7 assault, Smith had derided the school integrationists, including Watkins, calling them "disappointed office-seekers, brainless enthusiasts, fourth-class lawyers and broken-down clergymen."[10] Just six weeks before the attack, Watkins had publicly blamed Smith for the failure of the school desegregation campaign.[11] Moreover, at least according to local authorities, Smith's assailants had been

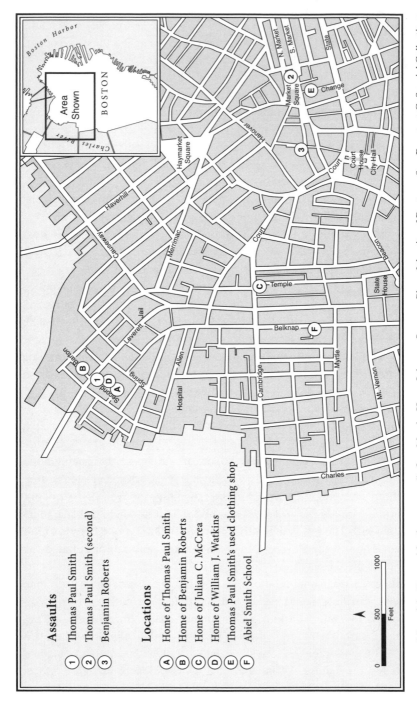

Assaults

1. Thomas Paul Smith
2. Thomas Paul Smith (second)
3. Benjamin Roberts

Locations

A. Home of Thomas Paul Smith
B. Home of Benjamin Roberts
C. Home of Julian C. McCrea
D. Home of William J. Watkins
E. Thomas Paul Smith's used clothing shop
F. Abiel Smith School

FIGURE 13. Map of the "tar and feathers scrape," 1851. Map by Harry Johnson. Sources: Plan of the city of Boston, 1844, Boynton, G. Special Collections and University Archives, W.E.B. Du Bois Library, University of Massachusetts, Amherst; Map of Boston, 1842. http://www.lib.utexas.edu.

commanded by another prominent black Bostonian, none other than Benjamin F. Roberts.[12]

No doubt, Roberts and Watkins wanted to punish Smith for the years of his vitriolic defense of separate schools. But the specifics of the assault imply that their motivations were more sophisticated and complex than mere revenge. Smith's assailants did not just beat him up. They covered his mouth with a "[p]laster made of tar and other substances."[13] Such a detail suggests they were tapping into a quintessentially American form of ritualistic violence: tarring and feathering. In their attack upon Smith, designed to symbolically and literally silence him, Roberts and Watkins were constructing a way to reaffirm blacks' status as Americans and to lay claim to the most Americanizing of all institutions: public schools. Against the backdrop of Boston, the epicenter of Revolutionary agitation, they sought to parody black exclusion from the body politic and to define Smith, along with his crusade for separate schools, as hostile to freedom. They also assumed that reclaiming their Revolutionary heritage in such a manner could excuse their "nonrespectable" behavior. The message of the assault was clear: school integrationists were the true Sons of Liberty. Smith, on the other hand, was no better than a tea-drinking, tax-enforcing king worshipper and no more American than his crusade for separate schools.[14]

The "tar and feathers scrape," as Roberts later dubbed the incident, exemplifies just how deeply the school desegregation movement had splintered Boston's black community by 1850.[15] It suggests, as well, a larger conflict among black leaders over how best to achieve their goals. Both Roberts and Watkins were born around the time John Brown Russwurm had helped to launch *Freedom's Journal,* a time when moral suasion trumped political militancy in the black activist tradition. But by the 1850s, the persistence of southern slavery and northern oppression tested blacks' faith in Garrisonian nonresistance. In the wake of the 1850 Fugitive Slave Law, which had denied accused black fugitives due process, a rising number of African Americans, including Roberts and Watkins, believed that the costs of an ideology of uplift were too great and the gains too meager. As Watkins remarked in 1854, "A timid man can no more make a Reformer, than can an ass become a lion."[16] Both Roberts and Watkins rejected the moral suasion of the 1830s, which demanded patience and eschewed violence, and the budding militancy of the 1840s and early 1850s, which urged African Americans to sever their ties to their country. Yet in contrast to their contemporaries like Henry Highland Garnet and

Martin Delany, Roberts and Watkins argued that blacks should look not to Africa but to America for liberation.[17] African Americans could agitate for civil rights, they maintained, and still remain loyal to their nation. By tarring and feathering their separatist rival, Roberts and Watkins were, then, committing the ultimate act of integration— ostracizing a member of their race to lay claim to what they deemed to be their rightful status within the nation.

*   *   *

By 1850, Boston was one of the most residentially segregated cities in the nation.[18] Its free black community (2,038) made up just 1.4 percent of the city's total population (144,517). Yet of that small subset, over 80 percent lived in the city's four "blackest" wards (1, 2, 5, and 6), and 60 percent lived in a single ward, Ward 6, located to the south of Cambridge Street and just east of the Charles River.[19] As of 1850, this district housed some 8,870 individuals, 7,651 of whom census takers described as white and 1,219 of whom they denoted as black, mulatto, or colored.[20] In total, more than 1,700 families lived in the district, 328 of which were headed by a person of color. As further evidence of the pervasiveness of residential segregation in Boston, most black families within this ward lived on just a handful of streets. Of the district's thirty-seven roads, eighteen including Western, Walnut, and Spruce, along with Louisburg Square, had no African American inhabitants whatsoever. Instead, just a few streets housed a disproportionate number of black people. Southack Street, for instance, included some 480 African American residents, almost a quarter of Boston's black community. Belknap Street reportedly had 274 black residents, 13 percent of the African Americans in the city.[21]

Several factors explain this extreme residential segregation. First, as manual laborers without steady employment, most African Americans preferred to reside within walking distance of the center of the city, where they were most likely to locate whatever work was available. Next, as Southack Street residents' resistance to the city's 1834 effort to build a black school attests, many whites resisted any move toward residential integration. At the same time, African Americans often preferred to live close to their family, friends, and institutions, especially churches and schools, the center of black life in the city. Both the Smith School and the Belknap Street African Baptist Church were located in Ward 6, for example. May Street, the location of the African Methodist Church, housed 167

black people, while West Center Street, the site of the African Methodist
Episcopal Zion Church, had 120.[22]

As in Baltimore, black churches like Belknap Street sustained black
Bostonians' educational activities, particularly those that took place outside of the public schools. Several self-improvement societies operated
out of the church's facilities during the antebellum period. Throughout
the 1830s, the Afric-American Female Intelligence Society assembled in
Belknap Street's basement once a month to study literature. Each session,
attendants surrendered twelve and one-half cents to purchase books for
the group and to create a fund for members in case of an emergency. Upon
"taking sick," women with memberships in good stead would receive one
dollar weekly.[23] The Boston Minor's Exhibition Society attracted "colored
lads and misses" eager to recite poetry and prose.[24] In 1831, Pulaski W.
Flanders also invited "colored Ladies and Gentlemen of Boston" to gather
every Sunday evening for "instruction in Sacred Music."[25] For twenty-six
lessons, he charged ladies a dollar and gentlemen two. Five years later, a
singing school moved into Belknap Street's basement.[26] This wide array of
educational activities attests to just how broadly black Bostonians concep-
tualized self-improvement in the antebellum period.

As many white lyceums in Boston often excluded black people or relegated them to segregated seating, Belknap Street also sponsored a variety of educational events open to the entire community.[27] In 1837, for
example, African Americans including William C. Nell and John T. Hilton
organized the Adelphic Union, an independent lecture society.[28] Among
its many public offerings, the group sponsored a speaking circuit to expose
black Bostonians to some of the city's best scientific and literary minds,
white and African American. For twelve and one-half cents and half of
that for children, attendants could hear lectures on subjects including
medicine, astronomy, history, and politics. Twenty-five cents secured an
individual entrance for the season.[29] These talks were often, although not
always, designed to be of especial interest to African Americans. Lectures
included, for instance, "The character of Touissant L'Overture," "Eli
Whitney, the inventor of the cotton gin," and a discussion of the question "Do separate churches and schools for colored people tend to foster
prejudice?"[30] In a like-minded spirit, William C. Nell spoke on "the importance of . . . acquiring Knowledge as a sure and distinct means of . . .
Elevation."[31] Typically sympathetic to African American efforts at uplift
and abolition, other speakers included Wendell Phillips, Charles Sumner,
Horace Mann, and future Smith School instructor Thomas Paul.[32]

As Belknap Street's sundry cultural and literary activities attested, Boston's black community evinced a profound commitment to intellectual inquiry and educational opportunity in the antebellum period. Consider, for instance, that by 1850 an overwhelming majority of African American adults in Ward 6 had learned to read and write. Although 95 percent of whites twenty years of age and older reported to the census marshal that they were literate, more than 80 percent of their black counterparts described themselves in such terms. To appreciate the significance of this figure, recall that in Baltimore's Ward 17, just over one-quarter of black adults reported having that ability.

When one examines the educational choices that black parents made for their children, African Americans' commitment to education also becomes apparent, especially in light of the many challenges segregation imposed. In Boston, as in other northern cities, segregated schooling galled many black parents precisely because of the added burden it placed upon their sons and daughters, who were often required to pass by several schoolhouses before arriving at the one institution that would accept them. Particularly for parents reluctant to allow their children to walk a long distance alone, whether the trip took one hour or ten minutes might make the difference between whether a child attended school daily or did not attend school at all.

Yet despite the many burdens that segregated schooling placed upon black families—burdens that it did not impose upon whites—only a modestly larger percentage of Ward 6's white parents sent their children to school. As of 1850, for example, while 72 percent of white children of school age (four to sixteen) attended school at some point in the year, so did 68 percent of their black counterparts (Figure 14). Similarly, of families in the ward with one or more school-age child, 74 percent of white parents sent at least one child to school, as did 66 percent of black parents.[33] To appreciate these numbers, it is again useful to put them into context; recall, for instance, that in Baltimore's Ward 17, just 17 percent of black children attended school in 1850, as did just 43 percent of their white counterparts.

Because Baltimore's public schools charged white students a modest tuition and excluded black children altogether, it is not surprising that school attendance rates for both white and black children in Boston would surpass those of their counterparts in Baltimore. In addition, because Boston, unlike Baltimore, provided schooling to white and black children free of charge, parents in the New England seaport were also not as hard pressed

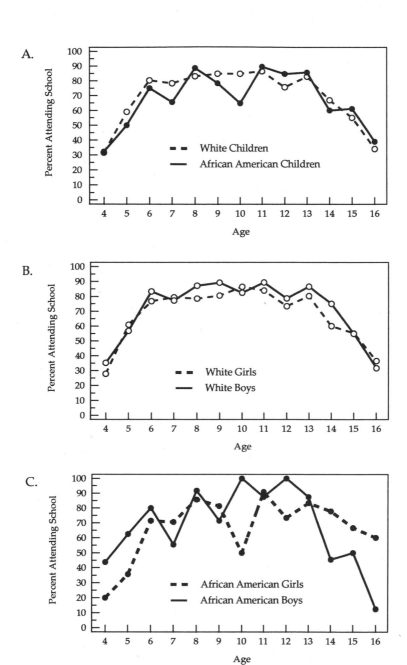

FIGURE 14. Children's school attendance by race, gender, and age in Boston Ward 6, 1850. (A) Percentage of white or African American children attending school, ages four to sixteen. (B) Percentage of white boys or girls attending school, ages four to sixteen. (C) Percentage of African American boys or girls attending school, ages four to sixteen. Source: Census Schedules, Boston, 1850.

to make difficult choices about which of their children to send to school and for how long they could remain. While in Baltimore's Ward 17, for example, black girls entered school later and left earlier than their brothers, in both white and black families in Boston's Ward 6, gender did not appear to influence parental decision making (Figure 14). Among white school-age children, for example, just a slightly higher percentage of boys (74 percent) attended school than girls (71 percent). Similarly, among African American children, boys' school attendance (71 percent) outpaced that of girls' (66 percent), but only by a modest percentage. If any gender difference can be asserted in Boston, it is that black girls tended to enter school later and exit later than boys.[34]

Similarly, if one peers within individual families it becomes apparent that in most instances, black parents in Ward 6 opted either to send all of their children to school or to send none whatsoever. For example, just 12 percent of the ward's 104 black families with one or more school-age child chose to keep one child at home while schooling another. And of those black families that did decide to school some but not all of their children, age appears to have been the most crucial consideration. Catherine Hix, for example, had four children between thirteen and sixteen years of age under her care; she opted to school her two youngest children, thirteen-year-old George and his fifteen-year-old brother Sam, but chose not to send her two sixteen-year-old children: Henry and his sister, A.M., who likely went to work instead.[35] Similarly, laborer Carter Judson and his wife Sarah shared six children between them, three between the ages of four and fourteen. The Judsons sent their two middle children, seven-year-old Sally and ten-year-old Thomas, to school but chose not to send Edwin, their sixteen-year-old.[36] In sum, despite the difficulties Boston's tradition of segregated schooling imposed upon black parents and their children, the overwhelming majority of African American families remained committed to educating their children in formal institutions. By extension, at least in the neighborhood that surrounded the Smith School, black parents valued schooling just as much for their sons as they did for their daughters.

Although Boston's policy of segregation did not dissuade African Americans from patronizing public schools, by the mid-1840s many black parents voiced a profound dissatisfaction with Boston's unwillingness to provide their children with an education equivalent to that offered to white students. As they noted, the Smith School itself stood in constant disrepair. In 1847, Charles Brooks, a white school committee member charged with inspecting its twelve-year-old structure, determined the building to be "perfectly deplorable." Brooks found himself "astonished [that] it should have been suffered to remain so long without enlargement or repairs" and took especial offense at the school's entryway ("through a dark and damp cellar") and its yard ("fifteen feet square . . . bounded on one side by the outhouses and favored on the other by a pump in questionable proximity"). "The old school houses, which have been abandoned, were palaces in comparison with this," he remarked.[37] One year after Brooks filed his report with the school committee detailing the Smith School's sorry condition, black parents echoed his appraisal to a tee; they too deemed the state of the Smith School "deplorable."[38]

By most measures, teachers at the Smith School also provided students with subpar instruction. In the mid-1840s, the Annual Examining Committee of the Boston Grammar and Writing Schools, which was charged with evaluating Boston's school system, administered a common exam to students, black and white, in each of the city schools' most advanced group. On every portion of the assessment, Smith School students finished last. On the definitions section, for example, only six black pupils completed the test, and not one managed to answer a question correctly. Although one might wonder whether the test was biased against black children, the extent of the Smith School students' failure suggests that, on the whole, they probably were not learning as much as their white counterparts.[39]

Beginning in 1844—spurred in part by African Americans' success in Nantucket and Salem—black Bostonians launched a formal campaign to end Boston's policy of segregated schooling. But after a series of petitions failed to move the school committee, integrationists concluded that the Smith School itself impeded their efforts. William J. Watkins, for example, considered the school to be "the sole barrier to the admission of our children into the several schools in the wards where they reside."[40] As he observed, the Smith School's very existence offered the city a viable alternative to desegregation. Fostering this view, the school committee rehabilitated the building's facilities and hired new instructors, which allowed it to appear sensitive to African Americans' concerns while stymieing integration. Integrationists, black and white, implored African American parents and children to boycott the separate institution, and they established an ad hoc system of protest schools in its stead. In 1849, they labeled the Smith School a "GREAT PUBLIC NUISANCE" and demanded it be "annihilated."[41]

But just as the integrationists were gaining ground in their campaign to close the Smith School, the soon to be assaulted Thomas Paul Smith initiated a movement to save it. In contrast to Benjamin Roberts and

William J. Watkins, Thomas Paul Smith had experienced both separate and integrated education firsthand. Born in 1827, he had attended the Smith School as a child. As a teenager, he had completed two terms at an elite white institution, Phillips Academy, in Andover, Massachusetts.[42] At some time in the early 1840s, while a student at the Smith School, Thomas Paul Smith joined William C. Nell's Young Men's Literary Society, an organization of "colored young men" that sponsored a lecture series, performed public elocutions, and established a library. At age sixteen, he departed to Albany to assist his uncle, Thomas Paul, in teaching at a local black school. William C. Nell took great pride in the young Smith's intellectual accomplishments. As Nell wrote to abolitionist Wendell Phillips in the aftermath of Smith's departure for Albany, "the active, enterprising members of the [Young Men's Literary Society] are stepping higher up the hill of Improvements."[43]

It is unclear when Smith left Albany and returned to Boston, although it was likely not long after he left for New York. In 1844, he was one of seventy-seven black Bostonians to file an appeal with the school committee for "the immediate and entire abolition of the colored schools in Boston." Separate schools by their very definition could not offer black children an education equivalent to that provided in integrated institutions, Smith and his fellow petitioners asserted. They contended, "The present exclusion of our children from the best schools and from competition in learning with white children is felt as a slight upon us and them, and is calculated to repress an honorable ambition."[44]

For at least the next four years, Smith, now a used-clothing dealer by profession, circulated among Boston's black abolitionist elite. In 1847, for example, he was elected to represent the city at the National Convention of Colored Americans in Troy, New York. His fellow delegates provide a useful illustration of the high esteem with which he was held within Boston's black community. The city's delegation included such activist luminaries as Frederick Douglass, Charles Lenox Remond, William C. Nell, and Robert Morris.[45] The fragmentary pieces of Smith's life that remain do not explain what drove him to sacrifice his social position by opposing the movement to close the Smith School just one year later.

During the first week of August 1848, Smith submitted a remonstrance to the school committee that made him the focus of the integrationists' indignation. While his memorial did not specifically address desegregation, it did call for the induction of a "coloured person" as "principal in the Smith School."[46] And for that post, Smith nominated "a gentlemanly man, a competent man, one in whose Literary Attainments, whose moral character, whose intellectual capabilities, we have perfect confidence, who was born and reared among us, who knows us and our wants and can most truly and naturally sympathize with us and we with him"—a man none other than his uncle, Thomas Paul.[47]

Like his nephew, Thomas Paul had also attended the Smith School, from age eight to fifteen. The son of Belknap Street's minister who bore the same name, the younger Paul had attempted to enroll in Boston's public high school as a teenager, but he withdrew at the mayor's urging. A year later, he traveled to Canaan, New Hampshire, to attend the integrated Noyes Academy, but local protest caused the institution to shut down. Undeterred, Paul went on to become one of the nation's first black collegians, graduating from Dartmouth College in 1841.[48] Upon completion of his advanced education, Paul returned to Boston to open a "school for colored youth." This institution proved short-lived; he soon abandoned it for "want of encouragement."[49] The school's failure, however, did little to lessen his estimation among some in the African American community. Some months later, for example, Paul encountered Jeremiah Sanderson, an African American abolitionist and close friend of William C. Nell. After the meeting, Sanderson recalled being so impressed with the young schoolteacher that he remarked to Nell, "I think Bostonians possess a jewel in him whose value they are slow to appreciate."[50] Soon after, Paul relocated to Albany to operate a school for black children. By the time of Smith's remonstrance on his behalf, Paul was comfortably installed as principal at Meeting Street, the only "African" grammar school in Providence, Rhode Island.[51]

But one day after Thomas Paul Smith filed his petition for Thomas Paul's instillation, thirty-nine individuals who signed their names to the appeal submitted a separate document that authorized Benjamin Roberts to erase them.[52] The following day, Roberts and his associates petitioned against Thomas Paul, claiming to have no confidence in his ability.[53] The group then organized a rally to oppose Paul's nomination. At the gathering, attendants invoked the rhetoric of school reformers like Horace Mann who envisioned education as a fundamental right of citizenship. "As common school privileges are the right of every inhabitant of this Commonwealth," they observed, "it is our duty to use every effort for the full enjoyment of that right." They continued, "As we belong to one common family, having one common cause . . . it is our belief that *separate schools* for the education of children are injurious in their effects upon society, and ought to be abolished."[54] Some individuals who had signed Smith's petition in support of Thomas Paul described Smith's appeal as a "misrepresentation and a deception" and charged Smith with doctoring the document without their knowledge or consent. They accused him of having no motivations beyond those of nepotism and "selfish gratification."[55]

Publicly, integrationists charged Smith with privileging family over community. Privately, however, they understood that Paul's appointment would severely damage, or even defeat, their efforts. The success of their campaign depended upon their ability to demonstrate that segregation was inherently unequal *and* that black Bostonians universally opposed it. The Smith School's former white headmasters, while usually qualified, had drawn the ire of black parents, who believed that the men treated their children with cruelty and indifference. Integrationists feared that an African American teacher as respected as Paul would entice black parents to return their children to the Smith School. The boycott they had mounted would collapse, and they would lose whatever leverage they had gained by forcing the school committee to choose between a school with no students or one meeting their demands.

Smith responded to these allegations by submitting a second document to the school committee. He informed the body that Roberts was concurrently circulating a memorial contesting Paul's nomination. He then accused his rival of opposing "all measures for the improvement of the Smith School" and in so doing, "disregarding the interests of the people living in its vicinity." In contrast to Roberts's indifference, Smith maintained, he had filed his appeal only after speaking with the parents of Smith School students. These men and women, he explained, were deeply disappointed with the quality of instruction their children received; in turn, they had turned to Smith to help them remedy the situation. At which point, according to Smith, he had consulted with Roberts and fellow integrationist John Robinson before organizing the petition. He hoped that the school committee would not dismiss his request solely on account of Roberts's machinations.[56]

Soon after, Smith authored an editorial in which he detailed his faith in the importance of independent black schools, controlled and operated by teachers who could identify personally with their students. Despite Roberts's and Watkins's claims to the contrary, Smith insisted that he did not object to integration but rather believed that African Americans should retain control over their neighborhood schools. That tension, between enforced integration and local control, would reverberate in the twentieth century, as black communities grappled with the consequences of desegregation. As he asserted, "the colored citizens of Boston, feeling the greatest anxiety that their children should be well educated, in order to make good citizens and good men, believe that their instructor should be one who is identified with themselves, who is well educated, who would naturally feel for and sympathize with them."[57] Further, instead of expecting black children, many new to freedom, to fight racial prejudice firsthand, Smith argued it was necessary to first cultivate their courage—an objective that could be achieved exclusively in a black-run institution. Only alongside "a band of brothers of their own complexion," he reasoned, could African American children discover their genius. And only after that realization, would they ever be able to "act well their part . . . as wise men and good citizens."[58]

Smith further recalled that he had served as secretary at the August meeting, believing it had been organized to demand the city remedy the Smith School's "deplorable condition."[59] According to Smith, Roberts, who chaired the meeting, stunned him and the audience by affirming his desire to see not the Smith School's improvement, but rather its destruction.[60] Another black Bostonian, Alexander Taylor, who also favored Paul's installation, confirmed Smith's version of events. Taylor added, however, that at the meeting in question, Roberts had attempted to stifle public discussion. At which point, at least according to Taylor, Roberts acknowledged his "full belief in the qualifications of Mr. Paul" and admitted that he only opposed his nomination "lest it should interfere with the abolition of the school."[61]

Smith reignited his efforts to secure Paul's installation at the Smith School one year later, in August 1849. This time, however, unlike the previous summer, the school committee endorsed Paul's nomination. And just as Roberts and his associates had feared from the start, the school committee framed its decision as a direct response to their request for desegregation. Two months earlier, in July 1849, Jonas Clark and 201 black Bostonians had appealed to the school committee to abolish the Smith School and grant African American children full access to the public schools.[62] In August 1849, William C. Nell, John T. Hilton, and other integrationists petitioned the school committee to close the Smith School.[63] Weeks later, it denied both appeals, rejecting integration as both "premature" and "impolitic."[64] In the same breath, it also relented to Smith's request for a black teacher, likely to retain the appearance that it was amenable to black demands.[65] Shortly thereafter, by a vote of fifteen to one, the school committee hired Thomas Paul as the Smith School's new master.[66]

Then, on what was to be Paul's first day on the job, integrationists encircled the Smith School and implored black students not to enter. The scene became so heated that someone called in a police officer to dispel the crowd. Patrols remained at the schoolhouse for two days.[67] Confrontation traveled from the schoolhouse steps to the Belknap Street Church later that evening. While integrationists resolved to keep "their children at home, or in temporary schools," Smith School supporters sought to make their voices heard. After another tense exchange, police were again called in to disperse the crowd while black rioters "assailed" the church with a "volley of stones and other missiles."[68] Integrationists including Roberts and Watkins thus interpreted Smith's decision to lobby for Paul's installation as a direct attempt to perpetuate segregation. In consequence, they cast him out as an enemy of the race.[69] According to one integrationist, Smith was a "young, ambitious bigot."[70] To another, he was, quite simply, an "ass."[71]

*   *   *

Given Benjamin Roberts's family history, it is not surprising that he found Boston's policy of separating children according to their skin color maddening. As historians James Brewer Stewart and George Price have documented, Roberts's lineage—English, African, and Native American—confounded the racial classification that "Euro-Americans enforced so ruthlessly" on people of color.[72] Roberts and his relatives opposed all attempts to categorize people by skin tone. Instead, his elders held up one promise of the Revolution: universal equality. Roberts's maternal grandfather, James Easton, served several years in the colonial militia, and James's son Hosea took his father's record as proof that the nation had failed to make good on one of its founding principles.[73]

Roberts's family instructed him that he had a personal responsibility to resist segregation and to promote education. In 1800, for example, galled by its decision to initiate segregated seating, grandfather Easton had refused to purchase a "negro" pew in Bridgewater's Fourth Church of Christ; instead, he procured seats in the "white" section of the gallery. The church's white congregants tarred the pew and then ejected him and his family.[74] Sometime around 1816, he opened a school for colored youth in Bridgewater, Massachusetts. The school survived for more than a decade.[75] Hosea Easton, Benjamin's uncle, and Robert Roberts, Benjamin's father, displayed the same devotion to educational opportunity. In 1831, they both lobbied on behalf of the failed movement to open an African college in New Haven.[76]

The Roberts family's devotion to activism, education, and integration influenced Benjamin's political formulations. At the early age of seventeen, in an 1834 *Liberator* editorial, Roberts had expounded on the question "Are Africans Americans?" Without hesitation, he proclaimed, "WE ARE AMERICANS!" He went on to defend blacks' claim to citizenship as he enumerated his ancestors' sacrifices and contributions. His forefathers, Roberts contended, had paid for his rights with their bodies and their blood. He affirmed, "This is the land of our birth; this is the land that our fathers fought, bled and died, to obtain liberty and independence, that our brethren now enjoy." He concluded his discussion by railing against all Americans, white and black, who fell prey to America's obsession with racial categorization. He took particular offense at black people, like Smith, who sustained this fixation by advocating separate schools and associations. Thus, as early as 1834, Roberts rejected separate schooling on the grounds that it underwrote America's nefarious fascination with racial classification.[77]

As Roberts's experience attests, in contrast to Baltimore and other slaveholding cities, few African Americans in Boston secured work in skilled professions. Even those with vocational training often lacked patronage and were forced to secure alternative, less lucrative, situations. Roberts experienced this difficulty first hand. Apprenticed as a shoemaker, he applied to scores of shops with "A good recommendation" in hand. Not one would hire him, he believed, because of his "dark stain of brow." Roberts expected his circumstance was not unique. There were "*Hundreds* of mechanics, in this city and vicinity, [who] are denied access to employment, for the very same crime." He knew two carpenters, five blacksmiths, two gold and silversmiths, one male tailor, eight shoemakers, at least eight female tailors, four milliners and dressmakers, and a host of brick makers, brush makers, coopers, and masons "who would, if any encouragement was offered, gladly embrace the opportunity of working at their trades."[78]

By 1850, as in Baltimore, the majority of African Americans in Boston supported themselves with unskilled and semiskilled manual labor; similarly, most of these individuals did not hold permanent positions but

TABLE 7 **Occupation of African American Men in Boston Ward 6 and Baltimore Ward 17, 1850**

	Boston, % ($n = 271$)	Baltimore, % ($n = 641$)
Nonmanual	7.5	0.9
Skilled	18.1	45.4
Unskilled/semiskilled	56.1	44.5
Service	8.5	4.4
None	2.2	—
Blank	7.4	4.8

Source: Census Schedules, Boston and Baltimore, 1850.

worked instead as day laborers, a situation that promised frequent, unpredictable periods of unemployment. In addition, while black Bostonians' exclusion from skilled trades was probably not as complete as Roberts had suggested, proportionally far fewer African Americans in Boston than in Baltimore performed skilled trades (Table 7). At the same time, however, in comparison with Baltimore, a greater percentage of black men in Boston supported themselves in nonmanual professions.[79]

Following along the path blazed by his grandfather, Benjamin Roberts worked diligently to expand black men's access to both mental and skilled occupations. As early as 1837, he had launched the *Anti-Slavery Herald,* which abolitionist Amos Phelps described as "a small anti-slavery paper, edited and published entirely by colored men," in an effort to provide vocational instruction to people of color. Less than a month later, however, his endeavor collapsed, and Roberts found himself embroiled in a messy dispute with Phelps, his former patron. For a time at least, Roberts believed that the *Anti-Slavery Herald* had failed because white abolitionists were reluctant to support him and also, by extension, black education. He fumed to Phelps:

> I am for *improvement* among this class of people, *mental* and *physical.* The arts and sciences have never been introduced to any extent among us—therefore they are of the utmost importance. If anti-Slavery men will not subscribe to the advancement of these principles, but *rail out* and *protest against* them when took up by those who have a darker skin, why we will go to the *heathen.* The principle grounds on which the anti-slavery cause is said to be founded (and *boasting* are not a few) *are the elevation of the free colored people here.* Now it is altogether useless to pretend to affect the welfare of blacks in this country, unless the chains of prejudice are broken. It is of no use [to] say with the mouth we are friends of the slave and not try to encourage and assist the free colored people in raising themselves. Here is sir the first efforts of the

colored man in this country of the kind, vis. the paper *published, printed* and *edited* by colored persons in Massachusetts—shall *this* be defeated?[80]

In the aftermath of the *Anti-Slavery Herald's* demise and his subsequent split with Phelps, Roberts withdrew from Boston and relocated to Lynn, Massachusetts, where he continued to work as a printer. He revived some of his connections in 1847, however, when he moved back to the Boston area and publicly entered the movement for school desegregation.[81]

In September 1847, Benjamin Roberts petitioned the primary school board to allow his daughter Sarah to enroll in the all-white Otis School. Like many young black Bostonians, Benjamin Roberts's daughter Sarah reportedly walked many blocks, past several schools, from her home in the city's West End before she reached the segregated Smith School in Beacon Hill.[82] It did not take the board long to deny Benjamin Roberts's application on the grounds of Sarah's skin color. Undeterred, Roberts sent his daughter to the primary school closest to their Andover Street residence in February 1848. The school's white instructor refused her admission. Under the terms of an 1845 statute that empowered pupils barred from city schools to request remuneration, Roberts sued the city for one thousand dollars in damages. The Court of Common Pleas ruled against him. Roberts then contacted African American attorney Robert Morris to file an appeal on Sarah's behalf. In October 1848, Morris submitted the document to the court and asked Charles Sumner to assist him at the trial.[83]

Sumner organized his closing arguments around the assertion that African Americans were citizens, and, therefore, the school committee lacked the authority to exclude them from public institutions. Yet contrary to Sumner's intentions, rather than reaffirming the rights African Americans believed they had earned, the *Roberts* verdict circumscribed their civil rights for a century. Ruling against Roberts, Chief Justice Lemuel Shaw dismissed Sumner's declaration that "*all men, without distinction of color or race, are equal before the law*" and settled on what would become the defining doctrine of Jim Crow segregation: separate but equal.[84] In denying African Americans the right to equal protection in favor of the city's authority to assign pupils to public schools, Shaw's ruling gave birth to the precedent that segregation in all arenas of public life—transportation, housing, and, most important, public schooling—did not contradict the Constitution. Five decades later, Shaw's concept of separate but equal reemerged in Henry Brown's ruling in *Plessy v. Ferguson* (1896).

Indeed, Shaw's verdict in *Roberts* proved so tenacious that Thurgood Marshall was battling it a half-century later in *Brown v. Board of Education* (1954).[85]

The justice system acted swiftly in the case of Roberts and Watkins. In June 1851, just three weeks after Smith's attack, their trial for assault and battery and false imprisonment opened in Boston's Municipal Court. Watkins advanced his own defense, while white attorney John C. Park appeared for Roberts. Park had long been sympathetic to the integrationists, and this was not the first time that he had spoken on their behalf. In 1844, he had represented African American parents in their efforts to remove white Smith School master Abner Forbes, whom they charged had inflicted "severe and unusual modes of punishment" on their children.[86] The following year, as he testified before the primary school committee, Park argued that the city lacked the legal authority to separate "colored" children from their white peers, noting that "if the colored man wishes to send his child to the nearest school, and within geographical limits, we have no right to deny him."[87] In light of the role that the desegregation debate had ostensibly played in Smith's attack, Park seemed a natural choice to lead the defense.[88]

As the trial proceeded, a number of witnesses were called to the stand. Watchman Jonathan B. Wheelock testified that Roberts and Watkins "did make an assault with great violence," seizing and holding "the said Smith with intent . . . to kill and murder."[89] But perhaps no one damned the defense more than Roberts. He denied that he had been the primary architect of Smith's attack, yet he acknowledged that he had known for some time that it was in the offing. As he explained, "For a number of days previous, it was hinted among several colored persons that on Wednesday evening last, a party would furnish themselves with a bucket of tar and a few feathers, and repair to a convenient location to *frighten* Thomas P. Smith." Having recently appeared before the state legislature to testify against integration, Roberts reported, Smith had "made himself extremely obnoxious to every respectable colored man, woman and child in this city." "It is bad enough, we think," Roberts went on, "for a white man to make statements like the above, but when a *black one* will voluntarily declare, in opposition to the feelings of an injured people, that these are the sentiments of a majority of them, he is utterly destitute of the principle of a man." And so, explained Roberts, a plan was devised. "The determination was not to *kill or feloniously assault* the said Smith, but to frighten him by a threat of tar and feathers." Although Roberts contended that—as "nothing more than a spectator and going there as a matter of curiosity"—he had stood "some 150 or 200 feet" away from Smith when "some half-a-dozen persons found their way to the upper part of Second Street, having with them tar and feathers, and succeeded in catching their victim," he acknowledged that the attack was successful. Smith had, in fact, been "frightened out of his wits."[90]

The particular form of the assault Roberts described should not be ignored. In an act both performative and commemorative, Roberts and Watkins, who had both come of age in an era in which black elites embraced virtues like respectability and order, inflicted a ritual of public humiliation while casting themselves as true patriots and marking Smith as a traitor to his race and nation. During the Revolutionary period, colonists—including free blacks—had seized upon the practice of tarring and feathering as a means of asserting their incipient identity as Americans. Although the ritual declined in popularity after independence, it occasionally emerged in the nineteenth century, largely as a means of defining a community's moral boundaries. Southern whites, for example, tarred and feathered accused black criminals and suspected abolitionists; in the North, antiabolitionist mobs tried to tar and feather antislavery advocates, including William Lloyd Garrison.[91] It is especially noteworthy that in 1835, black ministers in Baltimore threatened Watkins's father, William Watkins, "with a coat of tar and feathers" because he had spoken out in opposition to colonization.[92]

African Americans had struggled to participate in the public memory of the Revolution from the late eighteenth century and, by proxy, to lay claim to their role in their nation's creation.[93] As historian David Waldstreicher demonstrates, beginning in the late 1790s, antislavery whites and free blacks used July Fourth and other patriotic celebrations to condemn slavery and, in some northern communities, to commemorate its conclusion.[94] Such gestures were intended to recast the "peculiar institution" as an American problem at odds with the country's founding principles. These nationalist celebrations, Waldstreicher writes, also "became principal venues for political participation and for debates concerning what American identity was and what it meant." Accordingly, those whites who were uneasy with blacks' efforts to claim the democratic promises of the Revolution for themselves "hustled" African Americans from these nationalist spaces.[95]

It was no coincidence that some of the most vicious attacks by whites against free people of color occurred on the nation's anniversary. On July

4, 1834, for example, whites in New York City assailed an integrated celebration at Charles Finney's Chatham Street Church. Violence then spilled
over to St. Philip's African Episcopal Church, which white rioters burned
to the ground.[96] One year later, on July 4, 1835, a white mob attacked
an integrated school in Canaan, New Hampshire, which Thomas Paul
attended, eventually tearing the building down to its foundation. Some
African Americans responded to this intimidation by diverting their en-
ergies to racially focused observances: January First, the anniversary of
Haitian Independence, or August First, West Indian emancipation. Others, however, took Independence Day as an occasion for drawing attention to the hypocrisies inherent in American conceptions of freedom.[97]
Frederick Douglass, who delivered the stirring 1852 address in Rochester,
New York, "What to the American Slave Is Your Fourth of July?" was
prominent among them.[98]

Black Bostonian William C. Nell, one of the leaders in the movement
for school integration, saw the advantages of aligning African Americans'
struggle for equality with Boston's pivotal role in the events of the American Revolution. On March 5, 1851, just two months before Smith was assaulted and on the anniversary of the Boston Massacre, Nell organized a
campaign to persuade the city to erect a monument to Crispus Attucks,
"the first martyr" of the Revolution. That year, Nell also released his pamphlet *Service of Colored Americans in the Wars of 1776 and 1812,* a prelude
to his more extensive *Colored Patriots of the American Revolution* (1855).
Such activities, one may surmise, contributed to Roberts's and Watkins's
decision to assault Smith in the particular way that they did.[99]

We know far less than we should about why the Revolution assumed
a noticeable role in the civic culture of black Bostonians around the time
of the tar and feathers scrape. Several factors may have played a part:
the seventy-fifth anniversary of American independence; whites' desire
to reclaim national unity in the midst of increasing sectional tensions;
and abolitionists' attempts, in the aftermath of the Fugitive Slave Law,
to recast the Revolution as an epic conflict between liberty and slavery.
In Boston, speeches denouncing the legislative measure compared slave
catchers and the law's defenders with Tories, while characterizing fugitives and their antislavery allies as freedom-loving patriots. In October
1850, for example, soon after the law passed, free black Bostonians affirmed, "The example of the Revolutionary Fathers in resisting British
oppression, and throwing the tea overboard in Boston harbor, rather than
submit to a three penny tax, is a most significant one to us, when man is

likely to be deprived of his God-given liberty."[100] Four months later, as he called on Bostonians to resist the Fugitive Slave Law, Charles Sumner read excerpts from John Adams's 1765 diary, which reflected on popular resistance to the Stamp Act. Having fired up the crowd, Sumner then suggested they tar and feather marshals, judges, and other officials who by their actions or decisions assisted in the heinous deed of capturing escaped slaves.[101]

It is, indeed, impossible to overstate the trauma that the Fugitive Slave Law had inflicted upon Boston's black community. The statute put all African Americans in Boston at risk of being suspected fugitives and, therefore, noncitizens. Although it is unclear precisely how many black people fled the city because of it, the *Boston Evening Transcript* reported that "quite a number of families in this city, where either the father or mother are fugitives have been broken up, and the furniture sold off, with a view of leaving for safer quarters in Nova Scotia or Canada."[102] In this context, school integrationists may have concluded that it was all the more essential to demand equal access to public institutions, in particular, public schools. To their mind, all black residents of Boston were free, even if they had been born into slavery, so full and equal access to racially integrated schools could mark their status as free and full members of the body politic. Truly equal citizenship, they concluded, could not coexist with segregated educational institutions.[103] The furor surrounding the law likely convinced many black Bostonians, including Roberts and Watkins, that desperate measures were necessary to secure their claim to citizenship and, by extension, to American identity. Roberts's personal loss in his 1850 desegregation lawsuit no doubt intensified that belief.

In April 1851, just weeks before the tar and feathers scrape, unrest over the Fugitive Slave Law personally affected individuals on both sides of the school desegregation dispute. Two months earlier, in February 1851, abolitionists had succeeded in rescuing accused fugitive Shadrack Minkins and spiriting him to safety in Canada. Roberts, a printer by trade, distributed over one thousand broadsides throughout the city warning free blacks to remain vigilant (Figure 15). Vigilance did little to protect fugitive slave Thomas Sims, who was arrested during the first week of April and shipped south just two weeks later. Both Robert Morris, the black attorney who had argued Roberts's school desegregation case, and the separatist Smith were arrested and charged in the failed attempt to rescue Sims. The first Boston fugitive to have been captured and returned to slavery under the terms of the new law, Sims became a haunting symbol of African

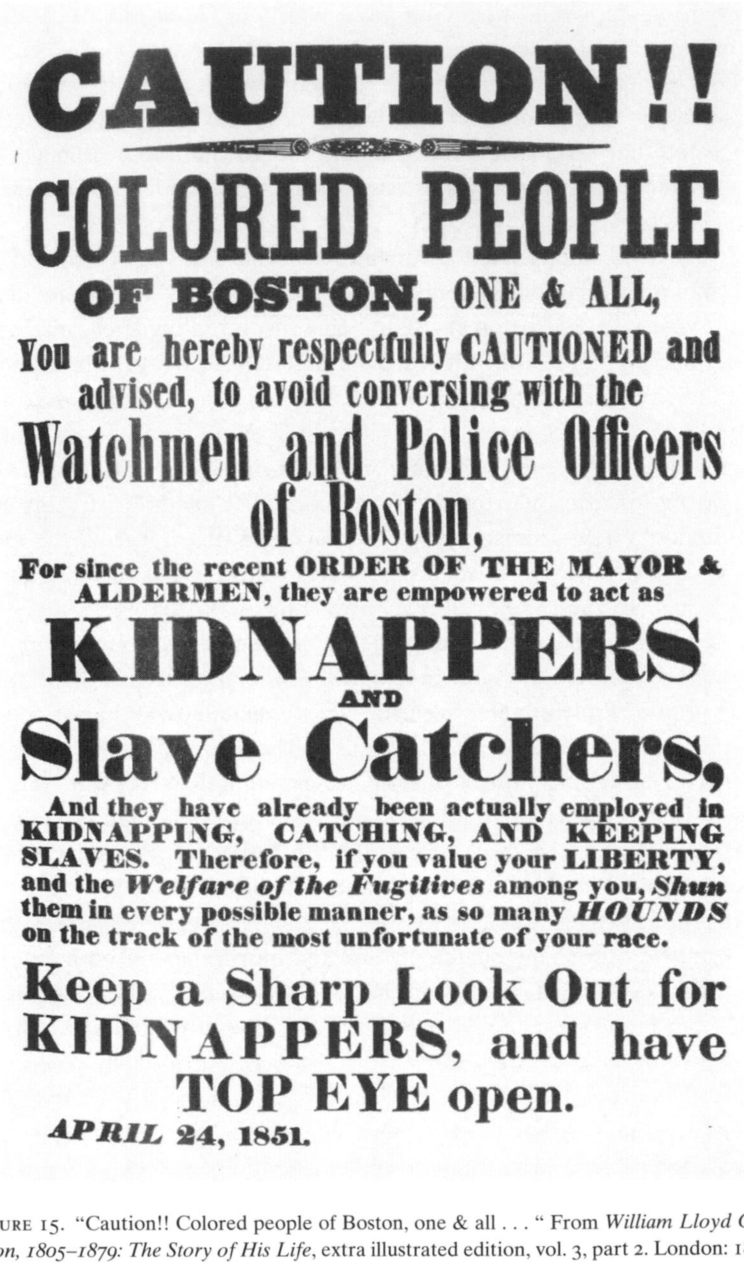

CAUTION!!

COLORED PEOPLE

OF BOSTON, ONE & ALL,

You are hereby respectfully CAUTIONED and advised, to avoid conversing with the

Watchmen and Police Officers of Boston,

For since the recent ORDER OF THE MAYOR & ALDERMEN, they are empowered to act as

KIDNAPPERS

AND

Slave Catchers,

And they have already been actually employed in KIDNAPPING, CATCHING, AND KEEPING SLAVES. Therefore, if you value your LIBERTY, and the *Welfare of the Fugitives* among you, *Shun* them in every possible manner, as so many *HOUNDS* on the track of the most unfortunate of your race.

Keep a Sharp Look Out for KIDNAPPERS, and have TOP EYE open.

APRIL 24, 1851.

FIGURE 15. "Caution!! Colored people of Boston, one & all . . . " From *William Lloyd Garrison, 1805–1879: The Story of His Life*, extra illustrated edition, vol. 3, part 2. London: 1889. Courtesy of the Massachusetts Historical Society.

Americans' continued vulnerability and exacerbated black Bostonians' anxieties over their inability to secure the full rights of citizenship.[104]

*   *   *

The jury hearing the case against Roberts found it difficult to believe that he had just happened to be standing two hundred feet away while "some half-a-dozen" unidentified persons assailed his long-time rival. And so, Roberts's peers found him "guilty of assaulting and beating Thomas P. Smith with intent to imprison him by force." At the same time, they rejected Roberts's attempt to elevate the attack to the level of Revolutionary protest and denied his tar-and-feathers defense. In treating the episode as just another case of assault and battery, the jury dismissed the symbolic importance that Roberts and Watkins had sought to bring to their intraracial attack. Although the colonists' battle for rights against their fellow Englishmen was viewed as heroic, Roberts's and Watkins's similarly internecine struggle was treated as no more than an act of street violence, devoid of effect and devoid of principle. The jury acquitted both Smith's brother Elijah, whom Roberts had accused of accosting him with an axe, and Watkins, about whose involvement they could not agree. The court then fined Roberts twenty-five dollars, plus costs, and ordered him to surrender a bond of two hundred dollars to be returned after one year's good behavior. If he violated either penalty, he could be "confined to Hard Labor in the House of Corrections" for up to three months.[105]

The tar and feathers scrape illustrates the degree to which an atmosphere of violence, symbolic and actual, saturated Boston's black community in 1851.[106] More than a century before white Bostonians resisted court-ordered desegregation of their public schools in the 1970s, the school desegregation movement had splintered the city's black community. This was not just an honest dispute among well-meaning men; it was bitter. And at least in May 1851, when Thomas Paul Smith returned home beaten and bruised and his brother went after his opponent, Benjamin Roberts, with an axe, it was ugly—perhaps more ugly than generations of historians have realized.

Given its absence from the African American and abolitionist press, it is not clear how Boston's black community responded to or remembered the tar and feathers scrape. But given the rhetorical ambiguity (or, in more positive terms, flexibility) of the American Revolution as a symbol of division as well as unity among the free black community, it is not entirely

FANEUIL HALL
COMMEMORATIVE
FESTIVAL,
March 5th, 1858.

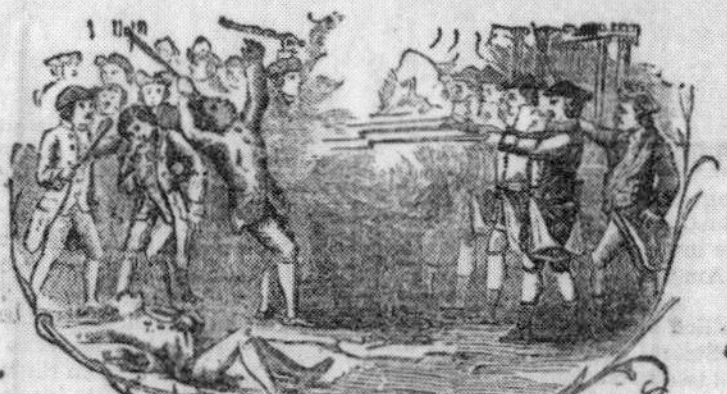

PROTEST
AGAINST THE
DRED SCOTT
"DECISION."

"BOSTON MASSACRE. MARCH 5th, 1770."

ON the 5th day of March, 1783, WILLIAM COOPER, Town Clerk, made a motion embracing the following clauses:

Whereas, The annual celebration of the Boston Massacre on the 5th of March, 1770, by the institution of a public oration has been found to be of eminent advantage to the cause of virtue and patriotism among her citizens, and * * * * * *

Whereas, The immediate motives which induced the commemoration of that day do now no longer exist in their primitive force * * * * * * * *

It is therefore

Resolved, That the Celebration of the 5th of March, from henceforth, shall cease, and that instead thereof, the anniversary of the fourth day of July, 1776 * * * * * shall be constantly celebrated by the delivery of a public oration * * * in which the orator shall consider the feelings, manners and principles, which led to this great national event, as well as the important and happy effects, whether general or domestic, which have already, and will forever, continue to flow from this auspicious epoch.

In accordance therewith, there has not been a public celebration of the 5th of March since 1783.

In view of the alarming spread of despotism in these United States — the suppression of Free Speech in one half of the Union — the subjugation of white citizens, and annihilation of the citizenship of Colored Americans by the Dred Scott Decision, the subscriber has, after mature deliberation, concluded, that now is the timely and significant hour for an application of that sentiment in the Constitution of Massachusetts, which declares *"that a frequent recurrence to its fundamental principles is absolutely n. cessary to preserve the advantages of liberty, and to maintain a free government.*

And, therefore, invites his fellow-citizens and friends to a Public Commemoration of the

88TH ANNIVERSARY OF THE BOSTON MASSACRE,

TO BE OBSERVED IN

FANEUIL HALL,

ON THURSDAY EVENING, MARCH 5th, 1858.

1858

FIGURE 16. William C. Nell, "Fanueil Hall Commemorative Festival, March 5, 1858. Protest against the Dred Scott Decision," 1858. Courtesy of the American Antiquarian Society.

surprising that those who lined up on either side of the incident rallied together under the Revolutionary banner seven years later. In yet another strange twist in a strange set of events, on March 5, 1858, as part of a public commemoration of the eightieth anniversary of the Boston Massacre organized to protest the Dred Scott decision, Benjamin Roberts and Thomas Paul Smith's brother Elijah shared the stage at Faneuil Hall (Figure 16).[107] Together they sang "Parody on 'Red, White, and Blue,' " written by Charlotte Forten:

> Oh, when shall each child of our Father,
> > Whatever his nation or hue,
> Be protected throughout thy dominions,
> > 'Neath the folds of the red, white and blue.
> > 'Neath the folds of the red, white and blue.[108]

What happened in the intervening years to bring Benjamin Roberts and Elijah Smith to the same political platform is a matter of speculation. Yet their verses that evening suggest that in the wake of the Dred Scott decision, they had found common cause, as William Nell had suggested: to protest "the annihilation of the citizenship of Colored Americans."[109] Three years earlier, in 1855, Boston had desegregated its public schools, but with Chief Justice Roger B. Taney's controversial ruling that African Americans were not—nor would they ever be—full and equal members of the nation, the constraints upon black citizenship seemed to be tightening each year. In the face of such an assault on their race, perhaps both Elijah Smith and Benjamin Roberts had independently concluded that, with a common enemy to connect them, they could – indeed, they must—join together.

Conclusion: The Great Equalizer?

Perhaps no maxim is engrained more deeply in America's educational imagination than Horace Mann's assertion that education, "beyond all other devices of human origin, is the great equalizer of the conditions of man. . . . "[1] By extension, the idea that public schools exist to alleviate inequality continues to resonate in conversations about educational opportunity—and for good reason. This mythology has a long history. The concept of a public school (or a common school, its antebellum antecedent) evokes images of inclusion, images that Mann himself promoted in an effort to entice Americans to finance the education of other people's children. A "[f]ree school system," Mann contended in 1848, "knows no distinction of rich and poor, of bond and free, or between those who, in the imperfect light of this world, are seeking, through different avenues, to reach the gate of heaven."[2] Whether he was pandering to America's worst fears about outsiders or appealing to its best sense of itself as a land of opportunity, his assertion that common schools could foster economic mobility and civic harmony continues to inform American expectations for public schools. Yet what Mann did not acknowledge, or what he did not acknowledge directly, was the cost of this ideology for the very ideals he invoked to drum up support for these institutions—for if, as he suggested, common schools could knit citizens together, they could exclude others just as easily.

The fact that public schools arguably have yet to become the "great equalizers" Mann imagined is not simply a consequence of failed reforms or misguided reformers. Rather, inequity was embedded into these institutions from the start. From the time European settlers built their first schoolhouses in America, many saw these institutions as central to key components of the colonial project: economic expansion, religious expression, political stability, and racial domination. While the form and function of schooling has evolved in multiple ways since the seventeenth century, Americans' faith in the awesome power of the schoolhouse to achieve an array of social, economic, and political objectives has remained omnipresent. Americans continue to look to these institutions to alleviate a range of ills: socioeconomic inequality; political and cultural fragmentation; and ethnic, religious, and class divisions, to name a few. Whether their faith is misplaced is not central to this story, but the premise at the heart of that devotion is. For just as many Americans see public schools as fundamental to the well-being of their children, their communities, and their country, so did their predecessors in the early nineteenth century. Even as they were inventing the concept of a common school, antebellum Americans, white and black, understood these institutions as gatekeepers of the good life—of socioeconomic mobility, civic inclusion, political participation, and vocational opportunity.

By juxtaposing white resistance to African American education with the movement for common school reform, I have sought to illuminate a contradiction inherent in America's educational mythology, one that feels particularly pronounced in the narratives of progress and democracy that suffuse scholarship on this period. Simply put, one cannot appreciate American educational history in all its complexity without integrating African Americans' divergent experiences. In saying this, I am not calling for historians to locate race at the center of America's educational master narrative in lieu of gender, class, culture, and other considerations, but I do believe that ideas about race are fundamental, and not tangential, to this history. Along similar lines, scholars seeking to understand how ideas about race and citizenship evolved in the antebellum period should take seriously access to public schools. The decisions that a society makes about educating its children say a great deal about how it imagines their future civic contributions. Of course, the individual priorities of students, parents, and localities can and often do exist in tension with the collective needs of the nation, but the decision to *deny* education to specific groups speaks volumes about their larger place within the body politic. Antebellum black educational activists appreciated this connection, interpreting their exclusion from common schools both as a barrier to individual advancement and to their collective ability to secure equal rights. As Benjamin Roberts noted in March 1851, a few months before he allegedly tried to tar and feather Thomas Paul Smith,

We have waged eternal war against exclusive schools, on account of their hindrance to our rights; and we believe them injurious in all communities where men, without

distinction of color, are equal before the laws. In Massachusetts, according to the
Constitution and the laws, the colored man is acknowledged equal. As this is the
fact, we wish, as law-loving and law-abiding citizens of this Commonwealth, to enjoy
perfectly and unqualifiedly all the rights and privileges we are entitled to. We wish
to have the blessings of common schools distributed without partiality—EQUAL.
These are our desires; and for the fulfillment of the same we shall continue to pray,
until the fact is established, that in Massachusetts, all men live in the full enjoyment
of their rights.[3]

By enacting antieducation statutes in Connecticut and enforcing de
facto school segregation in Massachusetts, by expelling a proposed African
college from New Haven and demolishing an integrated academy in Canaan, New Hampshire, white northerners exposed their profound discomfort with African American efforts to claim citizenship in the context of a
society still marked by slavery. Other factors also contributed to the emergence of white opposition to black education in this period. In New Haven, crumbling common schools, expanding access to higher education,
and white working-class concerns over social status combined to defeat
an effort to create a college for black men. While in actuality few black
people in New Haven displaced white workers from their jobs, the sting of
industrialization led many white working people to agree with Aristides
and link their precarious position to this phantom competition. Against
this backdrop, radical abolition eclipsed colonization as white reformers'
cause of choice, an ideological transformation that undercut white efforts
to literally and symbolically remove black people and reinforced African
American claims to an American identity. In the wake of a trio of arguably
abolitionist-induced traumas—David Walker's *Appeal,* William Lloyd
Garrison's *Liberator*, and Nat Turner's rebellion—a manual labor college
for black men appeared even more menacing.

While slavery fundamentally disconnected enslaved and free black Baltimoreans from citizenship, African Americans' educational experiences
in this slaveholding city suggest that here, as in New Haven, white attitudes
toward black schooling were rooted in economic self-interest. The relative
size of the city's free and enslaved black population led some whites to tolerate private black schools because they saw their own economic vitality as
dependent upon black labor. In this particular context, slavery's existence
actually worked to benefit African American efforts at self-education.
Despite the prevalence of gradual manumission agreements that replaced
the seaport's enslaved black population with the nation's largest free black

community, a complex system of race-based regulations continued to check black people's literal and socioeconomic mobility. While most African Americans in the city were free in name by 1830, slavery's enduring existence allowed some whites to feel more at ease with African Americans' educational institutions, even as the city excluded all black children from public schools. White Baltimoreans, in other words, tolerated African American education only in so far as it posed no real challenge to the established racial hierarchy and black people held no real prospect of becoming American citizens.

To modern-day Americans familiar with the nation's long struggle over desegregation, the notion of schools as sites of social, economic, and political conflict is neither new nor unfamiliar. But it might surprise some to learn that the promise of public schooling for all was a fiction from the start. While Mann eschewed overt discussions about race, the vision of public schooling he articulated was rooted in and reflective of Americans' evolving racial ideology. By conceptualizing common schools as citizen makers, Mann inadvertently provided ammunition for the devastating assertion that African Americans were neither citizens nor Americans. Black educational activists, in turn, appreciated the relationship between school reformers' rhetoric and their own efforts to abolish slavery and to claim citizenship. By extension, their resistance to segregated schooling stemmed not just from a belief that these institutions promoted inequality—although most held that opinion—but also from an understanding of the symbolic and symbiotic relationship between political inclusion and public schools. It was no coincidence that Boston's black educational activists invoked the egalitarian ethos of the Revolution in their desegregation campaign. They did so to remind white Bostonians, particularly in the aftermath of the Fugitive Slave Law, of America's failure to live up to the promises of the founding and to signal that *their* history and the nation's history were one in the same. Integrationists further understood white efforts to exclude black children from common schools as part and parcel of a larger impulse to expel all black people from the body politic, an impulse that sought—and failed—to construct a definition of American with whiteness at its core.

Despite Mann's assertion that education was the great equalizer, the power of racism in antebellum America and the inequitable structures to which it gave rise also prevented many black people from deriving a vocational benefit from their literary instruction. This assertion is not meant to suggest that education had no effect on African Americans' economic mobility, a question beyond the bounds of this study. Instead, it is intended to reiterate the importance of integrating race into discussions about educational opportunity. For those who continue to keep the faith in the power of public schools to make the American Dream available to everyone, it is worth noting that education could not empower antebellum African Americans to rise and fall by their own merits when so many other avenues of socioeconomic advancement remained closed to them.[4] For many black families, in fact, schooling entailed financial sacrifice. Those who elected to school their children not only had to pay for books and other supplies, they also had to compensate for their children's lost wages. These were not small sacrifices, particularly for men and women new to freedom, vacillating between poverty and stability.

But if literary instruction did not translate into vocational opportunity for many black people in the antebellum period, then why did African Americans in New Haven, Baltimore, and Boston devote so much energy to creating and sustaining educational institutions? Many did so, in part, because they genuinely believed in the unparalleled power of schools to lessen inequality and to promote civic inclusion—even if these institutions had yet to deliver on those promises. To Frederick Douglass, in fact, education was especially important to African Americans precisely because of their exclusion from other avenues of economic and political advancement. In 1849 he observed,

> Knowledge . . . is about the only power that at present can be wielded by the colored people. Political power they have not; the power of wealth they cannot reach—our only hope in this country at present, rests upon the improvement of our minds, and the elevation of our character. Knowledge is the preliminary step to all power, and for the want of this knowledge, the colored man is killed all day long. Our ignorance is pleaded as a reason for withholding our rights, while knowledge itself has been locked up from us.[5]

And he was not alone in this assessment. More than two decades before on his voyage to New Haven, John Brown Russwurm had uttered a similar sentiment about the importance of education. "Let every other thing be done to improve our condition," he observed, and "all our labor will be in vain."[6] While Douglass, Russwurm, and other black educational activists shared a common faith in the particular importance of schools to African Americans, many of the questions that divided them still resist easy answers. In what kind of environment will black students thrive? How should African American teachers' occupational concerns factor into discussions about desegregation? Do black people have a special responsibility to invest in educational institutions in light of their unique history? To what extent should they remain loyal to public schools, particularly when other institutions hold out the promise of superior academic and economic achievement? In raising such questions, I aim not only to provoke discussion, but to highlight just how many issues central to questions of race, citizenship, and educational opportunity have their roots in the antebellum period.

In the end, what mattered most to African American parents, teachers, students, and activists was not whether, in fact, public schools were actually the great equalizers Mann claimed they could be but their own ability to educate themselves in the face of indifference and hostility. African Americans' educational activism embodied the flexibility and creativity that also epitomized their opposition to slavery. Their actions defy a temptation to see militancy and accommodation as dichotomous and to link resistance with separatism. Recall Russwurm's devotion to elevating the African American community and his decision to leave for Liberia just a few years after his meeting with Aristides. Recall the persistence with which black Baltimoreans petitioned the city to be released from the school tax, employing a language of deference to launch radical appeals. Recall Benjamin Roberts's alleged decision to tar and feather Thomas Paul Smith and, in so doing, to use violence not to distance himself from America but to engage more fully with its institutions and traditions.

Likewise, the dispute between William Watkins and William Levington highlights the inherent challenge of linking political protest with educational opportunity. In this way, it presaged the debate more than a half century later between Booker T. Washington and W.E.B. Du Bois over the thorny relationships among education, civil rights, and economic mobility. Like Washington and Du Bois, Watkins and Levington pursued education because they saw it as linked to civic inclusion, even as they disagreed over the merits of militancy and compromise. But their activism raised a number of unresolved questions as it became clear that education alone could not break down other forms of economic and legal exclusion. Should parents ask—or allow—children to sacrifice in order to advance movements for social justice and equal rights? Should students, teachers, and families prioritize political uplift or educational opportunity? What kind of protest is best suited to alleviate educational inequity? Are separate institutions unequal inherently?

It is no coincidence that schools incited such effusive emotions from white and black Americans in this period. On the one hand, as Thomas Paul Smith and white residents of the Southack Street neighborhood affirmed, public schools were the most local of institutions, steeped in the politics of place, neighborhood, and community. But as black advocates of integration and common school reformers supposed, they were also the most national: they were uniquely able to affirm who could—and who could not—claim American identity. Imbued with all that responsibility, the wonder is not that schools created such deep divides within and across racial lines but that so many diverse individuals expected so much from the same institution.

Appendix 1

Index of Occupational Categories

Nonmanual	Skilled, Manual	Semi- and Unskilled, Manual
Accountant	Baker	Bell hanger
Actor	Barber/hair dresser	Collier
Agent	Bookbinder	Cook
Apothecary	Builder	Dyer
Artist	Butcher	Express
Bank Cashier	Carpenter	Expressman
Bath	Carpet	Hackman
Broker	Carriage	Hostler
City worker	Carriage trainer	Job wagon
Clerk	Carver	Job work
Collector	Cigar	Laborer
Custom house	Compass roof (roofer)	Lamp lighter
Dealer	Cooper	Marble
Dentist	Cushion, bench	Mash maker
Doctor	Cutter	Paper hanger
Druggist	Engineer	Pile driver
Dry goods	Engraver	Plasterer
Editor	Farmer	Porter
Express business	Fir	Railroad
Grocer	Founders/foundry	Rigger
Houses	Furniture	Seaman
Judge	Gardener	Slate keeper
Law/lawyer	Gilder	Slater
	Gold pen	
Matron	(manufacturing)	Teamster
Merchant	Hardware	Tender
Minister	Harness	Tin man
Music	Hatter	Truckman
Office/company	Housewright	Varnisher
Police/police officer	Iron holder	Vendor
		Worker (fur worker, iron
President	Iron moulder	worker, etc.)
Publisher	Japaner	
Sales	Jeweler	
Shops	Leather	

Index of Occupational Categories (*continued*)

Nonmanual	Skilled, Manual	Semi- and Unskilled, Manual
Stable Keeper	Lathe	
Stable	Maker	
Store	Manufacturing	
Superintendent reading		
room	Mason	
Teacher	Mechanics	
Toll man	Miller	
Trader	Painter (not artist)	
Watchman	Paper stainer	
	Plumber	
	Port painter	
	Printer	
	Sadler	
	Scissor grinder	
	Shoe	
	Sketchbook man	
	Smith	
	Tailor	
	Upholsterer	
	Wood wharf	

Service	None	Unknown
Coachman	None	M.U.S.C.
Domestic	Nonholder	Maine
Driver		
Hotel servant		
Waiter		

Appendix 2

Name, Occupation, and Address of Identifiable Petitioners Opposing the Proposal to Build a School for Black Children on Southack Street

Name	Occupation and Location (If Available)	Address
Allen, Francis	John Y. Champney and Francis Allen, Southack Street	Southack Street
Babcock, Abel	25 F. H. Market	House 44 Myrtle
Bartlett, John	Musician	19 Garden
Bayley, Benjamin	Housewright	15 South Russell
Beal, David	West Indies goods, 36 Belknap	36 Belknap
Beal, Madison	Grocer	Southack, corner of West Center
Bird, Asa	Cabinetmaker	House 6 North Russell
Blaney, Ambrose	Tinman, 81 Cambridge	House 18 Charles
Boles, Warren	Housewright, Sudbury	House 60 Myrtle
Bowker, Lazarus	Bricklayer	19 Myrtle
Briggs, Billings	Housewright	House 5 Myrtle Court
Carlton, William L.	Grocer, rear County Court House	Southack Street
Champney, John Y.	Housewright	House 5 Grove
Clark, Jonathan C.	Grocer, 10 Vine	House 3 Blossom Court
Crombie, Wm.	Tavern, 94 Cambridge	96 Cambridge
Cummings, Charls. W.	Smith, 135 Cambridge	House North Grove
Currier, J.T.	Bell hanger, Bromfield	House 17 May
Cushing, John	Housewright, Butolph	House 30 Garden
Cushing, Lemuel		32 Hancock
Daniels, Nath	Baker	38 Temple
Darling, Thos.	Darling and Pollard, soda, Frank Avenue	House 51 Allen
Davis, Jonathan	Paver	15 Garden
Dickinson, Dexter	Shipbuilder	House North Square
Dickinson, John		House 46 Bridge
Dunbar, Loring	(Mitchell and Dunbar)	House 50 Myrtle
Ellis, Rufus	Agent, Newton factory, 15 India wharf	House 2 Oak Place
Fay, Harrison	23 Fanueil Hall Market	House 34 Myrtle
Field, Wm. A.	Musician	West Center

Name, Occupation, and Address of Identifiable Petitioners Opposing the Proposal to Build a School for Black Children on Southack Street *(continued)*

Name	Occupation and Location (If Available)	Address
Fisher, Nathaniel	Beef	Garden
Forristall, Ezra	Truckman	House 6 Blossom
French, Samuel	Mason	Butolph
Frost, Reuben	Laborer	Rear 60 Myrtle
Fuller, Abrm. W.	Counselor	31 Court
Gay, James	Binder	House 35 Garden
Glover, Elisha V.	Constable, 2 Frank Avenue	House Southack Court
Greenwood, John	Housewright, S. Margin	House 33 Myrtle
Hadley, Moses	Toll gatherer, Cambridge	House 26 Charles
Hastings, Edm'd. T.	West Indies goods and sperm oil, 37 Commer	Garden
Hill, Elizabeth	Widow of Samuel	20 Myrtle
Hoppin, John	Laborer	House Garden
Hobart, Peter Jr.	Housewright, Hawley place	House North Russell
Jackson, Ward	Lumber, North Grove	House 12 McLean
Jermain, Roger	Paperhanger Harvard place	House Southack Court
Johnson, Abijah S.	Housewright, rear Charles	House 55 Belknap
Jones, David	Housewright	House South Russell
Judkins, Benjamin	Grocer, 91	House rear Cambridge
Kingsley, Elias	Mason, 25 Charles	House Charles
Lincoln, Ezra	Printer, 14 Congress	House 38 Myrtle
Low, John	Painter	South Russell
Lowell, Char. Russell	Clergyman, 83 Milk	House 3 Mount Vernon Place
Meads, Joseph	Grocer, 61 myrtle	House 65 Myrtle
Mitchel, Samuel H.	Mitchell (Sam. H.) and Dunbar (Loring), Housewrights, Lancaster	59 Myrtle
Mariner, Joseph	Clothing, 7 Congress square	House South
Norris, John	Housewright	Grove
Otis, H.G.		42 Beacon
Page, Calvin	Mason	House 21 Myrtle
Pike, Charles	Baker	George
Pike, William	Baker	104 Cambridge
Remick, Saml. H.	Housewright	Kennard Avenue
Richards, Wyatt	Mason	Garden
Roberts, Richard S.	Furniture, 114 Cambridge	House Fruit Street Court
Russell, John	Mason	Myrtle
Sargent, Ensign	Silverplater	House May
Shipley, Joel	Mason	39 Myrtle
Snow, William	Painter, Hawley place	House 24 Allen
Stevens, Franklin B.	Mahogany chairs, 113 Cambridge	House 60 Myrtle
Studley, Warren	Tailor	House South Russell
Templeton, John	Stonecutter, Charles	House George
Thomas, Mark W.	Painter, 44 Congress	House Southack Court
Tileston, Otis	Tileston (Otis), Samson (A.W.) and Co. (Peltiah Metcalf), dry goods, 174 Washington	House May
Titcomb, Stephen	32 Cornhill	House 6 Myrtle Court
Washburn, Theodore		House 32 Myrtle
Whitcomb, Asa	Whitcomb (Asa) and Bent (John P.), Grocers, Mt. Vernon	

Name, Occupation, and Address of Identifiable Petitioners Opposing the Proposal to Build a School for Black Children on Southack Street *(continued)*

Name	Occupation and Location (If Available)	Address
Whitney, Barnabas	Instructor, 22 Joy's building	House 35 Myrtle
Wiley, Thomas	Teller United States Bank of Boston	House Myrtle, corner of Butolph
Winter, F. B.	Mason	Corner of Myrtle Court and Center
Winthrop, Grenville T.	Counselor, 11 Court	House 7 Chestnut
Wood, Amos	Wood Amos and Son (Henry), lumber wharf	House 10 Charles
Wood, Henry	Housewright (A. Wood and Son)	House 20 Charles

Source: Ward 6 Tax Records (1834); Boston City Archives; Boston City Directory (1834).

Notes

Introduction

1. *Second Annual Report of the New-Hampshire Anti-Slavery Society* (Concord, N.H.: Elbridge G. Chase, 1836), 12–13; William Allen Wallace, *The History of Canaan, New Hampshire* (Concord, N.H.: Rumford Press, 1910), 268–69.

2. Craig Wilder, "Noyes Academy: The Struggle for a Black College in New Hampshire," lecture, Dartmouth College, Hanover, N.H., April 5, 2006, http://alumni.dartmouth.edu/media/ACE/chalktalk05wilderedit.mp3; "Not Quite a Riot," *Liberator*, August 8, 1835.

3. Alexander Crummell, *Africa and America: Addresses and Discourses* (Springfield, Mass.: Willey & Co., 1891), 280; "Coloured School in Canaan," *Connecticut Courant*, August 24, 1835.

4. George Kimball to David Lee Child, October 28, 1834, Anti-Slavery Collection, Boston Public Library.

5. George Kimball et al., "To the American Public," *Liberator*, October 25, 1834.

6. David L. Child and S. E. Sewall, "Noyes Academy," *Liberator*, February 28, 1835.

7. Crummell, *Africa and America*, 279.

8. Edward S. Abdy, *Journal of a Residence and Tour in the United States of North America, from April 1833, to October 1834*, vol. 3 (London: John Murray, 1835), 268.

9. Crummell, *Africa and America*, 280.

10. J. B. Wallace to William Allen Wallace, August 20, 1835, Papers of William Allen Wallace; Correspondence 1820–1840; New Hampshire Historical Society; William Allen Wallace, *History of Canaan*, 274–76.

11. Wallace, *History of Canaan*, 275.

12. Crummell, *Africa and America*, 280–1; Wallace, *History of Canaan*, 274–75.

13. Wallace, *History of Canaan*, 276.

14. *Fourth Annual Report of the Board of Managers of the Massachusetts Anti-Slavery Society* (Boston: Isaac Knapp, 1836), 27–8.

15. On the common school reform movement in antebellum America, see, for example, William J. Reese, *America's Public Schools: From the Common School to "No Child Left Behind"* (Baltimore: Johns Hopkins University Press, 2005); David Tyack, *Seeking Common Ground: Public Schools in a Diverse Society* (Cambridge: Harvard University Press, 2007); Carl Kaestle, *Pillars of the Republic: Common Schools and American Society:1760–1860* (New York: Hill and Wang, 1983); Lawrence A. Cremin, *American Education: The National Experience, 1783–1876* (New York: Harper and Row, 1982); and Michael Katz, *The Irony of Early School Reform: Educational Innovation in Mid-Nineteenth Century Massachusetts* (Boston: Beacon Press, 1968).

16. Linda Kerber, "The Meanings of Citizenship," *Journal of American History* 84 (December 1997): 834–36; Evelyn Nakano Glenn, *Unequal Freedom: How Race and Gender Shaped American Citizenship and Labor* (Cambridge: Harvard University Press, 2002), 19.

17. Paul Finkelman, "Prelude to the Fourteenth Amendment: Black Legal Rights in the Antebellum North," *Rutgers Law Journal* 17 (Spring and Summer 1986): 421–2, 480.

18. On free black education in the antebellum North see, for example, Stephen Kendrick and Paul Kendrick, *Sarah's Long Walk: The Free Blacks of Boston and How Their Struggle for Equality Changed America* (Boston: Beacon Press, 2004); Marian I. Hughes, *Refusing Ignorance: The Struggle to Educate Black Children in Albany, New York, 1816–1873* (Albany, N.Y.: Mount Ida Press, 1998); and Arthur O. White, "Blacks and Education in Antebellum Massachusetts: Strategies for Social Mobility" (Ed.D. dissertation, State University of New York at Buffalo, 1971).

19. On gradual emancipation in New England, see John Wood Sweet, *Bodies Politic: Negotiating Race in the American North, 1730–1830* (Baltimore and London: Johns Hopkins University Press, 2003), and Joanne Pope Melish, *Disowning Slavery: Gradual Emancipation and "Race" in New England, 1780–1860* (Ithaca: Cornell University Press, 1998).

20. Stephen T. Whitman, *The Price of Freedom: Slavery and Manumission in Baltimore and Early National Maryland* (Lexington: University Press of Kentucky, 1997).

21. I am indebted to Seth Rockman for this understanding of Baltimore's relationship to southern history. Peter Kolchin, *A Sphinx on the American Land: The Nineteenth-Century South in Comparative Perspective* (Baton Rouge: Louisiana State University Press, 2003), 4; Edward Pessen, "How Different from Each Other Were the Antebellum North and South?" *American Historical Review* 85 (December 1980): 1119–49; Thomas B. Alexander et al., "Antebellum North and South in Comparative Perspective: A Discussion," *American Historical Review* 85 (December 1980): 1150–66.

22. Seth Rockman, *Scraping By: Wage Labor, Slavery, and Survival in Early Baltimore* (Baltimore: Johns Hopkins University Press, 2009), 6–8. The concept of the "chattel principle" is articulated most fully in Walter Johnson, *Soul by Soul: Life inside the Antebellum Slave Market* (Cambridge, Mass.: Harvard University Press, 1999).

23. For this insight, I am indebted to Tracy Steffes.

24. On the history of African American education generally, see, for example, James D. Anderson, *No Sacrifice Too Great: The History of African American Education from Slavery to the Twenty-First Century* (Boston: Beacon Press, 2009); Adam Fairclough, *A Class of Their Own: Black Teachers in the Segregated South* (Cambridge, Mass.: Belknap Press, 2007); Heather Andrea Williams, *Self-Taught: African American Education in Slavery and Freedom* (Chapel Hill: University of North Carolina Press, 2005); Eric Anderson and Alfred A. Moss, Jr., *Dangerous Donations: Northern Philanthropy and Southern Black Education, 1902–1930* (Columbia, Mo.: University of Missouri Press, 1999); James D. Anderson, *The Education of Blacks in the South, 1860–1935* (Chapel Hill: University of North Carolina Press, 1988); Adam Fairclough, *Teaching Equality: Black Schools in the Age of Jim Crow* (Athens: University of Georgia Press, 2001); Robert A. Margo, *Race and Schooling in the South, 1880–1950* (Chicago: University of Chicago Press, 1990); Ronald E. Butchart, *Northern Schools, Southern Blacks, and Reconstruction: Freedmen's Education, 1862–1875* (Westport, Conn.: Greenwood Press, 1980); Jacqueline Jones, *Soldiers of Light and Love: Northern Teachers and Georgia Blacks, 1865–1873* (Chapel Hill: University of North Carolina Press, 1980); Vincent P. Franklin and James D. Anderson eds., *New Perspectives on Black Educational History* (Boston: G. K. Hall, 1978); Thomas L. Webber, *Deep Like the Rivers: Education in the Slave Quarter Community, 1831–1865* (New York: Norton, 1978); Henry Allen Bullock, *A History of Negro Education in the South: from 1619 to the Present* (Cambridge, Mass.: Harvard University Press, 1967); and Carter Woodson, *The Education of the Negro prior to 1861: A History of the Education of the Colored People of the United States from the Beginning of Slavery to the Civil War* (New York: G.P. Putnam's Sons, 1915).

25. Kaestle, *Pillars of the Republic*, x.

26. For this insight, I am indebted to Kate Masur.

27. Glenn, *Unequal Freedom*, 19.

28. Kerber, "The Meanings of Citizenship," 833–54.

29. On black self-improvement societies during this period see, for example, Elizabeth McHenry, *Forgotten Readers: Recovering the Lost History of African American Literary Societies* (Durham: Duke University Press, 2002), and Dorothy Porter, "The Organized Educational Activities of Negro Literary Societies, 1828–1846," *Journal of Negro Education* 5 (October 1936): 556–76.

30. The most complete discussion of southern white opposition to black literary education is Janet Duitsman Cornelius, *"When I Can Read My Title Clear": Literacy, Slavery, and Religion in the Antebellum South* (Columbia: University of

South Carolina Press, 1991). See also John S. Moore, "The Ban on Teaching Blacks to Read and Write," *Virginia Baptist Register* 37 (1998): 1872–76; and Edward F. Burrows, "The Literary Education of Negroes in Ante-Bellum Virginia, North Carolina, South Carolina, and Georgia with Special Reference to Regulatory and Prohibitive Laws (master's thesis, Duke University, 1940).

31. "African Free Schools in the United States," *Freedom's Journal,* June 1, 1827; Robert J. Cottrol, *The Afro-Yankees: Providence's Black Community in the Antebellum Era* (Westport, Conn.: Greenwood Press, 1982), 61; M. B. Goodwin, U.S. Bureau of Education, *Special Report of the Commissioner of Education on the Condition and Improvement of Public Schools in the District of Columbia, Government Printing Office* (Washington, 1871), 328.

32. On race and voting rights during this period see, for example, Christopher Malone, *Between Freedom and Bondage: Race, Party, and Voting Rights in the Antebellum North* (New York: Routledge, 2007); Jeffrey A. Mullins, "Race, Place, and African-American Disenfranchisement in the Early Nineteenth-Century American North," *Citizenship Studies* 10 (February 2006): 77–91; James Truslow Adams, "Disfranchisement of Negroes in New England," *American Historical Review* 30 (April 1925): 543–7; and Charles H. Wesley, "Negro Suffrage in the Period of Constitution-Making, 1787–1865," *Journal of Negro History* 32 (April 1947): 143–68.

33. On white efforts to exclude African Americans from the public sphere in the early republic, see, for example, Joanna Brooks, "The Early American Public Sphere and the Emergence of a Black Print Counterpublic," *William and Mary Quarterly* 62 (January 2005): 67–92; Richard S. Newman and Roy E. Finkenbine, "Forum: Black Founders in the New Republic: Introduction," *William and Mary Quarterly* 64 (January 2007): 83–94; Patrick Rael, *Black Identity and Black Protest in the Antebellum North* (Chapel Hill: University of North Carolina Press, 2002); James Oliver Horton and Lois E. Horton, *In Hope of Liberty: Culture, Community and Protest Among Northern Free Blacks* (New York: Oxford University Press, 1997); and Shane White, " 'It Was a Proud Day': African Americans, Festivals, and Parades in the North, 1741–1834," *Journal of American History* 81 (June 1994): 32–40.

34. *Bobolition of Slavery !!! Grand Selebrahum by De Africum Shocietee!!!* (Boston: 1818?), broadside, Boston Public Library.

35. David Waldstreicher, *In the Midst of Perpetual Fetes: The Making of American Nationalism, 1776–1820* (Chapel Hill: University of North Carolina Press, 1997), 328; White, " 'It Was a Proud Day,' " 13–50.

36. On the American Colonization Society, see, for example, Eric Burin, *Slavery and the Peculiar Solution: A History of the American Colonization Society* (Gainesville: University Press of Florida, 2005); Douglas R. Egerton, " 'Its Origin Is Not a Little Curious': A New Look at the American Colonization Society," *Journal of the Early Republic* 5 (Winter 1985): 463–80; Frankie Hutton, "Economic Considerations in the American Colonization Society's Early Effort to Emigrate Free Blacks

to Liberia, 1816–36," *Journal of Negro History* 68 (Autumn 1983): 376–89; David M. Streifford, "The American Colonization Society: An Application of Republican Ideology to Early Antebellum Reform," *Journal of Southern History* 45 (May 1979): 201–20; George M. Fredrickson, *The Black Image in the White Mind: The Debate on Afro-American Character and Destiny, 1817–1914* (New York: Harper and Row, 1971); and Phillip J. Staudenraus, *The African Colonization Movement, 1816–1865* (New York: Columbia University Press, 1961).

37. Peter Kolchin, "Whiteness Studies: The New History of Race in America," *Journal of American History* 89 (June 2002): 155–6.

Part 1

1. "To the Senior Editor—No. III," *Freedom's Journal*, August 17, 1827.

2. Floyd M. Shumway and Richard Hegel, "New Haven: A Topographical History," *Journal of the New Haven Colony Historical Society* 34 (Spring 1988): 6–11. On New Haven's early history, see also Michael Sletcher, *New Haven: From Puritanism to the Age of Terrorism* (Charleston, S.C.: Arcadia, 2004); Preston Maynard and Marjorie B. Noyes, eds., *Carriages and Clocks, Corsets and Locks: The Rise and Fall of an Industrial City—New Haven, Connecticut* (Hanover, N.H.: University Press of New England, 2004); Rollin G. Osterweis, *Three Centuries of New Haven, 1638–1938* (New Haven: Yale University Press, 1953); Mary Hewitt Mitchell, *History of New Haven County, Connecticut*, 3 vols. (Chicago: Pioneer Historical Publishing, 1930); and Edward E. Atwater, ed., *History of the City of New Haven to the Present Time* (New York: W. W. Munsell, 1887).

3. Rollin G. Osterweis, *The New Haven Green and the American Bicentennial* (Hamden, Conn.: Archon Books, 1976), 13–21.

4. Charles J. Hoadly, ed., *Records of the Colony or Jurisdiction of New Haven, from May, 1653, to the Union. Together with the Code of 1656* (Hartford, Conn.: Case, Lockwood, 1858), 191, 210, quoted in E. Jennifer Monaghan, *Learning to Read and Write in Colonial America* (Amherst: University of Massachusetts Press, 2005), 21–22.

5. Monaghan, *Learning to Read and Write in Colonial America*, 20–23.

6. Hoadly, *New Haven Colony Records, from May 1653*, 583–84, quoted in Monaghan, *Learning to Read and Write in Colonial America*, 24.

7. "Connecticut Legislature," *Connecticut Mirror*, May 7. 1831.

8. Hendrik D. Gideonse, *Common School Reform: Connecticut, 1838–1854* (Ed. D.dissertation, Harvard University, 1963), 390; Louise G. Wrinn, "The Development of the Public School System in New Haven, 1639–1930: A Problem in Historical Research," (Ph.D. dissertation, Yale University, 1933), 2. On education in late-nineteenth-century New Haven, see Stephen Lassonde, *Learning to Forget: Schooling and Family Life in New Haven's Working Class 1870–1940* (New Haven: Yale University Press, 2005).

9. Frederick Calvin Norton, "Negro Slavery in Connecticut," *Connecticut Magazine* 6, no. 5 (1899): 320.

10. Lorenzo Greene, *The Negro in Colonial New England: 1620–1776* (1942; Port Washington, N.Y.: Kennikat Press, 1966), 128–32.

11. As quoted in William C. Fowler, *The Historical Status of the Negro in Connecticut: A Paper Read before the New Haven Colony Historical Society* (Charleston, S.C.: Walker, Evans & Cogswell, 1901), 10.

12. Goucon Yang, "From Slavery to Emancipation: The African Americans of Connecticut: 1650s–1820s" (Ph.D. dissertation, University of Connecticut, 1999), 68–77.

13. *Connecticut Journal*, June 9, 1779.

14. *Connecticut Journal,* November 22, 1771.

15. "Twenty Dollars Reward," *Connecticut Journal,* October 11, 1783.

16. "Public Statute Laws of the State of Connecticut. May Session, 1833," *Connecticut Courant*, July 1, 1833; "Progressing Backwards," *Liberator,* July 20, 1833.

17. Truth, "Another Specimen!!" *Liberator,* November 2, 1833; Veritas, "The Reign of Prejudice," *Abolitionist,* November 1833. On this incident, see Robert Austin Warner, "Amos Gerry Beman—1812–1874, a Memoir on a Forgotten Leader," *Journal of Negro History* 22 (April 1937): 200–21.

18. "Fruits of Abolition," *Daily Herald*, September 5, 1835.

19. "Riot at Brookfield," *Colored American*, September 7, 1839.

20. William May, "Are Free Colored Men Citizens? The Opinions of Peter A. Jay, Chancellor Kent, Abraham Van Vecten, Rufus King, De Witt Clinton, and Others. Versus the Opinion of His Honor Judge Daggett," *Liberator*, October 26, 1833; "Judge Daggett's Charge," *Liberator*, October 26, 1833; *Connecticut Courant*, July 22, 1833; *Windham County Advertiser,* July 18, 1833; "The Canterbury Affair," *Genius of Universal Emancipation,* August 1833; "Canterbury Circular," *Liberator*, August 3, 1833; "Trial of Miss Crandall," *Liberator*, August 31, 1833; "Miss Crandall's Second Trial," *Abolitionist,* November 1833.

21. Andrew T. Judson, *Andrew T. Judson's Remarks to the Jury, on the Trial of the Case, State v. P. Crandall* (Hartford, Conn.: John Russell, 1833), 12.

22. Andrew T. Judson, *Andrew T. Judson's Remarks*, 15.

23. "Miss Crandall's Second Trial."

24. Samuel J. May, *The Right of Colored People to Education Vindicated* (Brooklyn, Conn.: Advertiser Press, 1833), 18.

Chapter One

1. "African Improvement Society," *Freedom's Journal*, April 20, 1827.

2. Hugh Davis, *Leonard Bacon: New England Reformer and Antislavery Moderate* (Louisiana State University Press: Baton Rouge, 1998), 57–59. On Leonard Bacon, see also Kenneth P. Minkema and Harry S. Stout, "The Edwardsean Tradition

and the Antislavery Debate, 1740–1865," *Journal of American History* 92 (June 2005): 47–74; Hugh Davis, "Northern Colonizationists and Free Blacks, 1823–1837: A Case Study of Leonard Bacon," *Journal of the Early Republic* 17 (Winter 1997): 651–75; David Brion Davis, "Reconsidering the Colonizationist Movement: Leonard Bacon and the Problem of Evil," *Intellectual History Newsletter* 14 (1992): 3–16; and Timothy J. Sehr, "Leonard Bacon and the Myth of the Good Slaveholder," *New England Quarterly* 49 (June 1976): 194–213.

3. Davis, "Northern Colonizationists and Free Blacks," 651, 654; Minkema and Stout, "The Edwardsean Tradition and the Antislavery Debate, 1740–1865," 63; Leonard Bacon, *A Plea for Africa; Delivered in New-Haven* (New Haven: T. G. Woodward, 1825); Davis, "Reconsidering the Colonizationist Movement," 10. On social reform movements during this period see, for example, Steven Mintz, *Moralists and Modernizers: America's Pre-Civil War Reformers* (Baltimore: Johns Hopkins University Press, 1995), and Robert H. Abzug, *Cosmos Crumbling: American Reform and the Religious Imagination* (New York: Oxford University Press, 1994).

4. "African Improvement Society," *Freedom's Journal*, April 20, 1827; *Third Annual Report of the African Improvement Society of New Haven* (New Haven, 1829); "African Improvement Society," *New Haven Chronicle,* April 14, 1827.

5. Davis, *Leonard Bacon: New England Reformer,* 57–58; Robert Austin Warner, *New Haven Negroes: A Social History* (New Haven: Yale University Press, 1940), 46.

6. Biars Stanley, William Lanson, Prince Cooper, Scipio C. Augustus, John P. Shields, and Wm. D. Pardy, "African United Ecclesiastical Society," *Connecticut Journal,* September 20, 1825.

7. *Third Annual Report of the African Improvement Society*, 10.

8. As quoted in "African Improvement Society," *Freedom's Journal,* April 27, 1827.

9. "African Improvement Society," *New Haven Chronicle,* April 14, 1827.

10. Aristides, "For the New Haven Chronicle," *New Haven Chronicle,* April 21, 1827.

11. Aristides, "For the New Haven Chronicle," *New Haven Chronicle,* April 21, 1827.

12. On the decline of colonization and the emergence of immediate abolition see, for example, Richard S. Newman, *The Transformation of American Abolitionism: Fighting Slavery in the Early Republic* (Chapel Hill: University of North Carolina Press, 2002); Ronald G. Walters, *The Antislavery Appeal: American Abolitionism after 1830* (Baltimore: Johns Hopkins University Press, 1976); Bruce Rosen, "Abolition and Colonization, the Years of Conflict: 1829–1834," *Phylon* 33 (2d Quarter, 1972): 177–92; and David Brion Davis, "The Emergence of Immediatism in British and American Antislavery Thought," *Mississippi Valley Historical Review* 49 (September 1962): 209–30. On the relationship between black education and colonization in the 1820s, see Vincent P. Franklin, "Education for

Colonization: Attempts to Educate Free Blacks in the United States for Emigration to Africa, 1823–1833," *Journal of Negro Education* 43 (Winter 1974): 91–103; and Charles A. Earp, "The Role of Education in the Maryland Colonization Movement," *Journal of Negro History* 26 (July 1941): 365–88.

13. Jacqueline Jones, "Race, Sex, and Self-Evident Truths: The Status of Slave Women during the Era of the American Revolution," in *Women in the Age of the American Revolution,* edited by Ronald Hoffman and Peter J. Albert (Charlottesville: University of Virginia Press, 1989), 293–337.

14. Lorenzo Greene, *The Negro in Colonial New England: 1620–1776* (Port Washington, N.Y.: Kennikat Press, 1966), 111.

15. Joanne Pope Melish, *Disowning Slavery: Gradual Emancipation and "Race" in New England, 1780–1860* (Ithaca, N.Y.: Cornell University Press, 1998), 18–23.

16. As of 1756, New Haven County contained 226 black residents, who made up 1.2 percent of the town's total population. Greene, *The Negro in Colonial New England,* 74, 90–92.

17. Greene, *The Negro in Colonial New England,* 98; Warner, *New Haven Negroes,* 301.

18. Jacqueline Jones, *American Work: Four Centuries of Black and White Labor* (New York: W. W. Norton & Company, 1998), 247; Warner, *New Haven Negroes,* 17–26.

19. "Scipio C. Augustus," *Freedom's Journal,* August 22, 1828.

20. Wm. Lanson, "African Boarding House," *Columbian Register,* November 19, 1831.

21. William Lanson, "Take Particular Notice," *Connecticut Journal,* July 8, 1828.

22. James Truslow Adams, "Disfranchisement of Negroes in New England," *American Historical Review* 30, no. 3 (1925): 545.

23. Evelyn Nakano Glenn, *Unequal Freedom: How Race and Gender Shaped American Citizenship and Labor* (Cambridge, Mass.: Harvard University Press, 2002), 1.

24. On the concept of "whiteness" in the nineteenth century see, for example, Bruce Dain, *A Hideous Monster of the Mind: American Race Theory in the Early Republic* (Cambridge, Mass.: Harvard University Press, 2002); Peter Kolchin, "Whiteness Studies: The New History of Race in America," *Journal of American History* 89 (June 2002): 154–73; Eric Arnesen, "Whiteness and the Historians' Imagination," *International Labor and Working-Class History* 60 (Fall 2001): 3–32; David R. Roediger, "The Pursuit of Whiteness: Property, Terror, and Expansion, 1790–1860," *Journal of the Early Republic* 19 (Winter 1999): 579–600; James Brewer Stewart, "The Emergence of Racial Modernity and the Rise of the White North, 1790–1840," *Journal of the Early Republic* 18 (Summer 1998): 181–217; Matthew Frye Jacobson, *Whiteness of a Different Color: European Immigrants and the Alchemy of Race* (Cambridge, Mass.: Harvard University Press, 1998); Noel

Ignatiev, *How the Irish Became White* (New York: Routledge, 1995); David R. Roediger, *The Wages of Whiteness: Race and the Making of the American Working Class* (New York: Verso, 1991); and Alexander Saxton, *The Rise and Fall of the White Republic: Class Politics and Mass Culture in Nineteenth-Century America* (New York: Verso, 1990).

25. Petition of Biars Stanley and William Lanson, record group 2, General Assembly Papers, African Americans, 1821–1869, box 2, folder 1, October 1815, Connecticut State Library.

26. Petition of Biars Stanley and William Lanson, record group 2, General Assembly Papers, African Americans, 1821–1869, box 2, folder 1, October 1815, Connecticut State Library.

27. Linda K. Kerber, "The Meanings of Citizenship," *Journal of American History* 84 (December 1997): 834. On citizenship in nineteenth-century America, see also Catherine O'Donnell Kaplan, *Men of Letters in the Early Republic: Cultivating Forums of Citizenship* (Chapel Hill: University of North Carolina Press, 2008); Mark Stuart Weiner, *Americans without Law: The Racial Boundaries of Citizenship* (New York: New York University Press, 2006); Susan Zaeske, *Signatures of Citizenship: Petitioning, Antislavery, and Women's Political Identity* (Chapel Hill: University of North Carolina Press, 2003); Glenn, *Unequal Freedom*; Michael Schudson, *The Good Citizen: A History of American Civic Life* (New York: Free Press, reprint 1998); Gary Gerstle, "Liberty, Coercion, and the Making of Americans," *Journal of American History* 84 (September 1997): 524–58; and Judith N. Shklar, *American Citizenship: The Quest for Inclusion* (Cambridge, Mass.: Harvard University Press, 1991).

28. Biars Stanley, Prince Cooper, Prince Duplex, James Ross, and John Williams, "African United Ecclesiastical Society," *New Haven Chronicle*, May 19, 1827; "African Congregations," *Connecticut Journal*, September 20, 1825; Biars Stanley, William Lanson, Prince Cooper, Scipio C. Augustus, John P. Shields, and Wm. D. Pardy, "African United Ecclesiastical Society," *Connecticut Journal*, September 20, 1825.

29. "To the Senior Editor—No. 2," *Freedom's Journal*, August 10, 1827.

30. Mary Beth McQueeny, "Simeon Jocelyn, New Haven Reformer," *New Haven Colony Historical Society Journal* 19 (September 1970): 63–68; Amos G. Beman, "Thoughts on the History of Temple Street," Amos Gerry Beman Scrapbooks, vol. 3, Beinecke Library, Yale University; Beman, "Sermon Notes," Amos Gerry Beman Scrapbooks, vol. 3, Beinecke Library, Yale University; "African Church and Ordination," *African Repository* V (1829): 252; *Connecticut Journal*, August 25, 1829. On Temple Street, see Kurt Schmoke, "The Dixwell Avenue Congregational Church, 1829–1896," *New Haven Colony Historical Society Journal* 20 (1971): 3–11.

31. Timothy Dwight, *A Statistical Account of the City of New Haven* (New Haven: Walter and Steele, 1811), 54; Andrew Kidston, Charles Bostwick, William

H. Ellis, James English, John Scott, Samuel Wadsworth, and Timothy Dwight, "Report of the Committee of the First School District, New Haven," *Connecticut Herald*, December 9, 1823.

32. G. "African Improvement Society, New Haven (Ct)," *Genius of Universal Emancipation*, January 1, 1830.

33. "To the Senior Editor—No. 2."

34. Sandra Sandiford Young, "A Different Journey: John Brown Russwurm, 1799–1851," (Ph.D. dissertation, Boston College, 2004), 61–62. On the classical curriculum of colleges in the early nineteenth century, see Caroline Winterer, *The Culture of Classicism: Ancient Greece and Rome in American Intellectual Life, 1780–1910* (Baltimore: Johns Hopkins University Press, 2002).

35. "Prospectus," *Freedom's Journal*, March 23, 1827.

36. Elizabeth McHenry, *Forgotten Readers: Recovering the Lost History of African American Literary Societies* (Durham: Duke University Press, 2002), 84–87; Philanthropos, "Education No. 1," *Freedom's Journal*, March 30, 1827; Philanthropos, "Education No. 2," *Freedom's Journal*, April 6, 1827; Philanthropos, "Education No. 3," *Freedom's Journal*, April 13, 1827; "Libraries," *Freedom's Journal*, October 5, 1827; "African Mutual Instruction Society," *Freedom's Journal*, April 4, 1828; "Lyceums," *Freedom's Journal*, January 24, 1829.

37. Philanthropos, "Education No. 3," *Freedom's Journal*, April 13, 1827.

38. On print culture in the early republic see, for example, Joanna Brooks, "The Early American Public Sphere and the Emergence of a Black Print Counterpublic," *William and Mary Quarterly* 62 (January 2005): 67–92; Robert A. Ferguson, *Reading the Early Republic* (Cambridge, Mass.: Harvard University Press, 2004); Jeffrey L. Pasley, *The Tyranny of Printers: Newspaper Politics in the Early American Republic* (Charlottesville: University Press of Virginia, 2001); and Michael Warner, *The Letters of the Republic: Publication and the Public Sphere in Eighteenth-Century America* (Cambridge, Mass.: Harvard University Press, 1990).

39. On black uplift ideology in the early nineteenth century see, for example, John Wood Sweet, *Bodies Politic: Negotiating Race in the American North, 1730–1830* (Baltimore: Johns Hopkins University Press, 2003); Dain, *A Hideous Monster of the Mind;* Patrick Rael, *Black Identity and Black Protest in the Antebellum North* (Chapel Hill: University of North Carolina Press, 2002); Tunde Adeleke, "Afro-Americans and Moral Suasion: The Debate in the 1830's," *Journal of Negro History* 83 (Spring, 1998): 127–42; Frederick Cooper, "Elevating the Race: The Social Thought of Black Leaders, 1827–1850," *American Quarterly* 24 (December 1972): 604–25; and Leon Litwack, *North of Slavery: The Negro in the Free States, 1790–1860* (Chicago: University of Chicago Press, 1961).

40. Shane White, *Stories of Freedom in Black New York* (Cambridge, Mass.: Harvard University Press, 2004), 13.

41. Patrick Rael, "The Long Death of Slavery," in *Slavery in New York*, edited by Ira Berlin and Leslie M. Harris (New York: New Press, 2005), 140. On slavery

and emancipation in New York state see, for example, David Gellman, *Emancipating New York: The Politics of Slavery and Freedom, 1777–1827* (Baton Rouge: Louisiana State University Press, 2006); Jill Lepore, *New York Burning: Liberty, Slavery, and Conspiracy in Eighteenth-Century Manhattan* (New York: Alfred A. Knopf, 2005); Leslie M. Harris, *In the Shadow of Slavery: African Americans in New York City, 1626–1863* (Chicago: University of Chicago Press, 2003); David Quigley and David Gellman, *Jim Crow New York: A Documentary History of Race and Citizenship, 1777–1877* (New York: New York University Press, 2003); and Shane White, *Somewhat More Independent: The End of Slavery in New York City, 1770–1810* (Athens, Ga.: University of Georgia Press, 1991).

42. "For the Freedom's Journal," *Freedom's Journal*, June 29, 1827.

43. "New Haven," *Freedom's Journal*, July 13, 1827.

44. *Freedom's Journal*, July 13, 1827. Many thanks to Jacqueline Bacon for this citation and for sharing her thoughts on Russwurm's visit to New Haven.

45. "To the Senior Editor—No. 1," *Freedom's Journal*, August 3, 1827.

46. "To the Senior Editor—No. 1."

47. Floyd M. Shumway and Richard Hegel, "New Haven: A Topographical History," *Journal of the New Haven Colony Historical Society* 34 (Spring 1988): 6.

48. "To the Senior Editor—No. 1"; Warner, *New Haven Negroes*, 28.

49. "To the Senior Editor—No. 2."

50. "To the Senior Editor—No. 2."

51. "To the Senior Editor—No. 2."

52. Warner, *The Letters of the Republic*, 113.

53. Pasley, *The Tyranny of Printers*, 35; Eran Shalev, "Ancient Masks, American Fathers: Classical Pseudonyms during the American Revolution and Early Republic," *Journal of the Early Republic* 23 (Summer 2003): 154.

54. Meyer Reinhold, *Classica Americana: The Greek and Roman Heritage in the United States* (Detroit: Wayne State University Press, 1984), 250–52.

55. David Sansone ed. *Plutarch: The Lives of Aristeides and Cato* (Warminster: Aris & Phillips Ltd., 1989), 37–39.

56. "For the New Haven Chronicle," *New Haven Chronicle*, April 28, 1827.

57. Clarkson, "African Improvement Society," *New Haven Chronicle*, May 22, 1827.

58. T. Z., "African Improvement Society," *New Haven Chronicle*, May 22, 1827.

59. Aristides, "For the Chronicle," May 26, 1827.

60. Aristides, "For the Chronicle."

61. Edward D. Griffith, "A Plea for Africa. A Sermon Preached October 26, 1817, in the First Presbyterian Church in the City of New York before the Synod of New York and New Jersey, at the Request of the Board of Directors of the African School established by the Synod," *Evangelical Guardian*, June 1818.

62. Lois Horton, "From Class to Race in Early America: Northern Post-Emancipation Racial Reconstruction," *Journal of the Early Republic* 19 (Winter 1999): 637–8.

63. "African School," *Genius of Universal Emancipation,* November 19, 1825; John Ford, "African School," *Religious Intelligencer,* March 20, 1824.

64. "African School," *Genius of Universal Emancipation,* November 19, 1825. On slavery and emancipation in New Jersey, see Graham Russell Hodges, *Slavery and Freedom in the Rural North: African Americans in Monmouth County, New Jersey, 1665–1865* (Madison, Wis.: University of Wisconsin Press 1997).

65. Edward D. Griffith, "A Plea for Africa."

66. "African School," *Religious Intelligencer,* January 1, 1820; John Ford, "African School," *Religious Intelligencer,* March 20, 1824.

67. John Ford, "African School," *Religious Intelligencer,* March 20, 1824.

68. "African School," *Genius of Universal Emancipation,* November 19, 1825; Edward D. Griffin, "A Plea for Africa"; "African School," *Religious Intelligencer,* January 1, 1820.

69. On the Foreign Mission School in Cornwall, Connecticut see, for example, Karen Sánchez-Eppler, "Copying and Conversion: An 1824 Friendship Album 'from a Chinese Youth,'" *American Quarterly* 59 (June 2007): 301–39; and John Andrew, "Educating the Heathen: The Foreign Mission School Controversy and American Ideals," *Journal of American Studies* 12, no. 3 (1978): 331–42.

70. "Society for the Education of African Youth," *Genius of Universal Emancipation,* August 19, 1826; "Kosciusko School," *American Journal of Education and Monthly Lyceum* (Boston) 1 (October 1826), 632; "Kosciusko School," *African Repository* 2 (September 1826): 223.

71. "African Education Society," *American Journal of Education and Monthly Lyceum* (Boston) 1 (June 1830): 267.

72. *Address of the Executive Committee of the African Mission School Society,* 19–20.

73. Jonathan Mayhew Wainwright, *A Discourse on the Occasion of Forming the African Mission School Society Delivered in Christ Church, in Hartford, Connecticut, on Sunday Evening, August 10, 1828* (Hartford, Conn., 1828).

74. *Address of the Executive Committee of the African Mission School Society, Together with the Record of the Proceedings at the Formation of Said Society* (Hartford, Conn.: H. & F. J. Huntington, 1828), 4–5.

75. A small number of Hartford students honored this agreement. Gustavus V. Cesar sailed from Connecticut for Liberia to work as a missionary in 1831. Edward Jones, who graduated from Amherst College in 1826, worked as a teacher and missionary in Sierra Leone. *Address of the Executive Committee of the African Mission School Society;* "African Mission School," *African Repository* IV (February 1829): 375–76; "Letter from Liberia," *Norwich Religious Messenger,* February 11, 1832; *Norwich Religious Messenger,* November 5, 1831.

76. Samuel E. Cornish, "To the Trustees and Faculty of the African Mission School Hartford," *Rights of All*, August 14, 1829.

77. Cornish, "To the Trustees and Faculty of the African Mission School Hartford."

78. On African American reactions to colonization see, for example, Marie Tyler-McGraw, *An African Republic: Black and White Virginians in the Making of Liberia* (Chapel Hill: University of North Carolina Press, 2007); Claude Clegg, *The Price of Liberty: African Americans and the Making of Liberia* (Chapel Hill: University of North Carolina Press, 2004); Christopher Phillips, "The Dear Name of Home: Resistance to Colonization in Antebellum Baltimore," *Maryland Historical Magazine* 91 (Summer 1996): 181–202; Ella Forbes, "African-American Resistance to Colonization," *Journal of Black Studies* 21 (December 1990): 210–23; and Floyd J. Miller, *The Search for a Black Nationality: Black Emigration and Colonization, 1787–1863* (Urbana: University of Illinois Press, 1975).

79. *Report of the Proceedings at the Formation of the African Education Society: Instituted at Washington, December 28, 1829 with an Address to the Public, by the Board of Managers* (Washington, D.C.: James C. Dunn, 1830), 3, 8.

80. "African Education Society," *American Journal of Education and Monthly Lyceum* 1 (June 1830): 266–67; "African Education Society," *African Repository* 6 (February 1830): 46–47. In 1831, soon to be abolitionist Amos Phelps also endorsed the African Education Society. Amos Phelps, "American Colonization and Af[Rican Education] Societies, Draft of a Sermon," July 10, 1831, *Anti-Slavery Collection*, Boston Public Library; "Connecticut Colonization Society Annual Meeting," *Connecticut Courant*, June 15, 1830; "Connecticut State Colonization Society," *African Repository* 6 (June 1830): 105–11; "African Education Society," *Connecticut Journal*, September 14, 1830; W. T. S. "From the New Haven Religious Intel.," *Liberator*, October 8, 1831; Franklin, "Education for Colonization," 96.

81. George M. Frederickson, *The Black Image in the White Mind: The Debate on Afro-American Character and Destiny, 1817–1914* (New York: Harper and Row, 1971), 16–21.

82. Frederickson, *The Black Image in the White Mind,* 16–21.

83. William Lloyd Garrison, *Thoughts on African Colonization or an Impartial Exhibition of the Doctrines, Principles and Purposes of the American Colonization Society. Together with the Resolutions, Addresses and Remonstrances of the Free People of Color* (Boston: Garrison and Knapp, 1832), 10.

84. "Public Meetings," *Liberator*, July 23, 1831.

85. As quoted in Garrison, *Thoughts on African Colonization.*

86. The ACS transported fewer than two hundred black people annually. Frankie Hutton, "Economic Considerations in the American Colonization Society's Early Effort to Emigrate Free Blacks to Liberia," *Journal of Negro History* 68 (Autumn 1983): 386.

87. "John B. Russwurm to [Edward Jones], March 20, 1830," Reprinted in the *Black Abolitionist Papers*, vol. 3, edited by C. Peter Ripley (Chapel Hill: University of North Carolina Press, 1985), 71–74.

88. "Liberia," *Connecticut Courant*, May 25, 1830.

89. C. D. T., "Mr. Russwurm," *Liberator*, April 30, 1831.

Chapter Two

1. "Extracts from a Letter from the Editor," *Liberator*, June 18, 1831.

2. James Forten et al., "Education—An Appeal to the Benevolent," *Philadelphia Chronicle*, September 5, 1831, quoted in *College for Colored Youth: An Account of the New-Haven City Meeting and Resolutions, with Recommendations of the College, and Strictures upon the Doings of New-Haven* (New York, 1831), 3.

3. *Boston Evening Transcript*, August 22, 1831; "Insurrection in Virginia," *Liberator*, September 3, 1831; "Virginia Insurrection," *Connecticut Mirror*, September 17, 1831; "Insurrection of the Blacks," *Niles' Register*, September 3, 1831.

4. "Negro Insurrection in Virginia," *Columbian Register*, September 3, 1831.

5. Kimberly had been in office for just three months when the proposed college came to his attention. As far as the historical record suggests, he did not subsequently demonstrate a proclivity for racial intolerance or antiabolitionism. To the contrary, in 1837 he represented Georgia bondswoman Nancy Jackson in her freedom suit against her master J. S. Bullock. Bullock had brought Jackson into Connecticut two years earlier while his daughters attended school in Hartford. Jackson sued him on the grounds that slaves could not be held in Connecticut. With Kimberly's help, she not only won her freedom but also set a critical precedent that prevented other slaveholders from holding their "property" in the state. Reverend Elisha L. D. D. Cleaveland, *An Address Delivered at the Funeral of the Hon. Dennis Kimberly, December 16, 1832* (New Haven: Tuttle, Morehouse & Taylor, 1863); Theodore Weld to Lewis Tappan, June 8, 1837, reprinted in *Letters of Theodore Dwight Weld, Angelina Grimke Weld, and Sarah Grimke, 1822–1844,* edited by Gilbert H. Barnes and Dwight L. Dumond, vol. 1. (1934; reprint, Gloucester, Mass.: Peter Smith, 1965), 398–99; *College for Colored Youth*, 4.

6. *Connecticut Journal*, September 13, 1831.

7. *College for Colored Youth*, 5.

8. Thomas Van Rensselaer to Gerrit Smith, March 13, 1834, Black Abolitionist Papers, microfilm collection, 1:0399, edited by George E. Carter et al., hereafter BAP.

9. Samuel E. Cornish, "Anomaly in Nature," *Liberator*, October 8, 1831; Simeon Jocelyn to William Lloyd Garrison, September 20, 1831, Anti-Slavery Collection, Boston Public Library, hereafter ASC.

10. James Forten to William Lloyd Garrison, October 20, 1831, ASC.

11. Hendrick D. Gideonse, "Common School Reform: Connecticut, 1838–1854" (Ph.D. dissertation, Harvard University, 1963), 382–83. In 1830, 2.8 percent of white males aged fifteen to twenty in Connecticut attended college. Rhode Island ranked second with 2.0 percent. Massachusetts followed with 1.6 percent. Colin B. Burke, *American Collegiate Populations: A Test of the Traditional View* (New York: New York University Press, 1982), 63. According to the 1840 census, only 0.003 percent of Connecticut residents were illiterate. New Hampshire ranked second with 0.006 percent, followed by Massachusetts with 0.01 percent. Lee Soltow and Edward Stevens, *The Rise of Literacy and the Common School in the United States: A Socioeconomic Analysis to 1870* (Chicago: University of Chicago Press, 1981), 159.

12. As quoted in Orwin Griffin, *Evolution of the Connecticut State School System, with Special Reference to the Emergence of the High School* (New York: Teacher's College, 1928), 29.

13. James M. Patten, *Patten's New Haven Directory, for the Year 1840 to Which Are Appended Some Useful and Interesting Notices* (New Haven: James M. Patten, 1840), 109.

14. On the evolution of abolitionism around 1830 see, for example, Matthew Mason, *Slavery and Politics in the Early American Republic* (Chapel Hill: University of North Carolina Press, 2006); Frederick J. Blue, *No Taint of Compromise: Crusaders in Antislavery Politics* (Baton Rouge: Louisiana State University Press, 2005); Bruce Laurie, *Beyond Garrison: Antislavery and Social Reform* (Cambridge: Cambridge University Press, 2005); Jonathan H. Earle, *Jacksonian Antislavery and the Politics of Free Soil, 1824–1854* (Chapel Hill: University of North Carolina Press, 2004); and Richard S. Newman, *The Transformation of American Abolitionism: Fighting Slavery in the Early Republic* (Chapel Hill: University of North Carolina Press, 2002).

15. In the midst of the movement, several individuals took credit for the idea. Garrison contended that he conceived of a black college in the late 1820s while editing the *Genius of Universal Emancipation* in Baltimore. Historian Bella Gross argues that Samuel Cornish promoted the notion as early as 1827. Cornish and John Brown Russwurm were corresponding with white philanthropist Gerrit Smith about a seminary for black youth in the late 1820s. Two years later, Cornish highlighted the need for black collegiate or professional education in the *Rights of All*. Gross, "*Freedom's Journal* and the *Rights of All*," *Journal of Negro History* 17(July 1932): 276–77; *Freedom's Journal,* March 23, 1827; *Rights of All,* September 28, 1829; Samuel E. Cornish and John Russwurm to Gerrit Smith, April 16, 1827, 16:0457, BAP.

16. African Americans were not permitted in the high school until Rhode Island desegregated its schools in 1865. "Summary," *Freedom's Journal,* February 8, 1828; Robert J. Cottrol, *The Afro-Yankees: Providence's Black Community in the Antebellum Era* (Westport, Conn.: Greenwood Press, 1982), 61,

90–91; "African Free Schools in the United States," *Freedom's Journal,* June 1, 1827.

17. Fewer than thirty black people earned college diplomas during the antebellum period. Faustine C. Jones-Wilson et al., *Encyclopedia of African-American Education* (Westport, Conn.: Greenwood Press, 1996), 431. On African American higher education in the antebellum period see Stephanie Y. Evans, *Black Women in the Ivory Tower, 1850–1954: An Intellectual History* (Gainesville: University Press of Florida, 2007); and Wanda Davis, "First Foundations: An Inquiry into the Founding of Three Selected African American Institutions of Higher Education" (Ed.D. dissertation, Pennsylvania State University, 1993). The first black colleges would not open for another decade: Cheney University (formerly the Institute for Colored Youth, 1840), Wilberforce University (1856), and Lincoln University (formerly Ashmun Institute, 1857).

18. Sandra Sandiford Young, " 'John Brown Russwurm's Dilemma: Citizenship or Emigration," in *Prophets of Protest: Reconsidering the History of American Abolitionism,* edited by John Stauffer and Timothy Patrick McCarthy (New York and London: New Press, 2006), 93.

19. *Freedom's Journal,* November 9, 1828.

20. Simeon S. Jocelyn, *New Haven Advertiser,* October 4, 1831, quoted in *College for Colored Youth,* 6.

21. Robert A. Gibson, "A Deferred Dream: The Proposal for a Negro College in New Haven, 1831," *New Haven Colony Historical Society Journal* 37, no. 2 (1991): 25–26.

22. Lewis Tappan, *The Life of Arthur Tappan* (1871; reprint New York: Arno Press, 1970), 77. *Report of the Proceedings at the Formation of the African Education Society Instituted at Washington, December 28, 1829* (Washington, D.C.: James C. Dunn, 1830), 3.

23. Simeon Jocelyn to William Lloyd Garrison, May 28, 1831, ASC. Carleton Mabee speculates that a black high school opened for a short time in 1831, although he acknowledges that evidence is "conflicting." *Black Education in New York State from Colonial to Modern Times* (Syracuse: Syracuse University Press, 1979), 57–58, 308n. On the New York African Free Schools, also see John L. Rury, "The New York African Free School, 1827–1836: Conflict over Community Control of Black Education," *Phylon* 44 (3d Quarter 1983): 187–97.

24. Peter Williams, "Education. A Sermon Delivered in St. Philip's Church on Sunday 27th April 1828, Continued," *Freedom's Journal,* June 13, 1828; "School Meeting," *Freedom's Journal,* January 11, 1828; Gross, "*Freedom's Journal* and the *Rights of All,*" 254–55, 275, 277.

25. Charles C. Andrews, *The History of the New York African Free Schools, from Their Establishment in 1787 to the Present Time; Embracing a Period of More Than Forty Years* (New York: Mahlon Day, 1830), 105–108.

26. Peter Williams, "To the Citizens of New York," *African Repository* 10 (August 1834), 137.

27. Burke, *American Collegiate Populations,* 63. On colleges in antebellum New England, see Michael S. Pak, "The Yale Report of 1828: A New Reading and New Implications," *History of Education Quarterly* 48 (February 2008): 30–57; Roger Geiger, ed., *The American College in the Nineteenth Century* (Nashville: Vanderbilt University Press, 2000); David F. Allmendinger Jr., *Paupers and Scholars: The Transformation of Student Life in New England* (New York: St. Martin's Press, 1975); and Donald G. Tewksbury, *The Founding of American Colleges and Universities before the Civil War* (New York: Bureau of Publications, Teachers College, Columbia, 1932).

28. Williams, "To the Citizens of New York," 187.

29. Jocelyn to Garrison, May 28, 1831, ASC; Mabee, *Black Education in New York State,* 57–58.

30. "Scipio C. Augustus," *Freedom's Journal,* August 22, 1828.

31. "College for the People of Color," *Liberator,* July 9, 1831; James Forten et al., "Education—An Appeal to the Benevolent," *Philadelphia Chronicle,* September 5, 1831, quoted in *College for Colored Youth,* 3.

32. "Report of the Manual Labor Academy of Pennsylvania," *American Journal of Education* I (August 1830): 366–67.

33. "Ruined by Hard Study," *Connecticut Courant,* January 18, 1831; L. F. Anderson, "The Manual Labor School Movement," *Educational Review* (1913): 369–86. On the ties between manual labor and abolition, see Paul Goodman, "The Manual Labor Movement and the Origins of Abolitionism," *Journal of the Early Republic* 13 (Autumn 1983): 355–88.

34. William Lloyd Garrison, *An Address Delivered before the Free People of Color in Philadelphia, New York, and Other Cities during the Month of June, 1831* (Boston: Stephen Foster, 1831), 10.

35. George R. Price and James Brewer Stewart, introduction to *To Heal the Scourge of Prejudice: The Life and Writings of Hosea Easton* (Amherst: University of Massachusetts Press, 1999), 8–10.

36. Garrison, *An Address Delivered before the Free People of Color*, 10.

37. "African Colonization," *Connecticut Courant,* July 4, 1836.

38. *Address to the Public by the Managers of the Colonization Society of Connecticut,* (New Haven: Treadway and Adams, 1828); "Connecticut Colonization Society Annual Meeting," *Connecticut Courant,* June 15, 1830.

39. "To the Senior Editor—No. 3," *Freedom's Journal,* August 17, 1827.

40. Elizur Wright Jr. and Beriah Green to Theodore Weld, February 1, 1833, in *The Letters of Theodore Dwight Weld, Angelina Grimke Weld and Sarah Grimke, 1822–1844,* edited by Gilbert H. Barnes and Dwight L. Dumond (Gloucester, Mass.: Peter Smith, 1965), 103.

41. Convention for the Improvement of Free People of Color, *Minutes and Proceedings of the Second Annual Convention, for the Improvement of the Free People*

of Color in These United States, Held by Adjournment in the City of Philadelphia, from the 4th to the 13th of June Inclusive, 1831 (Philadelphia, 1832), 34.

42. *Freedom's Journal,* March 23, 1827.

43. Philanthropos, "Education No. 1," *Freedom's Journal,* March 30, 1827.

44. Jonathan A. Glickstein, *Concepts of Free Labor in Antebellum America* (New Haven: Yale University Press, 1991), 32.

45. William J. Watkins, "Frederick Douglass in Boston," *Frederick Douglass' Paper,* August 12, 1853.

46. William Nell to [George T?] Downing, September 12, 1854, 9:0080–0082, BAP.

47. *Columbian Register,* October 13, 1831.

48. Simeon S. Jocelyn, *New Haven Advertiser,* October 4, 1831, quoted in *College for Colored Youth,* 7.

49. John Warner Barber, *Views in New Haven and Its Vicinity* (New Haven, 1825); Robert Warner, *New Haven Negroes: A Social History* (New York: Arno Press and the *New York Times,* 1969), 11–13.

50. New York housed 10,886 African Americans in 1820 and 13,977 in 1830. Philadelphia contained 7,582 African Americans in 1820 and 9,806 in 1830. According to the 1830 census, 1,481 "aliens" resided in Connecticut, of which 439 lived in New Haven County and 271 in New Haven City. Leonard P. Curry, *The Free Black in Urban America 1800–1850: The Shadow of a Dream* (Chicago: University of Chicago Press, 1981), 245; Mary H. Mitchell, *History of New Haven County, Connecticut,* vol. 1 (Chicago: Pioneer Historical Pub. Co., 1930), 863; Warner, *New Haven Negroes,* 301; "Census of the Town of New Haven," *Connecticut Journal,* January 4, 1831. On foreign immigration in 1831, see Charlotte Erickson, "Emigration from the British Isles to the U.S.A. in 1831," *Population Studies* 36 (July 1981): 175–97.

51. Rollin G. Osterweis, *Three Centuries of New Haven, 1638–1938* (New Haven: Yale University Press, 1953), 265–72; Barber, *Views in New Haven;* Warner, *New Haven Negroes,* 4.

52. *Liberator,* June 18, 1831.

53. *Minutes and Proceedings of the First Annual Convention of the People of Colour,* 6–7.

54. New institutions included the University of Vermont (1791), Bowdoin College (1784), Middlebury College (1800), Waterville College (1813), Amherst College (1821), and Washington College (1823); Allmendinger, *Paupers and Scholars,* 5.

55. *Connecticut Journal,* October 4, 1831.

56. The dividend from Connecticut's school fund yielded eighty-five cents per student. New Haven's Lancasterian school restricted enrollment to 280. Gideonese, "Common School Reform," v; "Literary Register: Or Annual View of the State and Progress of Education, and of Literary Institutions, Throughout the World," *American Quarterly Register* (May 1831)," 282; Edward E. Atwater, *History of the*

City of New Haven (New York, 1887), 152; "School Report," *Columbian Register*, September 10, 1831; Wm. W. Boardman, "School Report," *Connecticut Journal*, September 20, 1831; Alexander Harrison, "Lancasterian School," *Columbian Register*, November 12, 1831.

57. Barber, *Views in New Haven*, 4. John M. Garfield, "New Haven Female Seminary," *Connecticut Courant*, May 4, 1830; "Literary Register: Or Annual View of the State and Progress of Education," 299.

58. "New Haven," *Connecticut Journal*, October 11, 1831.

59. "From the New Haven Advertiser, Feb. 1," *Baltimore American and Commercial Daily Advertiser*, February 7, 1831.

60. On the socioeconomic insecurities plaguing antebellum white workingmen see, for example, Sean Wilentz, *Chants Democratic: New York City and the Rise of the American Working Class, 1788–1850* (New York: Oxford University Press, 1984); Susan G. Davis, *Parades and Power: Street Theatre in Nineteenth-Century Philadelphia* (Philadelphia: Temple University Press, 1986); Paul G. Faler, *Mechanics and Manufacturers in the Early Industrial Revolution: Lynn, Massachusetts, 1760–1860* (Albany: State University of New York Press, 1981); and David R. Roediger, *The Wages of Whiteness: Race and the Making of the American Working Class* (New York: Verso, 1991).

61. "Refuge of Oppression," *Liberator*, February 15, 1834.

62. Aristides, "For the New Haven Chronicle," *New Haven Chronicle*, April 21, 1827.

63. Roediger, *Wages of Whiteness*, 144–45.

64. Burke, *American Collegiate Populations*, 141, 146.

65. *Connecticut Herald*, October 4, 1831.

66. William A. Countryman, "Transportation," in *History of Connecticut in Monographic Form*, edited by Norris G. Osborn (New York, 1925); John Carroll Noonan, "Nativism in Connecticut: 1829–1860" (Ph.D. dissertation, Catholic University of America, 1938), 77–90; Osterweis, *Three Centuries of New Haven*, 281–82.

67. "New Haven," *Connecticut Journal*, March 25, 1831.

68. "Foreign Immigration" and "Influx of Immigrants," *Connecticut Observer*, October 27, 1834.

69. "Colonization," *Connecticut Journal*, July 6, 1830.

70. Warner, *New Haven Negroes*, 301; Noonan, "Nativism in Connecticut," 82–85.

71. Connecticut, for example, enacted a law in 1703 that prevented taverns from serving servants or slaves; in 1723, the legislature established a nine o'clock curfew for Native Americans and African Americans. Those in violation could be fined "ten stripes." Ralph Foster Weld, "Slavery in Connecticut," in *Tercentenary Commission of the State of Connecticut Committee on Historical Publications* (New Haven: Yale University Press, 1935), 9–10; Guocon Yang, "From Slavery

to Emancipation: The African Americans of Connecticut: 1650s–1820s" (Ph.D. dissertation, University of Connecticut, 1999), 41, 46–47, 140. On slavery in Connecticut, see also Denis Caron, *A Century in Captivity: The Life and Trials of Prince Mortimer, a Connecticut Slave* (Hanover: University Press of New England, 2006).

72. Alexis de Toqueville, *Democracy in America*, vol. 1 (New York: Knopf, 1945), 360 (originally published in 1835).

73. On African American exclusion from vocational instruction in the antebellum period see, for example, Curry, *The Free Black in Urban America;* Jacqueline Jones, *American Work: Four Centuries of Black and White Labor* (New York: W. W. Norton & Company, 1998); Roediger, *Wages of Whiteness;* and Shane White, "'We Dwell in Safety and Pursue Our Honest Callings': Free Blacks In New York City, 1783–1810" *Journal of American History* 75 (September 1988): 445–470.

74. Warner, *New Haven Negroes,* 23.

75. Specifically, of the sixty-six African Americans *Patten's* included, nearly two-thirds worked as laborers or had no occupation listed. The second largest subgroup (20 percent) performed some form of service. Craftspeople represented 12 percent of black entrants. *Patten's* described 7.5 percent of black people as storekeepers. It also listed one African American schoolteacher and one musician; Jacqueline Jones, *American Work,* 254–58; Warner, *New Haven Negroes,* 17–26.

76. Census Schedules, New Haven (1850).

77. Two other Connecticut towns had previously "warned out" Grimes. William Grimes, "Life of William Grimes the Runaway Slave, Brought Down to the Present Time, Written by Himself," in *Five Black Lives: The Autobiographies of Venture Smith, James Mars, William Grimes, the Rev. G. W. Offley, James L. Smith*, edited by Arna Bontemps (Middletown, Conn.: Wesleyan University Press, 1971; originally published in 1855), 120. See also *Life of William Grimes, the Runaway Slave*, edited by William L. Andrews and Regina E. Mason (New York: Oxford University Press, 2008).

78. Warner, *New Haven Negroes,* 29.

79. Yang, "From Slavery to Emancipation," 117–20; *Baltimore American and Commercial Daily Advertiser*, December 6, 1831.

80. George Wilson McPhail to Mary Venable (Carrington) Grisby, August 18, 1834, Carrington Family Papers, 1755–1839, Virginia Historical Society.

81. "Abolition," *New Haven Palladium*, October 5, 1833.

82. On Walker, see Peter P. Hinks, *To Awaken My Afflicted Brethren: David Walker and the Problem of Antebellum Slave Resistance* (University Park: Pennsylvania State University Press, 1997); Donald M. Jacobs, "David Walker: Boston Race Leader, 1825–1830," *Essex Institute Historical Collections* 107 (January 1971): 94–107; and Clement Eaton, "A Dangerous Pamphlet in the Old South," *Journal of Southern History* 2 (August 1936): 322–34.

83. "Walker's Pamphlet," *Liberator,* January 1, 1831.

84. "Education," *Liberator,* January 1, 1831.

85. For newspapers that printed stories of the proposed college and Turner's rebellion side by side, see, for example, *Columbian Register,* September 10, 1831, and *Columbian Register,* September 13, 1831. The September 13 edition also contained coverage of a black man who "dashed out" the "brains" of his infant son.

86. "Southampton Affair," *Columbian Register,* September 10, 1831.

87. Parker Pillsbury, "Letter from Parker Pillsbury," *Liberator*, March 26, 1852.

88. S. R. W., "Pennsylvania Quakerism," *Liberator*, July 4, 1851.

Part 2

1. Noah Davis, *A Narrative of the Life of Rev. Noah Davis, a Colored Man, Written by Himself, At the Age of Fifty-Four* (Baltimore: John F. Weishampel, Jr., 1859), 86.

2. Charles Varle, *A Complete View of Baltimore* (Baltimore: Samuel Young, 1833), 9; Christopher Phillips, *Freedom's Port: The African American Community of Baltimore, 1790–1860* (Urbana and Chicago: University of Illinois Press, 1997), 8.

3. As quoted in James T. Wright, *The Free Negro in Maryland, 1634–1860* (New York: Columbia University Press, 1921), 21.

4. Provincial law considered people of color without proof of freedom to be slaves. Ross M. Kimmel, "Free Blacks in Seventeenth-Century Maryland," *Maryland Historical Magazine* 71 (Spring 1976): 20–21.

5. Phillips, *Freedom's Port,* 11.

6. Phillips, *Freedom's Port,* 9.

7. Varle, *A Complete View of Baltimore,* 11; Tina Sheller, "Freemen, Servants and Slaves: Artisans and the Craft Structure of Revolutionary Baltimore Town," in *American Artisans: Crafting Social Identity, 1750–1850,* edited by Howard Rock, Paul Gilje, and Robert Asher (Baltimore: Johns Hopkins University Press, 1995), 18.

8. Phillips, *Freedom's Port,* 10.

9. Sheller, "Freemen, Servants, and Slaves," 18.

10. Varle, *A Complete View of Baltimore,* 68.

11. G. Terry Sharrer, "Flour Milling in the Growth of Baltimore, 1750–1830," *Maryland Historical Magazine* 71 (Fall 1976): 322–24; Tina H. Sheller, "Artisans, Manufacturing, and the Rise of a Manufacturing Interest in Revolutionary Baltimore Town," *Maryland Historical Magazine* 83 (Spring 1988): 3.

12. Seth Rockman, *Scraping By: Wage Labor, Slavery, and Survival in Early Baltimore* (Baltimore: Johns Hopkins University Press, 2009), 3. Phillips, *Free-*

dom's Port, 14–15; Tina H. Sheller, "Artisans, Manufacturing, and the Rise of a Manufacturing Interest, 3.

13. Barbara Jeanne Fields, *Slavery and Freedom on the Middle Ground: Maryland during the Nineteenth Century* (New Haven: Yale University Press, 1985), 4–6.

14. T. Stephen Whitman, *The Price of Freedom: Slavery and Manumission in Baltimore and Early National Maryland* (Lexington: University Press of Kentucky, 1997), 6.

15. Bettye Jane Gardner, "Free Blacks in Baltimore, 1800–1860" (Ph.D. dissertation, George Washington University, 1974), 38–41.

16. Anita Aidt Guy, "The Maryland Abolition Society and the Promotion of the Ideas of the New Nation," *Maryland Historical Magazine* 84 (Winter 1989): 342–44.

17. Gordon E. Finnie, "The Antislavery Movement in the Upper South before 1840," *Journal of Southern History* 35 (August 1969): 322–24. On antislavery sentiment in Maryland, see also Anita Aidt Guy, *Maryland's Persistent Pursuit to End Slavery, 1850–1864* (New York: Garland Publishing, 1997); and Roger Bruns and William Fraley, " 'Old Gunny': Abolitionist in a Slave City," *Maryland Historical Magazine* 68 (Winter 1973): 369–82.

18. Lorena S. Walsh, "Rural African Americans in the Constitutional Era in Maryland, 1776–1810," *Maryland Historical Magazine* 84 (Winter 1989): 336–38.

19. Whitman, *Price of Freedom,* 8–10.

20. Charles G. Steffen, "Changes in the Organization of Artisan Production in Baltimore, 1790 to 1820," *William and Mary Quarterly* 36 (January 1979): 105; Whitman, *Price of Freedom,* 18–19.

21. Steffen, "Changes in the Organization of Artisan Production in Baltimore," 103; Sheller, "Artisans, Manufacturing, and the Rise of a Manufacturing Interest," 3–5.

22. "Cook Wanted," *Baltimore Patriot and Mercantile Advertiser*, May 13, 1826.

23. Whitman, *Price of Freedom,* 61–63.

24. Robert Alcock, "25 Dollars Reward," *Baltimore Patriot and Mercantile Advertiser*, June 19, 1829.

25. D. H. White, "Five Hundred Dollars Reward," *Baltimore Sun*, November 14, 1837.

26. Harriet Jacobs, *Incidents in the Life of a Slave Girl* (New York: Signet Classic, 2000), 23.

27. Whitman, *Price of Freedom,* 100–103.

28. Phillips, *Freedom's Port,* 15.

29. Leonard P. Curry, *The Free Black in Urban America, 1800–1850: The Shadow of a Dream* (Chicago: University of Chicago Press, 1981), 245–48.

30. *Colored American*, October 19, 1839.

31. Davis, *A Narrative of the Life of Rev. Noah Davis,* 35.

Chapter Three

1. "Prospectus of a School for Coloured Girls," *Baltimore American and Commercial Daily Advertiser,* October 8, 1831.

2. "Prospectus of a School for Colored Girls." On the Oblates, see Diane Batts Morrow, *Persons of Color and Religious at the Same Time: The Oblate Sisters of Providence, 1828–1860* (Chapel Hill: University of North Carolina Press, 2002); M. Reginald Gerdes, "To Educate and Evangelize: Black Catholic Schools of the Oblate Sisters of Providence (1828–1880)," *U.S. Catholic Historian* 7 (Spring/Summer 1988): 183–99; Mary Carroll Johansen, "'Female Instruction and Improvement': Education for Women in Maryland, Virginia, and the District of Columbia, 1785–1835" (Ph.D. dissertation, College of William and Mary, 1996); and Grace H. Sherwood, *The Oblates' Hundred and One Years* (New York: Macmillan Co., 1931).

3. "Letter Anonymous Subject of Negroes," September 21, 1831, Mayor's Papers, box 7, item 464, Baltimore City Archives, hereafter BCA.

4. "Letter from an Anonymous person Subject of Negroes," n.d., Mayor's Papers, box 7, item 462, BCA. See also Sarah Katz, "Rumors of Rebellion: Fear of a Slave Uprising in Post–Nat Turner Baltimore," *Maryland Historical Magazine* 89 (Fall 1994): 328–33.

5. Scipio, "The Sisters of Providence," *Baltimore American and Commercial Daily Advertiser,* October 6, 1831.

6. Catherine Clinton, "Equally Their Due: The Education of the Planter Daughter in the Early Republic," *Journal of the Early Republic* 2 (Spring 1982), 42. On women's education in the early nineteenth century, see, for example, Anya Jabour, *Scarlett's Sisters: Young Women in the Old South* (Chapel Hill: University of North Carolina Press, 2007); Catherine Kerrison, *Claiming the Pen: Women and Intellectual Life in the Early American South* (Ithaca, N.Y.: Cornell University Press, 2006); Mary Kelley, *Learning to Stand and Speak: Women, Education, and Public Life in America's Republic* (Chapel Hill: University of North Carolina Press, 2006); Margaret A. Nash, *Women's Education in the United States, 1780–1840* (New York: Palgrave Macmillan, 2005); Catherine Hobbs, *Nineteenth-Century Women Learn to Write* (Charlottesville: University Press of Virginia, 1995); Christie Farnham, *The Education of the Southern Belle: Higher Education and Student Socialization in the Antebellum South* (New York: New York University Press, 1994); Linda M. Perkins, "The Impact of the 'Cult of True Womanhood' on the Education of Black Women," *Journal of Social Issues* 39 (1983): 17–28; and Maris A. Vinovskis and Richard M. Bernard, "Beyond Catharine Beecher: Female Education in the Antebellum Period," *Signs: A Journal of Women in Culture and Society* 3 (Summer 1978): 856–69.

7. On education and "republican motherhood," see Julie A. Reuben, "Patriotic Purposes: Public Schools and the Education of Citizens," in *The Public Schools*, edited by Susan Fuhrman and Marvin Lazerson (Oxford: Oxford University Press,

2005), 1–24; Rosemarie Zagarri, "Morals, Manners, and the Republican Mother," *American Quarterly* 44 (June 1992): 192–215; and Linda K. Kerber, *Women of the Republic: Intellect and Ideology in Revolutionary America* (Chapel Hill: University of North Carolina Press, 1980).

8. Scipio, "The Sisters of Providence."

9. Seth Rockman, "Mobtown U.S.A.: Baltimore," *Common-place* 3 (July 2003). http://www.common-place.org/vol-03/no-04/baltimore.

10. "Riots," *Baltimore Sun*, January 20, 1838.

11. "Row in a Church," *Liberator*, September 14, 1838.

12. "Mob and Riot," *Baltimore Sun*, August 28, 1838.

13. "Petition of Doct. Bond and others respecting a proclamation for the apprehension etc. of persons who attacked the African Meeting Home on Sunday night last 26th Augt. 1838," Mayor's Papers, Record Group 9, Series 2, correspondence, 1797–1923, box 17, item 402, BCA.

14. In addition to Bethel, Varle also listed public black schools on Sharp Street, Saratoga Street, and Richmond Street. Charles Varle, *A Complete View of Baltimore, with a Statistical Sketch* (Baltimore: Samuel Young, 1833), 33.

15. Jeffrey R. Brackett, *The Negro in Maryland: A Study of the Institution of Slavery* (Baltimore: Johns Hopkins University, 1889), 187.

16. "A Memorial from the Free People of Colour to the Citizens of Baltimore," *African Repository* II (1826): 295–96.

17. "Indenture of William Thompson to James Goth," November 27, 1826, Baltimore County Register of Wills (Indentures) 1829–1834, Maryland Hall of Records (hereafter cited as Register of Wills, MDHR), 37–38. On apprenticeship in the eighteenth and nineteenth centuries, see also Stephen T. Whitman, "Manumission and Apprenticeship in Maryland, 1780–1870," *Maryland Historical Magazine* 101 (Spring 2006), 55–71; John E. Murray and Ruth Wallis Herndon, eds., *Children Bound to Labor in Early America* (Ithaca, N.Y.: Cornell University Press, 2009); John E. Murray and Ruth Wallis Herndon, "Markets for Children in Early America: A Political Economy of Pauper Apprenticeship," *Journal of Economic History* 62 (June 2002): 356–82; Christine Daniels, "Alternative Workers in a Slave Economy: Kent County, Maryland, 1675–1810" (Ph.D. dissertation, Johns Hopkins University, 1989); and Helena Sorrell Hicks, "The Black Apprentice in Maryland Court Records from 1661 to 1865" (Ph.D. dissertation, University of Maryland, College Park, 1988).

18. Seth Rockman, "Working for Wages in Early Republic Baltimore: Unskilled Labor and the Blurring of Slavery and Freedom" (Ph.D. dissertation, University of California, Davis, 1999), 96. Baltimore County used this provision more frequently than Baltimore City. For examples of contracts with these substitutions see "Indenture of John Joseph to Elias C. Arieu," May 8, 1830, Register of Wills, MDHR, 97; "Indenture of Joshua Brown to David Polk," November 27, 1830, Register of Wills, MDHR, 200; "Indenture of Owen Green to Abraham Sellers," January 27,

1831 Register of Wills, MDHR, 231–32; "Indenture of Sarah Ann Augustine to Robert S. Hollins," December 15, 1830, Register of Wills, MDHR, 210; and "Indenture of Clarissa Jones to Asa Barrett," November 2, 1831, Register of Wills, MDHR, 363.

19. "Indenture of Samuel Ogle to Charles B. Green," July 27, 1826, Register of Wills, MDHR.

20. "Indenture of Catharine Jones to Charles McCann," October 22, 1829, Register of Wills, MDHR, 498.

21. "Indenture of Charles Barnes to William Hutson," July 22, 1829, Register of Wills, MDHR.

22. Samuel Jones had some exposure to reading and writing, as he and his father authorized the contract with their signatures as opposed to their marks. "Indenture of Samuel P. Jones to Patrick Hamilton," April 11, 1831, Register of Wills, MDHR.

23. Numbers are derived from the indentures located at the Maryland Hall of Records from 1826–30. Of this number, Baltimore's Orphans' Court apprenticed ninety black children; Trustees of the Poor apprenticed fifteen; black parents apprenticed twenty-three; one master apprenticed his slave; and one free black man bound out himself. The Trustees of the Poor also included listings for two children it described as "indigent." Forty-nine contracts made no provision for literary instruction—eleven involving girls and thirty-eight involving boys. Thirty-five contracts mentioned reading; twelve included reading and writing; and nineteen provided for reading, writing, and mathematics, usually phrased as ciphering to the rule of three.

24. Fourteen contracts mentioned schooling: one for a year of regular schooling, one for six months of day schooling, two for six months of night schooling, four for six months of schooling, two for three months of night school, one for three months of night school each year, and three for two quarters of night school.

25. "Indenture of Robert Barney to Elisha Barnett," May 8, 1829 Register of Wills, MDHR, 396.

26. "Indenture of Alexander Gibbs to John Durham," December 8, 1829, Register of Wills, MDHR, 335.

27. "Indenture of William Goulding to William Yearly," May 2, 1827, Register of Wills, MDHR, 93–94.

28. "Indenture of Milly Mills to Henry Trump," April 1, 1831, Register of Wills, MDHR, 257.

29. "Indenture of Edgar Butler to William Mills," September 1, 1828, Register of Wills, MDHR, 289–90.

30. African American girls were only offered training in domestic service. Thirty-seven contracts mentioned craft instruction for black boys. They included barber and hair dresser (2), biscuit making (3), blacksmith (2), bootblack (1), boot maker (1), carter (1), caulker (5), cigar maker (1), cooper (3), cordwainer (2), mari-

ner (1), miller (1), Morrocan leather tanning (1), oak cooper (2), ostler and carriage driver (1), rope maker (2), paper maker (1), sailor (3), seedsman (1), stove finisher (1), sugar maker (1), and whip sawyer (1).

31. Whitman, "Manumission and Apprenticeship in Maryland," 64.

32. Archibald Thompson endorsed the agreement with his mark. "Indenture of William Thompson to James Goth," November 27, 1826, Register of Wills, MDHR, 37–38.

33. "Indenture of William Jones to David Polk," February 26, 1829, Register of Wills, MDHR, 366.

34. "Indenture of Thomas Elliot to David Lomax," May 30, 1828, Register of Wills, MDHR, 256.

35. Rockman, *Scraping By: Wage Labor, Slavery, and Survival in Early Baltimore* (Baltimore: Johns Hopkins University Press, 2009), 2.

36. James M. Wright, *The Free Negro in Maryland, 1634–1860* (New York: Columbia University Press, 1921; reprint, New York: Octagon Books, 1971), 249; Leonard P. Curry, *The Free Black in Urban America, 1800–1850: The Shadow of the Dream* (Chicago: University of Chicago Press, 1981), 123.

37. Frank Harold Towers, "Ruffians on the Urban Border: Labor, Politics, and Race in Baltimore, 1850–1861" (Ph.D. dissertation, University of California, Irvine, 1993), 458–59.

38. Curry, *Free Black in Urban America,* 138; "Health Statistics," *Baltimore American and Commercial Daily Advertiser*, January 13, 1835; "Health Office—Report of Internments," *Baltimore American and Commercial Daily Advertiser*, January 16, 1833; "Local Matters," *Baltimore Sun*, January 6, 1852; "Filthy Alleys," *Baltimore Sun,* September 1, 1852; Christopher Phillips, *Freedom's Port: The African American Community of Baltimore, 1790–1860* (Urbana, Ill.: University of Illinois Press, 1997), 180–82. See also Christian Warren, "Northern Chills, Southern Fevers: Race-Specific Mortality in American Cities, 1730–1900," *Journal of Southern History* 63 (February 1997): 23–56.

39. Approximately 310 free black men and women listed an occupation, including seventy-four draymen, fifty-two carters, and forty-six porters. Fifteen black men were described as "hackmen." Other occupations included waiter (15), seamen (26), and whitewasher (19). Richard J. Matchett and Samuel Jackson, *Matchett's Baltimore Directory* (Baltimore: 1835).

40. According to the 1850 census, the average daily wage for an unskilled worker in Baltimore was $0.94. Joseph C. G. Kennedy, *History and Statistics of the State of Maryland According to the Returns of the Seventh Census* (Washington, D.C.: Gideon and Co., 1852), 63; William R. Sutton, *Journeymen for Jesus: Evangelical Artisans Confront Capitalism in Jacksonian Baltimore* (University Park, Penn.: Pennsylvania State University Press, 1998), 142. See also Donald R. Adams Jr., "Prices and Wages in Maryland, 1750–1850," *Journal of Economic History* 46 (September 1986): 625–45.

41. Kennedy, *History and Statistics of the State of Maryland,* 63.

42. There were twenty-nine caulkers, twenty-four brickmakers, and twenty-seven barbers or hairdressers.

43. According to Barbara Wallace, the percentage of black women residing in white homes fell modestly during the antebellum period, from approximately 29 percent in 1820 to 23.5 percent in 1850. " 'Fair Daughters of Africa': African American Women in Baltimore, 1790–1860" (Ph.D. dissertation, University of California, Los Angeles, 2001), 105–6.

44. Kennedy, *History and Statistics of the State of Maryland,* 63.

45. Jacqueline Jones, *Labor of Love, Labor of Sorrow: Black Women, Work, and the Family from Slavery to the Present* (New York: Basic Books, 1985), 125–26.

46. Washers accounted for 6 percent of black listings and were all female. "Huckster" was the second most frequently listed occupation. On black female domestic workers see, for example, Xiomara Santamarina, *Belabored Professions: Narratives of African American Working Womanhood* (Chapel Hill: University of North Carolina Press, 2005); Wallace, " 'Fair Daughters of Africa,' " and Stephanie Cole, "Servants and Slaves: Domestic Service in the Border Cities, 1800–1850" (Ph.D. dissertation, University of Florida, 1994).

47. Seth Rockman, *Scraping By,* 130.

48. Jonathan A. Glickstein, *Concepts of Free Labor in Antebellum America* (New Haven: Yale University Press, 1991), 32.

49. "Wanted," *Baltimore Sun,* September 26, 1844; "Wanted," *Baltimore Sun,* January 3, 1845; "Wanted to Hire," *Baltimore Sun,* April 19, 1849.

50. Paul A. Gilje and Howard B. Rock, " 'Sweep O! Sweep O!': African-American Chimney Sweeps and Citizenship in the New Nation," *William and Mary Quarterly* 51 (July 1994), 508; "Wanted," *Baltimore Sun,* December 14, 1855; "Wanted," *Baltimore Sun,* September 24, 1859.

51. "Wanted, a Stout Colored Boy to Work in a Printing Office," *Baltimore Sun,* August 20, 1851; "Roller Boy Wanted," *Baltimore Sun,* March 13, 1851.

52. According to the 1850 census, Lucas owned real estate valued at $3,000. *Baltimore Ward 5, Baltimore, Maryland,* roll M432_283, page 132, image 88. www.ancestrylibrary.com.

53. "Wanted—a White or Colored Roller Boy," *Baltimore Sun,* August 3, 1852. See also "Wanted," *Baltimore Sun,* February 12, 1856.

54. Basil Phillips, "10 Dollars Reward," *Baltimore Sun,* April 21, 1843.

55. "Wanted," *Baltimore Sun,* December 7, 1854.

56. Baltimore's 1819 City Directory also listed Benjamin Valentine, a black bill poster and printer. *The Baltimore Directory . . . By Samuel Jackson* (Baltimore: 1819).

57. "Wanted," *Baltimore Sun,* June 1, 1852.

58. "Wanted," *Baltimore Sun,* July 18, 1855.

59. "Wanted," *Baltimore Sun,* November 23, 1849.

60. "Wanted," *Baltimore Sun*, June 5, 1850.

61. "Wanted," *Baltimore Sun*, September 8, 1840.

62. "Wanted," *Baltimore Sun*, February 14, 1845.

63. "Wanted," *Baltimore Sun*, July 8, 1857.

64. "Wanted," *Baltimore Sun*, June 26, 1849.

65. "Wanted," *Baltimore Sun*, September 4, 1852.

66. "Wanted," *Baltimore Sun*, August 26, 1852; "Wanted," *Baltimore Sun*, August 20, 1852.

67. "Wanted," *Baltimore Sun*, October 24, 1839.

68. As the notice read, this master "Would prefer disposing of his time to a Quaker." "For Sale," *Baltimore Sun*, February 24, 1838.

69. "Wanted," *Baltimore Sun*, December 16, 1851.

70. "To Hire," *Baltimore Sun*, September 9, 1851.

71. Henry Bibb, *Narrative of the Life and Adventures of Henry Bibb, an American Slave* (New York: Published by the author, 1849), 101–2.

72. "Wanted," *Baltimore Sun*, June 14, 1845.

73. Curry, *Free Black in Urban America*, 268.

74. On using the manuscript census to survey patterns of educational opportunity in the nineteenth century, see, for example, Harvey J. Graff, "Notes on Methods for Studying Literacy from the Manuscript Census," *Historical Methods Newsletter* 5 (1971): 11–16; Michael B. Katz, "Who Went to School," *History of Education Quarterly* 12 (Autumn 1972): 432–54; and Lee Soltow and Edward Stevens, *The Rise of Literacy and the Common School in the United States: A Socioeconomic Analysis to 1870* (Chicago: University of Chicago Press, 1981).

75. Leonard Curry contends that as of 1850, in comparison with Boston, New York, and Philadelphia, Baltimore was one of the nation's least segregated cities. *Free Black in Urban America*, 56–57.

76. Charles Varle, *Complete View of Baltimore*, 9. According to Barbara Wallace, percentages of free blacks ranged from 7 percent in Ward 9 to 24 percent in Ward 17. Enslaved blacks (2,946) made up 1.7 percent of the city's total population and resided in every ward. The largest number of slaves (307) lived in Ward 15. Wallace, "Fair Daughters of Africa," 313.

77. Varle, *Complete View of Baltimore*, 9.

78. This number is derived from the skin color a census marshal assigned to the head of household. Census records distinguish between "blacks" and "mulattos." Marshals designated thirty-two household heads as "mulatto" and 365 as "black." In the ward as a whole, gender ratios were balanced evenly (4,889 men and 4,885 women). Women headed 14 percent of black households and 11 percent of white households in the district.

79. *Slave Schedules*, Ward 17, 1850.

80. *Matchett's* 1850 edition listed more than five hundred African Americans who worked in a skilled or semiskilled occupation. M. Ray Della Jr., "The

Problems of Negro Labor in the 1850s," *Maryland Historical Magazine* 66 (Spring 1971): 15–20.

81. Forty-two percent of blacks in the ward performed a skilled trade, as did 46 percent of whites.

82. As census takers did not list the trades of African Americans who lived inside white homes, "domestic" is noticeably absent from this analysis. In addition, census takers wrote "none" for the occupation of another fifteen white household heads. Women made up the overwhelming majority of white household heads with no trade listed (126 of 163). Census takers also counted four soldiers. The remaining occupations appearing on the Ward 17 census schedules were grouped into four categories: nonmanual labor, skilled labor, semi- and unskilled labor, and service. Those who listed no trade are referred to as "blank." Those whose trade was described as "none" are also recorded separately as "none" (Appendix 1). When possible, Michael Katz's occupational classification scale was used as a guide. Michael B. Katz, "Occupational Classification in History," *Journal of Interdisciplinary History* 3 (Summer 1972): 63–88. See also Donald J. Treiman, "A Standard Occupational Prestige Scale for Use with Historical Data," *Journal of Interdisciplinary History* 7 (Autumn 1976): 283–304.

83. While Cromwell was literate, census takers noted that his wife Eliza could not read. Year, census place Baltimore Ward 17, Baltimore, Maryland, roll M432_286, page 291, image 584, from www.ancestrylibrary.com.

84. "A Fair," *Baltimore Sun,* December 9, 1841.

85. *Baltimore Sun,* December 21, 1841.

86. Curry, *Free Black in Urban America,* 268–69.

87. As of 1840, the white illiteracy rate in the United States—illiteracy being defined by census takers as not being able to read and write—was around 9 percent. At 8 percent, Maryland's illiteracy rate was slightly lower than the U.S. average, but it ranked among the lowest of slaveholding states. A decade later, according to the 1850 census, only 5 percent of whites in Maryland twenty years of age and older reported that they could not read. Soltow and Stevens, *Literacy and the Common School,* 159; *Seventh Census of the United States* (1850), lxi.

88. "Baltimore Justice!!" *Freedom's Journal,* August 3, 1827.

89. Jacob Small, "Night Watch," *Baltimore Patriot and Mercantile Advertiser,* August 27, 1830. In 1845, Baltimore legislators also attempted to tie black curfews to a seasonal schedule. One proposal moved to prohibit African Americans from being out past ten at night between October and April but extended the curfew to eleven o'clock in the remaining months. "Report of the Joint Committee on Police, Relative to Persons of Color Perambulating the Streets after Certain Hours," February 10, 1845, City Council Papers, record group 16, series 1, box 75, item 709, BCA; "Proceedings of the City Council," *Baltimore Sun,* February 4, 1845.

90. "Petition of P. Laurenson for a Pass for David Roberts," December 6, 1838, Mayor's Papers, record group 9, series 2, box 19, item 1282, BCA.

91. "Petition of Thomas Walsh and Others for a Pass for Perry Boadley Coloured Man," November 16, 1838, Mayor's Papers, record group 9, series 2, box 19, item 1285, BCA.

92. Veritas, "Persecutions in Baltimore," *Weekly Anglo-African*, December 29, 1860.

93. "Petition of Abraham Williams for a Ball in Conway Street, between Charles and Hanover Street," February 1, 1839, Mayor's Papers, record group 9, series 2, box 20, item 328, BCA.

94. "Application of Wm. Watson for Daniel Kobourn to Have a Ball," December 4, 1838, Mayor's Papers, record group 9, series 2, correspondence, box 19, BCA.

95. "The Free Colored People's Convention," *Baltimore Sun*, July 29, 1852.

96. Wright, *Free Negro in Maryland,* 123.

97. "Look at This," *Baltimore Sun*, September 13, 1849.

98. "Colored Literary Festival," *Baltimore Sun*, May 24, 1853.

99. Paul Gilje, " 'Le Menu Peuple' in America: Identifying the Mob in the Baltimore Riots of 1812," *Maryland Historical Magazine* 81 (Spring 1986): 50–65.

100. On this trend, see Frank Towers, "Job Busting at Baltimore Shipyards: Racial Violence in the Civil War–Era South," *Journal of Southern History* 66 (May 2000): 221–56.

101. Frederick Douglass, *Life and Times of Frederick Douglass Written by Himself,* 1893. Reprint (New York: Library of America, 1996), 628–30.

102. As quoted in "A Colored Baltimorean, 'Carters and Draymen's Petition,' " *Genius of Universal Emancipation*, January 12, 1828.

103. Forbidden products included pork, beef, corn, wheat, rye, liquor, oats, and tobacco (Brackett, *The Negro in Maryland,* 210–13).

104. D. Dorsey, "Exchange Hotel," *Baltimore Sun*, February 18, 1850. In 1852, J. H. Luckett made a similar pronouncement: "I am . . . strongly in favor of the employment of the white laborer in the place of the negro labor . . . and I am substituting the white labor for the black labor in the public employment." J. H. Luckett, "A Card," *Baltimore Sun,* December 7, 1852.

105. "Petition of Franklin Brown and Others in Relation to Renting & Licensing Stalls in the Different Markets in This City," May 3, 1858, City Council Papers, record group 16, series 1, box 109, item 302, BCA.

106. Della Jr., "The Problems of Negro Labor," 26–27.

107. Brackett, *The Negro in Maryland,* 210.

108. Seth Rockman, *Scraping By,* 47.

109. Alexander Brown et. al., "Counter to the Memorial of sundry citizens of Baltimore praying that persons of color may be prohibited from driving hacks, carts and drays," January 23, 1828, City Council Papers, series 1, record group 16, box 34, item 425, BCA.

110. Della Jr., "The Problems of Negro Labor," 15–16.

111. Ethan Allen Andrews, *Slavery and the Domestic Slave Trade* (Boston: Light & Stearns, 1836), 51.

112. "Meeting in Opposition to the Bill Relating to the Colored Population," *Baltimore Sun*, March 5, 1842; "Abolition and State Legislation," *Baltimore Sun*, February 24, 1842.

113. As quoted in J. W. C. Pennington, "The Self-Redeeming Power of the Colored Races of the World," *Anglo-African Magazine* 1 (October 1859): 318.

Chapter Four

1. Frederick Douglass, *Narrative of the Life of Frederick Douglass, An American Slave, Written by Himself,* edited by David W. Blight (New York: Bedford St. Martin's, 1993), 57. On Douglass, see also James Oakes, *The Radical and the Republican: Frederick Douglass, Abraham Lincoln, and the Triumph of Antislavery Politics* (New York: Norton, 2008); William S. McFeely, *Frederick Douglass* (New York: Norton, 1991); David W. Blight, *Frederick Douglass' Civil War: Keeping Faith in Jubilee* (Baton Rouge: Louisiana State University Press, 1989); Waldo E. Martin, *The Mind of Frederick Douglass* (Chapel Hill: University of North Carolina Press, 1984); and Dickson J. Preston, *Young Frederick Douglass: The Maryland Years* (Baltimore: Johns Hopkins University Press, 1980).

2. Douglass, *Narrative of the Life of Frederick Douglass*, 58.

3. Douglass, *Life and Times of Frederick Douglass Written by Himself,* 1893. Reprint (New York: Library of America, 1996), 538.

4. Douglass, *My Bondage and My Freedom* , edited by John David Smith (New York: Penguin Books, 2003), 125 (reprint of 1855 edition).

5. Douglass, *Narrative of the Life of Frederick Douglass*, 63; Douglass, *Life and Times of Frederick Douglass*, 527.

6. Douglass, *Life and Times of Frederick Douglass,* 559; Charles Varle, *A Complete View of Baltimore* (Baltimore: Samuel Young, 1833), 54.

7. Douglass, *Life and Times of Frederick Douglass,* 633.

8. Douglass, *Life and Times of Frederick Douglass,* 559.

9. Carl Kaestle, *Pillars of the Republic: Common Schools in American Society* (New York: Hill and Wang, 1983), 192–94.

10. Vernon S. Vavrina, "The History of Public Education in the City of Baltimore, 1829–1956" (Ph.D. dissertation, Catholic University of America, 1958), 2. On the early history of public schooling in Baltimore see also Tina H. Sheller, "The Origins of Public Education in Baltimore, 1825–1829," *History of Education Quarterly* 22 (Spring 1982): 23–44; and William R. Johnson, " 'Chanting Choristers': Simultaneous Recitation in Baltimore's Nineteenth-Century Primary Schools," *History of Education Quarterly* 34 (Spring 1994): 1–23.

11. "Property of Colored Persons," *Baltimore Sun*, May 8, 1852.

12. Using the 1850 census, Leonard Curry estimated that 22 percent of free black children between the ages of five and fourteen attended school in Baltimore. Because the 1850 census did not separate Baltimore City from Baltimore County, the percentage in Baltimore City alone was probably higher. In contrast, nearly 60 percent of white children in Baltimore County attended school. To contextualize these numbers, Curry also found that 21 percent of free black children in Washington, D.C., and 43 percent of free black children in New Orleans and Louisville attended school. At the other end of the geographic spectrum, 78 percent of free black children in Boston attended school, as did 76 percent of those in Providence, 70 percent of those in Buffalo, 59 percent of those in New York, and 57 percent of those in Philadelphia. Curry, *The Free Black in Urban America, 1800–1850: The Shadow of the Dream* (Chicago: University of Chicago Press, 1981), 169.

13. On black literacy in the colonial and antebellum South, see Antonio T. Bly, "Breaking with Tradition: Slave Literacy in Early Virginia, 1680–1780 (Ph.D. dissertation, College of William and Mary, 2006); Heather Andrea Williams, *Self Taught: African American Education in Slavery and Freedom* (Chapel Hill: University of North Carolina Press, 2005), chapter 1; John S. Moore, "The Ban on Teaching Blacks to Read and Write," *Virginia Baptist Register*, no. 37 (1998): 1872–76; Janet Duitsman Cornelius, *"When I Can Read My Title Clear": Literacy, Slavery, and Religion in the Antebellum South* (Columbia, S.C.: University of South Carolina Press, 1991); Edward F. Burrows, "The Literary Education of Negroes in Ante-Bellum Virginia, North Carolina, South Carolina, and Georgia with Special Reference to Regulatory and Prohibitive Laws (Master's thesis, Duke University, 1940); and Carter Godwin Woodson, *The Education of the Negro prior to 1861: A History of the Education of the Colored People from the Beginning of Slavery to the Civil War* (New York: G. P. Putnam's Sons, 1915).

14. Burrows, "Literary Education of Negroes," 81–83.

15. "Is It Possible?" *Liberator*, July 16, 1831; H. E. Sterkx, *The Free Negro in Ante-Bellum Louisiana* (Rutherford, N.J.: Farleigh Dickenson University Press, 1972), 98–99; Woodson, *The Education of the Negro*, 99.

16. Burrows, *Literary Education of Negroes*, 40–41.

17. As quoted in Clement Eaton, "A Dangerous Pamphlet in the Old South," *Journal of Southern History* 2 (August 1936): 332.

18. Moore, "Ban on Teaching," 1874.

19. Tommy L. Bogger, *Free Blacks in Norfolk, Virginia, 1790–1860: The Darker Side of Freedom* (Charlottesville: University Press of Virginia, 1997), 41.

20. For more on this episode see Philip Sheldon Foner and Josephine Pacheco, *Three Who Dared: Prudence Crandall, Margaret Douglass, Myrtilla Miner: Champions of Antebellum Black Education* (Westport, Conn.: Greenwood Press, 1984); and Margaret Douglass, *Educational Laws of Virginia; the Personal Narrative of Mrs. Margaret Douglass, a Southern Woman, Who Was Imprisoned for One Month*

in the Common Jail of Norfolk, under the Laws of Virginia, for the Crime of Teaching Free Colored Children to Read (Boston: J. P. Jewitt, 1854).

21. Douglass, *Life and Times of Frederick Douglass,* 559.

22. Douglass, *Life and Times of Frederick Douglass,* 599–600.

23. This was not the first time the 1841 law was enforced. In 1848, an eighty-year-old white Harford County man and former slaveholder with the surname of Grover was tried and acquitted for sending a copy of Frederick Douglass's narrative in the mail. A Methodist, "A Preacher in the Maryland Penitentiary," *Liberator,* October 22, 1858; H. Mattison, "That Imprisoned Colored Exhorter," *Liberator,* November 19, 1858; Richard Albert Blondo, "Samuel Green: A Black Life in Antebellum Maryland" (Master's thesis, University of Maryland College Park, 1988); "Incendiarism," *Liberator,* January 28, 1848.

24. Brackett, *The Negro in Maryland,* 198.

25. Delphic, "Our Baltimore Letter," *Weekly Anglo-African,* February 18, 1860.

26. One hundred thirty-seven of 868 free blacks in New Haven County age twenty and older—sixty-nine men and sixty eight women—reported to the census taker that they could not read. To put those numbers into context, whites in New Haven County had around a 2 percent illiteracy rate, while African Americans' illiteracy rate was around 16 percent. African Americans' illiteracy in Suffolk County was around 15 percent. In Baltimore County, 59 percent of free African Americans twenty years of age and older described themselves as illiterate (*Seventh Census* 1850, 82, 77, 219, 225, 56, and 49).

27. Douglass, *Life and Times of Frederick Douglass,* 625.

28. Kaestle, *Pillars of the Republic,* 192–94; William Reese, *America's Public Schools: From the Common School to "No Child Left Behind"* (Baltimore: Johns Hopkins University Press, 2005), 27, 44.

29. "Meeting for the Preservation of the Public Schools," *Baltimore Sun,* April 12, 1853.

30. "Convention of Delegates on the Subject of Public Education," *Baltimore American and Commercial Daily Advertiser,* January 27, 1825.

31. Sheller, "The Origins of Public Education in Baltimore," 26–27.

32. "Public Education. An Act for the Establishment and Support of Public Schools in the City of Baltimore," *Baltimore American and Commercial Daily Advertiser,* February 7, 1825.

33. "To the Mayor and City Council of Baltimore," *Baltimore American and Commercial Daily Advertiser,* February 9, 1825; "Public Education," *Baltimore American and Commercial Daily Advertiser,* February 8, 1825.

34. Another S., "For the American," *Baltimore American and Commercial Daily Advertiser,* February 8, 1825.

35. Robin L. Einhorn, *American Taxation, American Slavery* (Chicago: University of Chicago Press, 2006), 7–8.

36. "School Bill," *Baltimore American and Commercial Daily Advertiser*, February 23, 1825; Sheller, "The Origins of Public Education in Baltimore," 37; "City of Baltimore. A Supplement to the Ordinance Relating to Public Schools," *Baltimore Patriot and Mercantile Advertiser*, May 11, 1829; Vavrina, "History of Public Education in the City of Baltimore," 2.

37. Curry, *The Free Black in Urban America,* 169.

38. "The Advantages of the Lancasterian System of Education," *The Almoner* (September 1814): 145.

39. "Report of Randolph Fossmall—Teacher in Baltimore Public School at Jones Falls," December 21, 1829, Papers of the Baltimore City Council, record group 16, series 1, item 728, hereafter BCA.

40. "Harriet D. Randolph—First Female Teacher in Public School in Baltimore," December 17, 1829, Papers of the Baltimore City Council, record group 16, series 1, item 739, BCA.

41. "William Coffin—First Male Teacher of Public School in Baltimore West of Jones Falls," December 1829, Papers of the City Council, record group 16, series 1, item 729, BCA.

42. Johnson, "'Chanting Choristers': Simultaneous Recitation in Baltimore's Nineteenth Century Primary Schools," 1–23.

43. "William Coffin—First Male Teacher of Public School in Baltimore West of Jones Falls."

44. H., "Read and Think," *Baltimore Sun*, January 7, 1839.

45. "Report in Relation to Admission of Orphan Children into Public Schools," February 16, 1837, Papers of the City Council, record group 16, series 1, box 57, item 1273, BCA.

46. As John C. Eastman points out, Maryland's Constitution did not affirm a right to public schooling. "When Did Education Become a Civil Right? An Assessment of State Constitutional Provisions for Education, 1776–1900," *American Journal of Legal History* 42 (January 1998): 3.

47. Anne M. Boylan, *Sunday School: The Formation of an American Institution, 1790–1880* (New Haven: Yale University Press, 1988), 23–26.

48. "Condition of the Coloured Population of the City of Baltimore," *Baltimore Literary and Religious Magazine* IV (1838).

49. Sabbath schools were equally popular among whites in Baltimore. As of 1850, the city housed sixty such institutions. "Sabbath School Statistics," *Baltimore Sun,* May 16, 1850; Wright, *The Free Negro in Maryland,* 202; Bettye J. Gardner, "Free Blacks in Baltimore, 1800–1860" (Ph.D. dissertation, George Washington University, 1974), 110.

50. As quoted in Gardner, "Free Blacks in Baltimore, 1800–1860," 55.

51. Bettye J. Gardner, "Antebellum Black Education in Baltimore," *Maryland Historical Magazine* 71 (Fall 1976): 362–63; Christopher Phillips, "'Negroes and Other Slaves': The African-American Community of Baltimore, 1790–1860"

(Ph.D. dissertation, University of Georgia, 1992), 242. On Coker, see also James Sidbury, *Becoming African in America: Race and Nation in the Early Black Atlantic* (New York and Oxford: Oxford University Press, 2007); and Daniel E. Payne, ed. *History of the African Methodist Episcopal Church* (Nashville, Tenn.: Publishing House of the A. M. E. Sunday School Union, 1891), 89.

52. "Union Seminary," *Freedom's Journal*, July 4, 1828; W. M. Lively, "Union Seminary at the Back of the African Church, Sharp Street," *Genius of Universal Emancipation*, July 26, 1828; Lively, "Union Seminary at the Back of the African Church, Sharp-Street," *Genius of Universal Emancipation*, July 12, 1828; G., "African School," *Genius of Universal Emancipation*, November 6, 1829.

53. According to Mary Caroll Johansen, 26 percent of white schools in her sample that enrolled female students were coeducational, in contrast to 79 percent of comparable African American institutions. Johansen, "'Female Instruction and Improvement': Education for Women in Maryland, Virginia, and the District of Columbia, 1785–1835" (Ph.D. dissertation, College of William and Mary, 1996), 259–60.

54. Ethan Allen Andrews, *Slavery and the Domestic Slave Trade* (Boston: Light & Sterns, 1836), 85–86; William M. Lively, "Sabbath School," *Genius of Universal Emancipation*, February 18, 1826; "African Oration," *Genius of Universal Emancipation*, March 1825; Lively, "Education," *Genius of Universal Emancipation*, October 8, 1825. Lively probably moved to New York during the 1830s, as a W. M. Lively operated a similar institution there at that time. W. M. Lively, "Union Seminary at the Back of the African Church, Sharp-Street," *Genius of Universal Emancipation*, May 3, 1828; Jacob Richardson, "Colored Schools," *Colored American*, January 26, 1839; James H. Henderson, "Evening School," *Colored American*, October 17, 1840; Gardner, "Free Blacks in Baltimore," 63.

55. Andrews, *Slavery and the Domestic Slave Trade*, 87.

56. "A Fair," *Baltimore Sun*, December 21, 1846; "The Ladies of the Sharp Street Church," *Baltimore Sun*, December 23, 1852; "Baltimore, July 13," *National Era*, July 20, 1854.

57. *Baltimore American and Commercial Daily Advertiser*, May 2, 1834.

58. Andrews, *Slavery and the Domestic Slave Trade*, 92.

59. "African Free School," *Freedom's Journal*, August 22, 1828; "African Free School," *Genius of Universal Emancipation*, July 19, 1828; "Free School," *Genius of Universal Emancipation*, September 25, 1829.

60. "African Orphaline School," *Baltimore Patriot and Mercantile Advertiser*, November 22, 1828.

61. Mary F. Hollon, "Fair," *Baltimore Sun*, October 14, 1841.

62. Diane Batts Morrow, *Persons of Color and Religious at the Same Time: The Oblate Sisters of Providence, 1828–1860* (Chapel Hill: University of North Carolina Press, 2002), 1, 16–17; G., "School for Girls of Color," *Genius of Universal Emancipation*, January 8, 1830; "Prospectus of a School for Coloured Girls," *Baltimore*

American, October 8, 1831; Scipio, "The Sisters of Providence," *Baltimore American,* October 6, 1831.

63. Morrow, *Persons of Color and Religious at the Same Time,* 239.

64. As quoted in Morrow, *Persons of Color and Religious at the Same Time,* 254.

65. Morrow, *Persons of Color and Religious at the Same Time,* 239–40, 254, 265–67.

66. Baltimore black women's fundraising went beyond education. See, for example, "Fair at the Bethel Church," *Baltimore American and Commercial Daily Advertiser,* December 25, 1827; "The Ladies of the Sharp St. and Asbury Station," *Baltimore Sun,* December 21, 1844; "A Fair—a Fair—a Fair," *Baltimore Sun,* May 8, 1846; "The Colored Ladies," *Baltimore Sun,* April 8, 1846; and "Fair! Fair! Fair!" *Baltimore Sun,* May 25, 1847.

67. Webb, "Notice," *Baltimore Sun,* December 24, 1838.

68. Mary Wells, Lydia Bowser, Mary Ridgly, Hester Hughes, and Mary Ann Chubs, "Fair for the Benefit of the Colored People's Public School," *Baltimore Sun,* December 18, 1838; "Notice," *Baltimore Sun,* December 27, 1838.

69. "A Fair," *Baltimore Sun,* December 21, 1846; "A Fair," *Baltimore Sun,* January 4, 1847.

70. "The Ladies of the Sharp Street Church," *Baltimore Sun,* December 23, 1852.

71. "Proceeds of the Fair of the Ladies of Strawberry Alley Church," *Baltimore Sun,* January 6, 1842.

72. "The Female Members of St. James' First A. Prot. E. P. Church," *Baltimore Sun,* May 7, 1859.

73. "Christmas Fair, for the Benefit of the Methodist Protestant Church of Color," *Baltimore Sun,* December 24, 1838.

74. "Colored Fairs," *Baltimore Sun,* December 25, 1850.

75. William Levington, "Notice," *Genius of Universal Emancipation,* November 15, 1828.

76. One visitor noted that Levington's students were "almost exclusively the children of free parents," a comment that suggests that at least some of his students were enslaved. Andrews, *Slavery and the Domestic Slave Trade,* 57; Gardner, "Free Blacks in Baltimore," 94; "African Church," *Genius of Universal Emancipation,* March 1825; H. W., "Obituary," *Colored American,* August 5, 1837; "African Church," *Genius of Universal Emancipation,* March 1825; Terry D. Bilhartz, *Urban Religion and the Second Great Awakening: Church and Society in Early National Baltimore* (Rutherford, N.J.: Farleigh Dickinson University Press, 1986), 33; "Notice," *Genius of Universal Emancipation,* November 15, 1828; Edward S. Abdy, *Journal of a Residence and Tour in the United States of North America, from April, 1833, to October, 1834,* vol. 1 (London: John Murray, 1835), 157.

77. Abdy, *Journal of a Residence and Tour,* 157–58.

78. "Notice," *Liberator*, July 27, 1833.

79. "Notice," *Liberator*, July 27, 1833; "The Rev. Wm. Levington," *Liberator*, August 3, 1833; Abdy, *Journal of a Residence and Tour,* 1:157.

80. *Connecticut Courant*, October 7, 1833.

81. Abdy, *Journal of a Residence and Tour,* 2:53.

82. Andrews, *Slavery and the Domestic Slave Trade*, 55–57; "Condition of the Coloured Population of the City of Baltimore," *Baltimore Literary and Religious Magazine* 4 (1838), 3; "Died," *Liberator*, May 26, 1837; H. W., "Obituary," *Colored American*, August 5, 1837. Financial difficulties persisted, however, for one year later, the "Ladies attached to St. James 1st African Protestant Episcopal," advertised a "Fair, consisting of Staple and Fancy Articles" "to aid in liquidating a heavy debt, yet resting on the Church." "A Fair," *Baltimore Sun*, May 31, 1838.

83. Year 1850; census place Baltimore, Ward 17, Baltimore, Maryland; roll M432_286; page 196; image 392. www.ancestrylibrary.com.

84. Year 1850; census place Baltimore Ward 17, Baltimore, Maryland; roll M432_286; page 190; image 380. www.ancestrylibrary.com.

85. While Benjamin Smith was literate, his thirty-one-year-old wife Ellen was not. They sent all four of their children to school: fourteen-year-old Thomas, eight-year-old Eliza, seven-year-old Susan, and five-year-old George. Year 1850; census place Baltimore Ward 17, Baltimore, Maryland; roll *M432_286;* page 190; image 381. www.ancestrylibrary.com.

86. Year 1850; census place: Baltimore Ward 17, Baltimore, Maryland; roll M432_286; page 194; image 388. www.ancestrylibrary.com.

87. A White Citizen, "The Colored People of Baltimore," *Niles' Register*, October 3, 1835.

88. Evelyn Nakano Glenn, *Unequal Freedom: How Race and Gender Shaped American Citizenship and Labor* (Cambridge: Harvard University Press, 2002), 22–23.

89. A White Citizen, "The Colored People of Baltimore," *Niles' Register*, October 3, 1835.

90. Bettye J. Gardner, "William Watkins: Antebellum Black Teacher and Anti-Slavery Writer," *Negro History Bulletin* 39 (September/October 1976): 623–25.

91. "Poems by Francis Ellen Watkins," *Liberator*, September 18, 1857.

92. Year 1850; census place Baltimore Ward 16, Baltimore, Maryland; roll M432_286; page 124; image: 249. www.ancestrylibrary.com.

93. A Colored Baltimorean, "American Colonization Society (Continued)," *Freedom's Journal*, July 18, 1828.

94. A Colored Baltimorean, "An Able Reply," *Liberator*, June 4, 1831. For examples of his anticolonizationist editorials, see "A Voice from Baltimore!" *Liberator*, April 2, 1831; A Colored Baltimorean, "Colonization Society," *Freedom's Journal*, July 6, 1827; A Colored Baltimorean, "American Colonization Society

(Continued)"; "Colonization of the Free Blacks," *Liberator*, March 4, 1831; "A Voice from Baltimore!" *Liberator*, April 2, 1831.

95. William Watkins to William Lloyd Garrison, September 30, 1835, Anti-Slavery Collection, Boston Public Library.

96. William J. Watkins, *Philanthropist*, November 4, 1836.

97. Linda Kerber, "The Republican Mother: Women and the Enlightenment—An American Perspective," *American Quarterly* 28 (Summer 1976): 203.

98. As Susan Zaeske observed in her discussion of women's antislavery petitions, "At its core a petition is a request for redress of grievances sent from a subordinate (whether an individual or a group) to a superior (whether a ruler or a representative) . . . characterized by a humble tone and an acknowledgement of the superior status of the recipient." Zaeske, *Signatures of Citizenship: Petitioning, Antislavery, and Women's Political Identity* (Chapel Hill: University of North Carolina Press, 2003), 3; Michael Schudson, *The Good Citizen: A History of American Civic Life* (New York: Free Press, 1998), 108.

99. David M. Ricci, *Good Citizenship in America* (Cambridge: Cambridge University Press, 2004), 7.

100. Harold B. Hancock, "Not Quite Men: The Free Negroes in Delaware in the 1830s," *Civil War History* 17 (December 1971): 323.

101. Kent County made this determination in 1834, Montgomery County in 1838, and Anne Arundel County in 1860. Wright, *The Free Negro in Maryland*, 126.

102. "Property of Colored Persons," *Baltimore Sun*, May 8, 1852.

103. Ira Berlin, *Slaves without Masters: The Free Negro in the Antebellum South* (New York: Vintage Books, 1974), 305.

104. "An Ordinance to Release Certain Property from the Payment of the Public School Tax," February 27, 1838, Papers of the City Council, record group 16, series 1, box 60, item 1194, BCA.

105. "An Ordinance to Exempt the property of Persons of Colour from the Payment of the Public School Tax," April 6–8, Papers of the City Council, record group 16, box 60, item 1194, BCA.

106. "Petition of James Corner and Others," January 24, 1839, Papers of the City Council, record group 16, series 1, box 61, item 706, BCA.

107. "Proceedings of the City Council," *Baltimore Sun*, January 28, 1839; "Proceedings of the City Council," *Baltimore Sun*, February 6, 1839; "Proceedings of the City Council," *Baltimore Sun*, February 8, 1839; "Report of Joint Committee of Ways and Means on the Petition of D. Grieves and Others," February 4, 1839, City Council Papers, record group 16, series 1, box 63, item 1161, BCA.

108. "Proceedings of the City Council," *Baltimore Sun*, February 2, 1844.

109. "Petition of Daniel Kilbourn and Others Relative to the Coloured Schools," January 30, 1844, Papers of the City Council, record group 16, series 1, box 72, item 448, BCA.

110. According to census records, sailor Daniel Myers owned $1,200 of property in 1850. Unlike Samuel Hiner, neither he nor his wife Charlotte could read. At the time of the petition, the couple had three school-aged children: Hester, Daniel, and Robert. Moses Clayton, a carpenter, owned $1,000 of property in 1850. Although he could read and write, his wife, Susan, could not. The couple had two school-aged children, one daughter and one son. William Winsey, a brick maker, owned real estate valued at $1,000 and like Clayton, could read and write. As of 1844, Winsey did not have children, but as of 1850, he and his twenty-four-year-old wife Maria had two sons. Ship carpenter, Jas. Morris, owned $800 of property. Neither he nor his wife Ann could read or write. They had two children of school age at the time he signed the appeal. Year 1850; census place Baltimore Ward 3, Baltimore, Maryland; roll M432_283; page 330; image 88, www.ancestrylibrary.com; Year 1850; census place Baltimore Ward 6, Baltimore, Maryland; roll M432_283; page 245; image 315; Year 1850; census place Baltimore Ward 5, Baltimore, Maryland; roll M432_283; page 138; image 100; www.ancestrylibrary.com; Year 1850; census place Baltimore Ward 3, Baltimore, Maryland; roll M432_283; page 330; image 89; Year 1850; census place Baltimore Ward 7, Baltimore, Maryland; roll M432_283; page 305; www.ancestrylibrary.com.

111. "Petition of Joseph Cook and Others for a Portion of the School Fund for Colored Children in Hartford," General Assembly Papers, record group 002, African Americans, box 1, folder 8, April 29, 1830; "Resolve on Petition of Joseph Cook and Others for a Portion of the School Fund for Colored Children in Hartford," General Assembly Papers, record group 002, African Americans, box 1, folder 8, May 28, 1830, Connecticut State Library.

112. "Proceedings of the City Council," *Baltimore Sun*, February 24, 1844; *Baltimore Sun*, February 16, 1844; "An Ordinance to Exempt Coloured People from Payment of the School Tax," January 29, 1844, Papers of the City Council, record group 16, series 1, box 74, item 1071, BCA; "Report of the Committee of Ways and Means Recommending That the Coloured People of Balt. Be Exempt from the School Tax," February 19, 1844, City Council Papers, record group 16, series 1, box 73, item 709, BCA; "Proceedings of the City Council," *Baltimore Sun*, February 20, 1844.

113. Aristides, "Taxation of the Colored People," *Liberator*, February 23, 1844.

114. "Public Schools for Colored Children," *Baltimore Sun,* February 16, 1850.

115. The 1850 petition is missing from the BCA. Its contents are briefly discussed in the *Baltimore Sun*. See "Public Schools for Colored Children," *Baltimore Sun*, February 16, 1850; "Proceedings of the City Council," *Baltimore Sun*, February 20, 1850. The school is mentioned in "Meeting of Colored People," *National Era*, August 12, 1852; Gardner, "Antebellum Black Education in Baltimore," 361.

116. "Memorial of Jas. Wilson and others in favor of the establishment of Public Schools by the colored population," February 7, 1850, Papers of the City Council, record group 16, box 87, item 457, BCA.

117. Many thanks to Frank Towers for sharing his findings. According to Towers, identifiable petitioners averaged the "remarkably high figure of $37,460 in taxable wealth." Frank Harold Towers, "Ruffians on the Urban Border: Labor, Politics, and Race in Baltimore" (Ph.D. dissertation, University of California-Irvine, 1993), 547–49, 782.

118. "Public Schools for Colored Children," *Baltimore Sun*, February 16, 1850; "Report of the Joint Committee on Education in Memorial of Elias Williams and Others for the Public Schools for Colored Children," City Council Papers, record group 16, box 88, item 822, BCA.

119. M. J. Kerney, "Report of the Committee of Education, Establishing a Uniform System of Instruction in the Public Schools of This State, Reported in the House of Delegates April 16, by M. J. Kerney, Chairman." *Baltimore Sun*, April 29, 1852.

120. "Proceedings of the City Council," *Baltimore Sun*, May 12, 1852; "Proceedings of the City Council," *Baltimore Sun*, May 27, 1852; "An Ordinance to Exempt from Taxation for Public School Purposes the Property Owned by Colored Persons in the City of Balt.," May 11, 1852, City Council Records, record group 16, series 1, box 95, item 1371, BCA; "Property of Colored Persons," *Baltimore Sun*, May 8, 1852.

121. "The Public School Bill," *Baltimore Sun*, May 5, 1852.

122. On Catholics' relationship with public education see, for example, Benjamin Justice, "The Blaine Game: Are Public Schools Inherently Anti-Catholic?" *Teachers College Record* 109 (November 2007): 2171–206; Chris Beneke, " 'Mingle with Us': Religious Integration in Eighteenth and Nineteenth-Century American Education," *American Educational History Journal* 33 (2006): 29–37; Justice, *The War That Wasn't: Religious Conflict and Compromise in the Common Schools of New York State, 1865–1900* (Albany: State University of New York Press, 2005); Joan DelFatorre, *The Fourth R: Conflicts over Religion in America's Public Schools* (New Haven: Yale University Press, 2004); John T. McGreevy, *Catholicism and American Freedom: A History* (New York: W. W. Norton, 2003); James W. Fraser, *Between Church and State: Religion and Public Education in a Multicultural America* (New York: St. Martin's Press, 1999); Jay P. Dolan, *In Search of an American Catholicism: A History of Religion and Culture in Tension* (Oxford: Oxford University Press, 2002); and Dolan, "Catholic Education in the Early Republic," *History of Education Quarterly* 21 (Summer 1981): 205–11.

123. M. J. K., "Citizens of Baltimore," *Baltimore Sun*, April 26, 1852.

124. As of 1860, Kerney, a forty-one-year-old attorney, owned $4,000 of property. Together with his wife, Mary, also a native of Ireland, Kerney had two sons, thirteen-year-old John and nine-year-old Peter, who both attended school. Year 1860; census place Baltimore Ward 5, Baltimore, Maryland; roll M653_460; page 314: image 315, www.ancestrylibrary.com.

125. M. J. Kerney, "Citizens of Baltimore," *Baltimore Sun*, April 26, 1852.

126. "The New School Bill before the Legislature," *Baltimore Sun,* April 26, 1852.

127. "Maryland Legislature," *Baltimore Sun*, May 7, 1852.

128. "Proceedings of the City Council," *Baltimore Sun,* April 29, 1852.

129. Baltimorean, "The Public School Question—Mr. Kerney's Bill," *Baltimore American and Commercial Daily Advertiser*, April 29, 1852.

130. Aristides, "The School Question," *Baltimore Sun*, May 4, 1852; Anti-Humbug, "Mr. Kerney's School Bill," *Baltimore Sun*, October 13, 1852; "The Public School System of Baltimore," *Baltimore Sun*, April 29, 1852; "The School Bill and the City Council," *Baltimore Sun*, April 29, 1852. Debate over Kerney's proposal persisted in the state legislature for two years.

131. "Threatened Destruction of the Public Schools," *Baltimore Sun*, April 11, 1853; "Meeting for the Preservation of the Public Schools," *Baltimore Sun*, April 12, 1853.

132. "The Public School Bill," *Baltimore Sun*, May 5, 1852.

Part 3

1. *Twelfth Annual Report of the [Massachusetts] Board of Education with the Twelfth Annual Report of the Secretary of the Board* (1848); reprinted in Lawrence A. Cremin, ed., *The Republic and the School: Horace Mann on the Education of Free Men* (New York: Teachers College Press, 1957), 103.

2. On the history of Boston see, for example, John Hanson Mitchell, *The Paradise of all These Parts: a Natural History of Boston* (Boston: Beacon Press, 2008); Thomas H. O'Connor, *The Athens of America: Boston, 1825–1845* (Amherst: University of Massachusetts Press, 2006); O'Connor, *The Hub: Boston Past and Present* (Boston: Northeastern University Press, 2001); Jacqueline Barbara Carr, *After the Siege: A Social History of Boston* (Boston: Northeastern University Press, 2005); Thomas O'Connor, James M. O'Toole, and David Quigley, *Boston's Histories: Essays in Honor of Thomas H. O'Connor* (Boston: Northeastern University Press, 2004); Jack Tager, *Boston Riots: Three Centuries of Social Violence* (Boston: Northeastern University Press, 2001); Walter Muir Whitehill and Lawrence W. Kennedy, *Boston: A Topographical History* (Cambridge: Belknap Press of Harvard University Press, 2000); Oscar Handlin, *Boston's Immigrants, 1790–1880; A Study in Acculturation* (Cambridge: Belknap Press of Harvard University Press, 1959); Peter R. Knights, *The Plain People of Boston, 1830–1860: A Study in City Growth* (New York: Oxford University Press, 1971); and Roger Lane, *Policing the City: Boston, 1822–1885* (Cambridge: Harvard University Press, 1967).

3. Lee Soltow and Edward Stevens, *The Rise of Literacy and the Common School in the United States: A Socioeconomic Analysis to 1870* (Chicago: University

of Chicago Press, 1981), 11; E. Jennifer Monaghan, *Learning to Read and Write in Colonial America* (Amherst: University of Massachusetts Press, 2005), 37–39. On literacy in colonial New England, see Edward E. Gordon and Elaine H. Gordon, *Literacy in America: Historic Journey and Contemporary Solutions* (Westport, Conn.: Praeger, 2003); Hilary Wyss, *Writing Indians: Literacy, Christianity, and Native Community in Early America* (Amherst: University of Massachusetts Press, 2000); E. Jennifer Monaghan, *Reading for the Enslaved, Writing for the Free: Reflections on Liberty and Literacy* (Worcester, Mass.: American Antiquarian Society, 2000); Ruth Wallis Herndon, "Research Note: Literacy among New England's Transient Poor, 1750–1800," *Journal of Social History* 29 (Summer 1996): 963–65; Joel Perlmann and Dennis Shirley, "When Did New England Women Acquire Literacy?" *William and Mary Quarterly* 48 (January 1991): 50–67; Monaghan, "Literacy Instruction and Gender in Colonial New England," *American Quarterly* 40 (March 1988): 18–41; Carl F. Kaestle, "The History of Literacy and the History of Readers," *Review of Research in Education* 12 (1985): 11–53; William J. Gilmore, *Elementary Literacy on the Eve of the Industrial Revolution: Trends in Rural New England, 1760–1830* (Worcester, Mass.: American Antiquarian Society, 1982); Linda Auwers, "Reading the Marks of the Past: Exploring Female Literacy in Colonial Windsor, Connecticut," *Historical Methods* 13 (Fall 1980): 204–14; and Kenneth A. Lockridge, *Literacy in Colonial New England: An Enquiry into the Social Context of Literacy in the Early Modern West* (New York: Norton, 1974).

4. Joel Spring, *The American School, 1642–1993,* 3d ed. (Boston: McGraw-Hill, 1994), 63.

5. As of 1845, 37,289 foreign immigrants and their children made up 32 percent of Boston's total population. Josiah Curtis, *Report of the Joint Special Committee on the Census of Boston, May, 1855* . . . (Boston: Moore and Crosby, 1856), 3; Lemuel Shattuck, *Report to the Committee of the City Council Appointed to Obtain the Census of Boston for the Year 1845* (Boston: John H. Eastburn, 1846), 37; Knights, *Plain People of Boston,* 20, 35.

6. "Address of Hon. Horace Mann at the National Common School Convention," *Boston Evening Transcript,* October 26, 1849.

7. Lorenzo Johnston Greene, *The Negro in Colonial New England: 1620–1776* (New York: Atheneum, 1971), 16–17.

8. As quoted in Robert M. Spector, "The Quock Walker Cases (1781–1783): Slavery, Its Abolition, and Negro Citizenship in Early Massachusetts," *Journal of Negro History* 53 (January 1968), 17.

9. James J. Allegro, "Law, Politics and Slavery in Massachusetts Bay Colony, 1686–1738" (Master's thesis, Tufts University, 1997), 73–78.

10. Cotton Mather, *The Negro Christianized. An Essay to Excite and Assist the Good Work, the Instruction of Negro Servants in Christianity* (Boston: B. Green, 1706). On Mather's ideas about slaveholding, see Daniel K. Richter, "'It Is God Who Has Caused Them to Be Servants': Cotton Mather and Afro-American Slav-

ery in New England," *Bulletin of the Congregational Library* 30 (Spring–Summer 1979): 4–12.

11. As early as 1693, Mather created the Society of Negroes to teach enslaved and free black people the catechism and to read the Bible. While he did not provide writing instruction, every Sunday evening Mather invited black men and women into his home to listen to sermons, to pray, and to study. He also supplied his three bondsmen, Onesimus, Obediah, and Ezer, with lessons in reading and religion. Mather, *The Negro Christianized;* Mather, *Rules for the Society of Negroes* (Boston: B. Green, 1714); E. Jennifer Monaghan, "Family Literacy in Early 18th-Century Boston: Cotton Mather and His Children," *Reading Research Quarterly* 26 (Autumn 1991): 364.

12. Charles W. Akers, " 'Our Modern Egyptians': Phillis Wheatley and the Whig Campaign against Slavery in Revolutionary Boston," *Journal of Negro History* 60 (July 1975): 399. On Wheatley, see also Cedrick May, *Evangelism and Resistance in the Black Atlantic, 1760–1835* (Athens: University of Georgia Press, 2008); Kathrynn Grace Seidler Engberg, "The Right to Write: Anne Bradstreet and Phillis Wheatley" (Ph.D. dissertation, University of Alabama, 2006); Jennifer Rene Young, "Marketing a Sable Muse: The Cultural Circulation of Phillis Wheatley," *1767–1865* (Ph.D. dissertation, Howard University, 2004); and Henry Louis Gates, *The Trials of Phillis Wheatley: America's First Black Poet and Her Encounters with the Founding Fathers* (New York: Basic Civitas Books, 2003).

13. Robert Desrochers, "Slave-for-Sale Advertisements and Slavery in Massachusetts, 1704–1781," *William and Mary Quarterly* 59 (July 2002), 636–37; Greene, *The Negro in Colonial New England,* 84; James Oliver Horton and Lois E. Horton, *In Hope of Liberty: Culture, Community and Protest among Northern Free Blacks, 1700–1860* (New York: Oxford University Press, 1997), 4.

14. Emily V. Blanck, "Reaching for Freedom: Black Resistance and the Roots of a Gendered African-American Culture in Late Eighteenth Century Massachusetts" (Master's thesis, College of William and Mary, 1998), 33–34; Gary B. Nash, *The Urban Crucible: Social Change, Political Consciousness, and the Origins of the American Revolution* (Cambridge: Harvard University Press, 1979), 320–21.

15. Spector, "Quock Walker Cases," 25–26.

16. Jesse Chickering, *A Statistical View of the Population of Massachusetts, from 1765 to 1840* (Boston: Charles Little and James Brown, 1846), 113. On the end of slavery in Massachusetts, see Thea K. Hunter, "Publishing Freedom, Winning Arguments: Somerset, Natural Rights and Massachusetts Freedom Cases, 1772–1836" (Ph.D. dissertation, Columbia University, 2005); Emily Blanck, "Seventeen Eighty-Three: The Turning Point in the Law of Slavery and Freedom in Massachusetts," *New England Quarterly* 75 (March 2002), 24–51; T. H. Breen, "Making History: The Force of Public Opinion and the Last Years of Slavery in Revolutionary Massachusetts," in Ronald Hoffman, Mechal Sobel, and Fredrika J. Teute, eds., *Through a Glass Darkly: Reflections on Personal Identity in Early America*

(Chapel Hill: University of North Carolina Press, 1997), 67–95; Elaine MacEacheren, "Emancipation of Slavery in Massachusetts: A Reexamination, 1770–1790," *Journal of Negro History* 55 (October 1970): 289–306; Arthur Zilversmit, "Quok Walker, Mumbet, and the Abolition of Slavery in Massachusetts," *William and Mary Quarterly* 25 (October 1968): 614–24; and William O'Brien, "Did the Jennison Case Outlaw Slavery in Massachusetts?" *William and Mary Quarterly* 17 (April 1960): 219–41.

17. As quoted in Mary Ann Connolly, "Boston Schools in the New Republic, 1776–1840," (Ed.D. dissertation, Harvard University, 1963), 147–48.

18. Linda K. Kerber, "The Meanings of Citizenship," *Journal of American History* 84 (December 1997): 834.

19. "Meeting of Colored Citizens," *Liberator,* August 10, 1849.

20. Patrick Rael, *Black Identity and Black Protest in the Antebellum North* (Chapel Hill: University of North Carolina Press, 2002), 5.

Chapter Five

1. In the mid–1840s, Boston spent $241,860 on 200 public schools that served 21,000 students (or $11.52 per pupil). While Baltimore's population surpassed Boston's by 34,000, it spent $45,352 to sustain 34 public schools collectively enrolling 7,093 students (or $6.39 per pupil). *Seventh Census of the United States* (1850), 147.

2. According to Leonard P. Curry, 90 percent of white children and 79 percent of African American children between the ages of five and fourteen attended school in Boston "during the 1849–1850 School Year." By comparison, 22 percent of black children attended school in Baltimore in 1850, all at private institutions. In Connecticut, 1,264 black children between the ages of six and twenty attended school in 1850, or 52 percent of that subset of the population, as did 72 percent of similarly aged white children. *The Free Black in Urban America, 1800–1850: The Shadow of the Dream* (Chicago: University of Chicago Press, 1981), 169; Paul Finkelman, "Prelude to the Fourteenth Amendment: Black Legal Rights in the Antebellum North," *Rutgers Law Journal* 17 (Spring/Summer 1986): 472–73.

3. As quoted in Justin Winsor, ed., *The Memorial History of Boston, Including Suffolk County, Massachusetts. 1630–1880,* vol. 4 (Boston: James R. Osgood and Company, 1881), 236.

4. Winsor, *Memorial History of Boston,* 236.

5. Mary Ann Connolly, "The Boston Schools in the New Republic, 1776–1840" (Ed.D. dissertation, Harvard University, 1963), 3–18; Lemuel Shattuck, *Report to the Committee of the City Council Appointed to Obtain the Census of Boston for the Year 1845 . . .* (Boston: John H. Eastburn, 1846), 2–3; Stanley K. Schultz, *The Culture Factory: Boston Public Schools, 1789–1860* (New York: Oxford University Press, 1973), 5–7.

6. Connolly, "Boston Schools in the New Republic," 17–19.

7. Schultz, *Culture Factory,* 8.

8. As quoted in James G. Carter, *Letters to the Hon. William Prescott, LL. D. on the Free Schools of New England, with Remarks upon the Principles of Instruction* (Boston: Cummings, Hilliard & Co., 1824), 24; Schultz, *Culture Factory,* 11.

9. As quoted in James G. Carter, *Letters to the Hon. William Prescott,* 24–25.

10. Winsor, *Memorial History of Boston,* 242.

11. Joseph Wightman, comp., *Annals of the Boston Primary School Committee, from Its First Establishment in 1818, to Its Dissolution in 1855* (Boston: Rand and Avery, 1860), 8.

12. Schultz, *Culture Factory,* 14–15.

13. Linda Kerber, "The Republican Mother: Women and the Enlightenment— An American Perspective," *American Quarterly* 28 (Summer 1976): 187–205.

14. James G. Carter, *Essays upon Popular Education, Containing a Particular Examination of the Schools of Massachusetts, and an Outline of an Institution for the Education of Teachers* (Boston: Bowles & Dearborn, 1826; reprint New York: Arno Press & The New York Times, 1969), 20.

15. As quoted in Carter, *Letters to the Honorable William Prescott,* 49.

16. On schooling in nineteenth-century Boston, see, for example, Rachel Remmel, "The Origins of the American School Building: Boston Public School Architecture, 1800–1860" (Ph.D. dissertation, University of Chicago, 2006); Amy Earhart, "Boston's 'Un-Common' Common: Race, Reform, and Education, 1800– 1865" (Ph.D. dissertation, Texas A&M University, 1999); Robert L. Osgood, "Undermining the Common School Ideal: Intermediate Schools and Ungraded Classes in Boston, 1838–1900," *History of Education Quarterly* 37 (Winter 1997): 375–98; and James W. Fraser, Henry L. Allen, and Sam Barnes, eds. *From Common School to Magnet School; Selected Essays in the History of Boston's Schools* (Boston: Public Library of the City of Boston, 1979).

17. Prince Hall et al., "Petition of Prince Hall, October 17, 1787," reprinted in *Equal Protection and the African American Constitutional Experience: A Documentary History,* edited by Robert P. Green, Jr. (Westport, Conn.: Greenwood Press, 2000), 38–39.

18. On Hall and Boston's free black community at the end of the eighteenth century, see Chernoh Momodu Sesay, Jr., "Freemasons of Color: Prince Hall, Revolutionary Black Boston, and the Origins of Black Freemasonry, 1770–1807" (Ph.D. dissertation, Northwestern University, 2006).

19. Details of the school's history are culled from the School Committee Minutes (1792–1854) and the School Committee Loose Papers (1830–56), both located at the Boston Public Library (hereafter SCM and SCLP). October 15, 1833, SCM.

20. "Petition of George Middleton referred to Sub-Committee," March 20, 1800, SCM; Arthur Owen White, "Blacks and Education in Antebellum Massachusetts: Strategies for Social Mobility" (Ed.D. dissertation, State University of New York at Buffalo, 1971), 98–99.

21. White, "Blacks and Education in Antebellum Massachusetts," 99–101.

22. James Horton, "Generations of Protest: Black Families and Social Reform in Ante-Bellum Boston," *New England Quarterly* 49 (June 1976), 245; George A. Levesque, *Black Boston: African American Life and Culture in Urban America, 1750–1860* (New York: Garland Publishing, 1994), 266.

23. "Public Meeting," *Liberator,* July 16, 1831.

24. J. F. Bumstead, "Annual Visit," *Liberator*, April 14, 1837.

25. Chas. V. Caples, "Proposals for Opening an Evening School," *Liberator*, September 19, 1835.

26. "Colored Infant School, Belknap Street," May 24, 1834.

27. On Sabbath school instruction in the nineteenth century, see Anne M. Boylan, *Sunday School: The Formation of an American Institution, 1790–1880* (New Haven: Yale University Press, 1988).

28. William Minot, *Mr. Minot's Address Delivered at the Smith School House in Belknap Street, March 3, 1835, to Which Are Added a Few Friendly Suggestions to the Colored People of Boston* (Boston, 1835), 2.

29. October 15, 1833, SCM.

30. George A. Levesque, "Before Integration: The Forgotten Years of Jim Crow Education in Boston," *Journal of Negro Education* 48 (Spring 1979): 122.

31. James G. Barbadoes et al., "Memorial of the People of Color for the Removal of Mr. Bascom from the African School," December 24, 1833, SCLP; David Child, "Committee Report on Immoral Conduct of William Bascom, Master of African School" 1833, SCLP.

32. In 1821, Boston became the first city in the nation to open an English high school for boys. While it gave white girls educational parity with boys in primary and grammar schools, it did not permit girls to advance to high school. In 1825, the school committee agreed to open a girls' high school, also the first of its kind in the nation, hoping to train female students to become primary school teachers. The new institution enrolled qualified girls between the ages of eleven and fifteen for a three-year period. This experiment proved to be short-lived. Troubled by the expense and its pretense to offer girls a "professional" education, Mayor Josiah Quincy lobbied for its closure. The subcommittee appointed to study the issue agreed with Quincy's concerns and concluded that "girls are not like boys." By 1829, impoverished white girls were in much the same predicament as African American children. The city refused to provide all of them advanced education. Josiah Quincy, *Report of a Sub Committee of the School Committee Recommending Various Improvements in the System of Instruction in the Grammar and Writing Schools of this City* (Boston: Nathan Hale, 1828); Connolly, "Boston Schools in the New Republic," 141–45.

33. September 7, 1824, SCM; Edward S. Abdy, *Journal of a Residence and Tour in the United States of North America, from 1833 to October 1834,* 3 vols., vol. 1 (London: John Murray, 1835), 169.

34. March 22, 1825, SCM.

35. July 5, 1825, SCM.

36. November 17, 1826, SCM; January 13, 1827, SCM; March 23, 1827, SCM.

37. March 26, 1833, SCM.

38. October 15, 1833, SCM.

39. "Evening School for People of Color," *Liberator*, February 1, 1834.

40. "Petition from the Citizens of Southack Street to the Board of Alderman," July 28, 1834, SCLP.

41. Harrison Gray Otis to Capt. Shaw, July 26, 1834, SCLP.

42. "Petition from the Citizens of Southack Street."

43. Nathaniel Fisher et al., "Petition against the Building of a Coloured School on Garden Street," August 18, 1834, SCLP.

44. "Remonstrance against the African School," 1834, SCLP.

45. Special thanks go to Heather Wilson for compiling and analyzing this data and for generously sharing her ideas. All addresses and occupations are culled from *Stimpson's 1835 Boston Directory* (Boston: C. Stimpson, 1835). Thomas Darling owned three houses on West Center Street, which he rented to African American laborers Ralph Roberts, Joseph Sanders, and Henry Carroll. He also owned two homes on Southack Street, which he rented to black laborers George Bradford and John Williams. Darling owned 21 other properties on Southack Street and West Center Street in addition. Business partners John Low and Elias Kingsley owned one home on Butolph Street, which they rented to black laborer Aaron Gall, and four homes that they rented to white tenants. Mitchel and Dunbar rented a home on Southack Street to black seaman Thomas Robbins and were in the process of building two additional houses on Pickney Street at the time of the petition.

46. "Removed," *Boston Daily Atlas*, July 6, 1833.

47. "Remonstrance of Residents of Garden Street against African School," SCLP, 1833.

48. In addition, seventeen of the ninety-five African Americans identified had no occupation listed in the city directory.

49. At least eleven African Americans owned homes in the vicinity, defined here as Belknap, Cambridge, Southack, South Russell, Washington, May, Butolph, George, Grove, and West Center streets and North Square. In total, tax records recorded ninety-five black household heads in this area, seventy-four of which resided in single-family homes and twenty-one of which lived in shared residences.

50. Jonas W. Clarke, Lewis Smith, Joseph Sprague, and Oliver Nash, for example, lived on May Street; Thomas Dalton resided on South Russell; Primus Hall, Joseph Woodson, and John Robinson resided on George Street; William Riley and Henry Thacker lived on Southack Street; finally, George Putnam lived on Belknap Street. Clarke, Riley, and Robinson each owned a used-clothing business, which they set up outside the immediate neighborhood, on 18 Brattle Street, 22 Brattle Street, and 42 Brattle Street, respectively.

51. According to tax records, Titcomb, who signed the first and second petitions, owned $10,000 in real property, for which he paid $62.60 in taxes. He rented his property on 60 Myrtle Street to three men who also petitioned in opposition to the proposed school. The first, Reuben Frost, a drain digger, had no personal property and paid $1.50 in taxes in 1834. Frost's housemate, Warren Boles, a housewright, owned $200 in personal property and paid $3.38 in taxes. Boles signed only the third petition. Finally, Stephen B. Franklin, a furniture maker, had $200 in personal property and paid $3.38 in taxes. Ward 6 Tax Records (1834), Boston City Archives.

52. This phrase comes from Leonard L. Richards, *"Gentlemen of Property and Standing": Anti-Abolition Mobs in Jacksonian America* (New York: Oxford University Press, 1970).

53. H. G. Otis to Capt. Shaw, July 26, 1834, SCLP. Otis lived at 42 Beacon Street, just north of the Common. *Stimpson's 1835 Boston Directory*, 285.

54. There were thirty-four black barbers and seventeen black purveyors of used clothes.

55. "The Colored Population of the United States, No. 2." *Liberator*, January 22, 1831.

56. "Letter—No. VI to Rev. Samuel E. Cornish," *Freedom's Journal*, November 9, 1827.

57. "Colored People of Boston," *Liberator*, November 22, 1834.

58. The 1850 census, for example, noted forty-eight black domestic servants, nearly all of whom were women. In Ward 6, the seven African American female domestics whom census takers counted lived in white households. Census Schedules (1850).

59. "A Colored Woman," *Boston Evening Transcript*, September 18, 1845.

60. Levesque, *Black Boston,* 89.

61. Many thanks to William Walker for this observation.

62. For this insight, I am indebted to Benjamin Justice.

63. "Petition from the Citizens of Southack Street."

64. Kevin Fox Gotham, "Urban Space, Restrictive Covenants and the Origins of Racial Residential Segregation in a US City, 1900–50," *International Journal of Urban and Regional Research* 24 (September 2000): 617–18. The literature on race, schooling, and residential segregation in the twentieth century is rich and evolving. See, for example, David M. Freund, *Colored Property: State Policy and White Racial Politics in Suburban America* (Chicago: University of Chicago Press, 2007); Jack Dougherty, "The Rise of 'Shopping for Schools' in Suburbia," paper delivered at the History of Education Society meeting, October 2007, in the possession of the author; Michael Clapper, "School Design, Site Selection, and the Political Geography of Race in Postwar Philadelphia," *Journal of Planning History* 5 (August 2006): 241–63; Kevin Michael Kruse and Thomas J. Sugrue, eds. *The New Suburban History* (Chicago: University of Chicago Press, 2006); Matthew D. Lassiter, *The Silent*

Majority: Suburban Politics in the Sunbelt South (Princeton, N.J.: Princeton University Press, 2006); Kevin Michael Kruse, *White Flight: Atlanta and the Making of Modern Conservatism* (Princeton, N.J.: Princeton University Press, 2005); Kevin Fox Gotham, *Race, Real Estate, and Uneven Development: The Kansas City Experience, 1900–2000* (Albany: State University of New York Press, 2002); and Ansley T. Erikson, "Schooling the Metropolis: Growth Ideology and Educational Inequity, Nashville, TN, 1950–2000" (Ph.D. dissertation in progress, Columbia University). Special thanks go to Ansley Erikson for her guidance on this literature.

65. "Petition from the Citizens of Southack Street."

66. Nathaniel Fisher et al., "Petition against the Building of a Coloured School on Garden Street."

67. Petitioners suggested the school should remain near its original location. Southack Street residents proposed, for example, that the "Belknap St. [facility] be enlarged, or land procured near it to erect a new building upon, in the center of a population of coloured people who would no doubt be pleased with its location there, and where there is not a White population to be affected by it." "Petition from the Citizens of Southack Street"; Minot, *Mr. Minot's Address*.

68. Abner Forbes to the Boston School Committee, November 14, 1837, SCLP.

69. May 8, 1838, SCM; August 7, 1838, SCM.

70. Quarterly Report of the Smith School, November 4, 1839, SCLP.

71. Quarterly Report of the Smith School, May 5, 1840, SCLP; Annual Report of the Committee for the Examination of the Grammar Schools, August 4, 1840, SCLP.

72. Quarterly Report of the Smith School, August 2, 1842.

73. M. Minot to the Boston School Committee, August 4, 1836, SCLP.

74. For further explication of these arguments see, for example, Michael B. Katz, *The Irony of Early School Reform: Educational Innovation in Mid-Nineteenth Century Massachusetts* (Cambridge: Harvard University Press, 1968); and Schultz, *Culture Factory*.

75. November 20, 1840, SCM; February 2, 1841, SCM; February 23, 1841, SCM; March 9, 1841, SCM.

76. "Annual Examination of Grammar Departments," 1843, SCLP.

77. "Petition of Thomas Dalton et al. to have the Smith School abolished and that their children be permitted to attend other schools," May 7, 1844, SCLP.

78. On Mann's involvement with the common school movement see, for example, William Hayes, *Horace Mann's Vision of the Public Schools: Is It Still Relevant?* (Lanham, Md.: Rowman & Littlefield Education, 2006); Gabriel G. Compayré and Mary D. Frost, *Horace Mann and the Public School in the United States* (Honolulu, Ha.: University Press of the Pacific, 2002); Thomas Michael Buck, "Horace Mann: Enigmatic Leader in Change and Conflict" (Ph.D. dissertation, Marquette University, 1999); Jonathan Messerli, *Horace Mann; a Biography* (New York: Knopf,

1972); Maris A. Vinovskis, "Horace Mann on the Economic Productivity of Education," *New England Quarterly* 43 (December 1970): 550–71; and B. A. Hinsdale, *Horace Mann and the Common School Revival in the United States* (New York: Charles Scribner's Sons, 1898).

79. P., "Horace Mann and Colored Schools," *Liberator,* December 24, 1847.

80. Horace Mann, "Reply of Hon. Horace Mann to Wendell Phillips, Esq.," *Liberator*, April 8, 1853; Carlton Mabee, "A Negro Boycott to Integrate Boston Schools," *New England Quarterly* 41 (September 1968): 346.

81. Horace Mann to Elizabeth Peabody, August 24, 1833, Horace Mann Papers, Massachusetts Historical Society (hereafter MHS).

82. Horace Mann, "Reply of Hon. Horace Mann to Wendell Phillips, Esq.," *Liberator*, April 8, 1853.

83. On Mann's abolitionist activities in the US House of Representatives, see Ernest Cassara, "Reformer as Politician: Horace Mann and the Anti-Slavery Struggle in Congress, 1848–1853," *Journal of American Studies* 5 (December 1971): 247–63. For Mann's own writings on the subject, see "Slavery Letters and Speeches," Burt Franklin Research and Source Works Series, 350 (New York: B. Franklin, 1969).

84. Wendell Phillips, "Reply of Wendell Phillips, Esq. to Hon. Horace Mann," *Liberator*, March 25, 1853.

85. "Reply of Hon. Horace Mann to Wendell Phillips, Esq.," *Liberator,* April 8, 1853.

86. On the school desegregation movement in Nantucket, see Francis Ruley Karttunen, *The Other Islanders: People Who Pulled Nantucket's Oars,* (New Bedford, Mass.: Spinner Publications, 2005), chapter 2; Barbara White, "The Integration of Nantucket Public Schools," *Historic Nantucket* 40 (Fall 1992): 59–62; Kristi Kraemer, "The Background and Resolution of the Eunice Ross Controversy," *Historic Nantucket* 28 (April 1981): 11–18; Barbara Linebaugh, *The African School and the Integration of Nantucket Public Schools, 1825–1847* (Boston: Afro-American Studies Center, Boston University, 1978); and Lorin Lee Cary and Francine C. Cary, "Absalom F. Boston, His Family, and Nantucket's Black Community," *Historic Nantucket* 25 (Summer 1977): 15–23.

87. William Bentley, ed., *The Diary of William Bentley, D. D. Pastor of the East Church of Salem, Massachusetts,* vol. 3, January 1803–December, 1810 (Salem, Mass.: Essex Institute, 1911), 273.

88. Arthur Owen White, "Salem's Antebellum Black Community; Seedbed of the School Integration Movement," *Essex Institute Historical Collections* 108 (April 1972): 99–118; "African Free Schools in the United States," *Freedom's Journal*, June 1, 1827; "Colored People of Salem," *Liberator*, January 7, 1832; "Costly Prejudice," *Liberator*, August 23, 1834; Charles B. Ray, "For the Colored American," *Colored American*, July 28, 1838.

89. White, "Salem's Antebellum Black Community," 108–109.

90. H. C. Wright, "First Free School—A Lie," *Liberator*, September 9, 1842.

91. "The Colored School," *Salem Register*, March 7, 1844.

92. "Reply of Hon. Horace Mann to Wendell Phillips, Esq.," *Liberator,* April 8, 1853.

93. C. C. "Public Schools," *Salem Register*, March 21, 1844.

94. Richard Fletcher, "Rights of Colored Citizens," *Liberator*, July 12, 1844.

95. Thomas Dalton, et al., "Petition of Thomas Dalton et al."

96. June 12, 1844, SCM.

97. "The Smith School," *Liberator*, July 19, 1844; "Meeting of the Colored Citizens of Boston," *Boston Evening Transcript*, June 28, 1844.

98. "Smith School—Report of Committee of Investigation," June 12, 1844, SCLP.

99. William B. Fowle to Horace Mann, July 11, 1844, Horace Mann Papers, MHS.

100. Horace Mann to Samuel Gridley Howe, May 11, 1845, Horace Mann Papers, MHS.

101. September 4, 1845, SCM.

102. "Meeting of the Primary School Committee," *Liberator*, June 27, 1845.

103. "Intolerance of the Primary School Committee," *Liberator,* June 27, 1845.

104. H. I. B, "Educational Spirit of Caste," *Liberator*, July 10, 1846.

105. *Report to the Primary School Committee, June 15, 1846, on the Petition of Sundry Colored Persons, for the Abolition of the Schools for Colored Children with the City Solicitor's Opinion* (Boston: J. H. Eastburn, 1846), 2.

106. *Twelfth Annual Report of the Board of Education Together with the Twelfth Annual Report of the Secretary of the Board of Education* (Boston: Dutton and Wentworth, 1849), 79.

107. *Eighth Annual Report of the Board of Education Together with the Eighth Annual Report of the Secretary of the Board* (Boston: Dutton and Wentworth, 1845), 135–36.

108. On race and voting rights in the early nineteenth century see, for example, James Truslow Adams, "Disfranchisement of Negroes in New England," *American Historical Review* 30 (April 1925): 543–47; and Charles H. Wesley, "Negro Suffrage in the Period of Constitution Making, 1787–1865," *Journal of Negro History* 32 (April 1947): 143–68.

109. "Prospectus," *Common School Journal* I (1838), 7.

110. Massachusetts's Democratic governor, Marcus Morton, led an effort to close the school board and the state normal schools in 1840. In Connecticut, Whig Henry Barnard endured a similar Democratic campaign in the 1840s to overturn many of his efforts to reform common schools. By 1841, public funding for education represented one of the key differences between the two parties statewide. Hendrick D. Gideonse, "Common School Reform: Connecticut, 1838–1854" (Ed.

D. dissertation, Harvard University, 1963), 92, 126–28; Vinovskis, "Horace Mann on the Economic Productivity of Education," 560.

111. Peter R. Knights, *The Plain People of Boston, 1830–1860: A Study in City Growth* (New York: Oxford University Press, 1971), 33–36; Richard A. Meckel, "Immigration, Mortality, and Population Growth in Boston, 1840–1880," *Journal of Interdisciplinary History* 15 (Winter 1985), 400; Lemuel Shattuck, *Report to the Committee of the City Council Appointed to Obtain the Census of Boston for the year 1845* (Boston: J. H. Eastburn, 1846), 37; Josiah Curtis, *Report of the Joint Special Committee on the Census of Boston, May, 1855* (Boston: Moore & Crosby, 1856), 3.

112. "Taxes against Immigration," *Boston Evening Transcript*, September 27, 1847.

113. "Changes in Boston," *Boston Evening Transcript*, January 22, 1852.

114. "Naturalization of Irishmen," *Boston Evening Transcript*, October 21, 1851.

115. "Immigration and Education," *Common School Journal* 14 (September 1852): 266.

116. "Address of Hon. Horace Mann at the National Common School Convention," *Boston Evening Transcript*, October 26, 1849.

117. "Crime in Boston," *Boston Evening Transcript*, October 9, 1848.

118. On this transformation, see Jacqueline S. Reinier, *From Virtue to Character: American Childhood, 1775–1850* (New York: Twayne, 1996).

119. Henry Barnard, *Legal Provision Respecting the Education and Employment of Children in Factories, &c; with Examples of Improvement in Manufacturing Districts* (Hartford: Case, Tiffany & Burham, 1842), 3.

120. "Immigration and Education," 266.

121. For further explication of Mann's views on this subject see Vinovskis, "Horace Mann on the Economic Productivity of Education."

122. *Fifth Annual Report of the Board of Education Together with the Fifth Annual Report of the Secretary of the Board* (Boston: Dutton and Wentworth, 1842), 82.

123. *Fifth Annual Report of the Board of Education*, 88.

124. *Fifth Annual Report of the Board of Education*, 90.

125. *Fifth Annual Report of the Board of Education*, 94–95.

126. Vinovskis, *Horace Mann on the Economic Productivity of Education*, 556–60. On the impact of the panic on Boston specifically, see William H. Pease and Jane H. Pease, *The Web of Progress: Private Values and Public Styles in Boston and Charleston, 1828–1843* (Athens: University of Georgia Press, 1991); and Jessica M. Lepler, "1837: Anatomy of a Panic" (Ph.D. dissertation, Brandeis University, 2008). For its effect on common schools, see William H. Pease and Jane H. Pease, "Paternal Dilemmas: Education, Property, and Patrician Persistence in Jacksonian Boston," *New England Quarterly* 53 (June 1980): 147–67.

127. Jacqueline Jones, *American Work: Four Centuries of Black and White Labor* (New York: W. W. Norton & Company, 1998), esp. chapter 8.

Chapter Six

1. "Letter to the Editor," unidentified newspaper clipping, Boston Municipal Court Records, Loose Papers No. 992 (1851), Massachusetts State Archives, Boston, Mass, hereafter MSA.

2. *Commonwealth of Massachusetts vs. Julian McCrea, Benjamin F. Roberts, and William J. Watkins, Assault and Battery, False Imprisonment, etc.*, Loose Papers 992 (1851), MSA.

3. "Letter to the Editor," Loose Papers No. 992.

4. *Commonwealth on Complaint of Benjamin F. Roberts vs. Elijah Smith, Assault and Battery,* Loose Papers 994 (1851), MSA.

5. "The Trouble among Colored Persons," *Boston Daily Atlas,* May 10, 1851.

6. "Daring Assault," *Boston Daily Atlas,* May 9, 1851.

7. "Meeting of Friends of Separate Colored Schools," *Boston Courier,* May 19, 1851; "A Meeting of Colored Persons," *Boston Evening Transcript,* May 19, 1851.

8. "William J. Watkins to Editor, *Boston Herald,* April 22, 1853," reprinted in *The Black Abolitionist Papers*, edited by C. Peter Ripley, vol. 4 (Chapel Hill: University of North Carolina Press, 1991), 153–56. On Watkins, see also Bettye J. Gardner, "William Watkins: Antebellum Black Teacher and Anti-Slavery Writer," *Negro History Bulletin* 39 (September/October 1976): 623–24.

9. Watkins resided at 8 Second Street, Smith at 9 (see *The Directory of the City of Boston* [Boston: George Adams, 1851]).

10. Thomas P. Smith, *An Address Delivered before the Colored Citizens of Boston in Opposition to the Abolition of the Colored Schools, on Monday Evening, Dec. 24, 1849* (Boston: Bela Marsh, 1850), 8.

11. W. C. N., "Equal School Rights," *Liberator,* February 8, 1850.

12. Arrested alongside Watkins, hairdresser Julian McCrea was less involved in the school integration dispute. He would later sue the city in 1856 to outlaw segregation in places of "public entertainment." *Commonwealth vs. Wm. J. Watkins, Recog. of Accused; Commonwealth of Massachusetts vs. McCrea, Benjamin F. Roberts, and William J. Watkins, Assault and Battery, False Imprisonment, etc.;* Thomas P. Smith, "Vindication," *Liberator,* October 5, 1849.

13. *Commonwealth on Complaint of Jona B. Wheelock vs. Julian B. McCrea et al.*

14. Roberts's version of the events is culled from his "Letter to the Editor," May 10, 1851, unidentified clipping in Boston Municipal Court Records, MSA.

15. Benjamin F. Roberts, "Letter to the Editor."

16. "William J. Watkins to Editor, *Boston Herald,* April 7, 1854," reprinted in *The Black Abolitionist Papers*, vol. 4, edited by C. Peter Ripley (Chapel Hill: University of North Carolina Press, 1991), 212.

17. On Henry Highland Garnet, see, for example, James Arthur Holmes, "Black Nationalism and Theodicy: A Comparison of the Thought of Henry Highland Garnet, Alexander Crummell, and Henry McNeal Turner" (Ph.D. dissertation, Boston University, 1997); Martin B. Pasternak, *Rise Now and Fly to Arms:*

The Life of Henry Highland Garnet (New York: Garland, 1995); Joel Schor, *Henry Highland Garnet: A Voice of Black Radicalism in the Nineteenth Century* (Westport, Conn.: Greenwood Press, 1977); and Earl Ofari Hutchinson, *Let Your Motto Be Resistance: The Life and Thought of Henry Highland Garnet* (Boston: Beacon Press, 1972). On Delany, see, for example, Robert S. Levine, *Martin Delany, Frederick Douglass, and the Politics of Representative Identity* (Chapel Hill: University of North Carolina Press, 1997). On the literature of black nationalism in this period more generally, see John Ernest, *Liberation Historiography: African American Writers and the Challenge of History, 1794–1861* (Chapel Hill: University of North Carolina Press, 2004); Patrick Rael, *Black Identity and Black Protest in the Antebellum North* (Chapel Hill: University of North Carolina Press, 2002) esp. chapter 6; and Eddie S. Glaude, *Exodus!: Religion, Race, and Nation in Early Nineteenth-Century Black America* (Chicago: University of Chicago Press, 2000).

18. According to Peter Knights and Leo Schnore, for black people to be dispersed evenly throughout the city in 1830, 44 percent would need to relocate to another ward. Three decades later, 62.3 percent of African Americans would have to reposition themselves to eliminate segregation. From these indices, Knights and Schnore concluded that it was not the size of Boston's black population but rather the stigma of its color that caused segregation to tighten. "Residence and Social Structure: Boston in the Antebellum Period," in *Nineteenth Century Cities: Essays in the New Urban History,* edited by Stephan Thernstrom and Richard Sennett (New Haven: Yale University Press, 1969), 252; George Adams, ed., *Report and Tabular Statement of the Censors . . . State Census of Boston, May 1850,* Boston City Documents No. 42 (Boston: J. H. Eastburn, 1850), 23; Josiah Curtis, *Report of the Joint Special Committee on the Census of Boston, May, 1855* (Boston: Moore and Crosby, 1856), 3.

19. Eighty-four percent lived in four wards: 1, 2, 5, and 6. 60.9 percent lived in Ward 6. George A. Levesque, *Black Boston: African American Life and Culture in Urban America, 1750–1860* (New York: Garland, 1994), 256.

20. Census of 1850, 52.

21. By 1850, Southack Street alone would contain more than 480 African Americans, 23 percent of Boston's total black population. George Adams, ed., *Report and Tabular Statement of the Censors . . . State Census of Boston, May 1850,* Boston City Docs. No. 42 (Boston: J. H. Eastburn, 1850), 23.

22. Adams, *Report and Tabular Statement of the Censors,* 23.

23. "Constitution of the Afric-American Female Intelligence Society of Boston," *Liberator,* January 7, 1832; "Female Associations," *Liberator,* May 5, 1832; "Notice," *Liberator,* September 1, 1832.

24. "Boston Minor's Exhibition," *Liberator,* May 21, 1831.

25. "Notice," *Liberator,* January 21, 1832.

26. "Singing School," *Liberator,* September 17, 1836.

27. Lyceums in New Bedford and Nantucket, for instance, became embroiled in

integration controversies. "Protest," *Liberator*, November 28, 1845; "Ralph W. Emerson and Charles Sumner," *Liberator*, January 16, 1846; "The Prejudice of Color," *Liberator*, February 6, 1846, "New Bedford Lyceum," *Liberator*, October 30, 1846; "Triumph over Color-Phobia," *Liberator*, April 30, 1847; "Letter from a Member of the Athenaeum to a Friend," *Nantucket Islander*, January 16, 1841.

28. "Scientific Lectures," *Liberator*, January 7, 1837.

29. "Notice," *Liberator*, February 4, 1837; "Lectures for People of Color," *Liberator*, March 24, 1837; "Self Improvement," *Liberator*, November 3, 1837.

30. "Adelphic Union," *Liberator*, December 29, 1837; "Notice," *Liberator*, February 23, 1838; "Adelphic Union Lectures," *Liberator*, February 21, 1840; "Adelphic Union," *Liberator*, January 8, 1841; Adelphic Union Library Association," *Liberator*, October 21, 1842; "Adelphic Union Library Association," *Liberator*, January 27, 1843.

31. Nell copied portions of that speech in his correspondence. William C. Nell to Wendell Phillips, August 31, 1840, 3:0596–3:0597, *Black Abolitionist Papers,* microfilm collection, edited by George E. Carter et al., 17 reels, hereafter BAP. Nell to Phillips, April 15, 1841, 3:986–3:989, BAP.

32. "Notice," *Liberator*, March 11, 1837; "Adelphic Union Lectures," *Liberator*, January 3, 1840; William C. Nell to Charles Sumner, December 29, 1845, 5:0131, BAP.

33. Five hundred ninety-seven of 804 white households with one or more children between the ages of four and sixteen sent at least one child to school. Of the 160 black households with one or more school-age children, 104 sent at least one child to school. Within these groupings, certain patterns emerge. For example, within black households, slightly more illiterate than literate household heads schooled their children (71.4 versus 65.3 percent). Black female household heads were also more likely to school their children than their male counterparts (72 versus 64 percent). Of literate black male household heads, 62.2 percent schooled their children, in comparison with 70 percent of illiterate black male household heads. Of literate black female household heads, 71.4 percent schooled their children, as did 77 percent of illiterate black female household heads.

34. While 44 percent of black four-year-old boys attended school, just 20 percent of their female counterparts did so. Similarly, while 63 percent of five-year-old black boys attended school, only 36 percent of black five-year-old girls had that opportunity. By age seven, however, while 70 percent of black girls attended school, 56 percent of black boys did so. At the other end of the chronological spectrum, while 67 percent of sixteen-year-old black girls attended school, only 50 percent of sixteen-year-old black boys had that opportunity. Even more dramatically, while 60 percent of black sixteen-year-old girls attended school, just 12.5 percent of sixteen-year-old black boys did so.

35. Year 1850; census place Boston Ward 6, Suffolk, Massachusetts; roll M432_336; page 407; image 168. www.ancestrylibrary.com.

36. Year 1850; census place Boston Ward 6, Suffolk, Massachusetts; roll M432_336; page 406; image 167. www.ancestrylibrary.com.

37. "Report of the Sub-Committee to Consider the Expediency of Erecting a New School House for the Smith School," May 19, 1847, School Committee Loose Papers, Boston Public Library (1836–56; hereafter SCLP).

38. John Robinson et al., "Petition to Have Thos. Paul Be Considered a Candidate for the Master of the Smith School," August 2, 1848, SCLP.

39. "Boston Grammar and Writing Schools (Cont.)," *Common School Journal* 7, no. 21 (1845): 326–37.

40. William J. Watkins, "Hints to the Free People of Color," *Liberator*, January 9, 1852.

41. "Meeting of Colored Citizens," *Liberator,* August 10, 1849.

42. Nell identifies Smith as a member of the Young Men's Literary Society in his correspondence. William C. Nell to Wendell Phillips, August 28, 1843, 4:0655–4:0659, BAP.

43. William C. Nell to Wendell Phillips, August 28, 1843, 4:0655–4:0659, BAP.

44. Joshua B. Smith et al., "Petition on Separate Schools to the Boston School Committee," 1844, 4:0722, BAP.

45. "National Convention of Colored Americans and Their Friends," *Liberator*, September 10, 1847.

46. August 9, 1848, School Committee Minutes, Boston Public Library (hereafter SCM).

47. John Robinson et al., "Petition of John Robinson et al. to have Thos. Paul be considered a candidate for the master of the Smith School."

48. "Dartmouth College—A Noble Example," *Colored American,* April 29, 1837.

49. *Liberator*, November 19, 1841.

50. Jeremiah Sanderson to William C. Nell, January 13, 1842, 4:0346, BAP.

51. "Thomas Paul," *Liberator,* November 29, 1839; "Speech of Thomas Paul, a Colored Student of Dartmouth College, Delivered before the Massachusetts Anti-Slavery Society, January 27th, 1841, in the Representatives' Hall, Boston," *Liberator,* February 19, 1841; "Report of the Examining Committee of Candidacy for the Instructorship of the Smith School," September 12, 1849, SCLP. On the Paul family in Boston, see also J. Marcus Mitchell, "The Paul Family," *Old Time New England* 63 (1975): 73–77; and Susan Paul, *The Memoir of James Jackson, The Attentive and Obedient Scholar, Who Died in Boston, October 31, 1833, Aged Six Years and Eleven Months,"* edited by Lois Brown, (Cambridge: Harvard University Press, 2000).

52. Wm. Lawson et al., "Request to Erase Our Names from the Petition of Thos. P. Smith," August 3, 1848, SCLP.

53. Jonas W. Clark et al., "Petition Opposing the Appointment of Thomas Paul," August 10, 1848, SCLP.

54. J. J. De Bois and Thomas P. Smith, "The Smith School—Meeting of Colored Citizens," *Liberator,* August 18, 1848.

55. J. J. De Bois and Benjamin F. Roberts, "Proceedings of a Meeting of Colored Citizens for the Purpose of Expressing an Opinion in Relation to the Petition Asking That Thomas Paul Be Appointed Principal in the Smith School," August 5, 1848, SCLP.

56. Thomas P. Smith, "To the Boston School Board," August 10, 1848, SCLP.

57. Thomas P. Smith, "City Intelligence," n.d., SCLP.

58. Smith, *An Address Delivered before the Colored Citizens of Boston.*

59. Smith, "City Intelligence."

60. J. J. De Bois and Thomas P. Smith, "The Smith School—Meeting of Colored Citizens"; Smith, "City Intelligence."

61. Alexander Taylor, "To the Committee of the Smith School," August 10, 1848, SCLP.

62. *Report of a Special Committee of the Grammar School Board Presented August 29, 1849, on the Petition of Sundry Colored Persons, Praying for the Abolition of the Smith School* (Boston: J. H. Eastburn, 1849).

63. "Meeting of Colored Citizens," *Liberator,* August 10, 1849.

64. August 29, 1849, SCM.

65. "School Committee," *Boston Evening Transcript,* August 30, 1849.

66. September 12, 1849, SCM.

67. *Report of a Special Committee of the Grammar School Board,* 70; Smith, *An Address Delivered before the Colored Citizens of Boston.*

68. W. C. N., "The Smith School," *Liberator,* September 21, 1849.

69. W. C. N., "Equal School Rights," *Liberator,* February 8, 1850; William C. Nell to Charles Sumner, January 12, 1850, BAP, 6:0348.

70. De Bois and Roberts, "Proceedings of a Meeting of Colored Citizens for the Purpose of Expressing an Opinion."

71. "Caste Schools," *Boston Chronotype,* December 29, 1849. For more on divisions over school desegregation in Boston, see, for example, Scott Hancock, "The Elusive Boundaries of Blackness: Identity Formation in Antebellum Boston," *Journal of Negro History* 84 (Spring 1999): 115–29; George A. Levesque, "White Bureaucracy, Black Community: The Contest over Local Control of Education in Antebellum Boston," *Journal of Educational Thought* 11 (August 1977): 140–55; Arthur O. White, "Antebellum School Reform in Boston: Integrationists and Separatists," *Phylon* 34 (June 1973): 203–17; Donald M. Jacobs, "The Nineteenth Century Struggle over Segregated Education in the Boston Schools," *Journal of Negro Education* 39 (Winter 1970): 76–85; Carleton Mabee, "A Negro Boycott to Integrate Schools," *New England Quarterly* 41 (September 1968): 341–61.

72. George R. Price and James Brewer Stewart, "The Roberts Case, the Easton Family, and the Dynamics of the Abolitionist Movement in Massachusetts, 1776–1870," *Massachusetts Historical Review* 4 (2002): 101–102.

73. Price and Stewart, "The Roberts Case, the Easton Family, and the Dynamics of the Abolitionist Movement in Massachusetts, 1776–1870," 100–104. On Hosea Easton, see also Easton's *To Heal the Scourge of Prejudice: The Life and Writings of Hosea Easton,* edited by George R. Price and James Brewer Stewart (Amherst: University of Massachusetts Press, 1999). On the Easton family more generally, see George R. Price, "The Easton family of Southeast Massachusetts: the Dynamics Surrounding Five Generations of Human Rights Activism, 1753–1935" (Ph.D. dissertation, University of Montana, 2006). James Easton's school also appears in the Records of the New England Anti Slavery Society, vol. 1, April 30, 1832, Boston Public Library.

74. Price and Stewart, "The Roberts Case," 94–95.

75. B. F. Roberts, "Our Progress in the Bay State," *New Era,* March 30, 1870.

76. *Minutes and Proceedings of the First Annual Convention of the People of Colour: Held by Adjournments in the City of Philadelphia, from the Sixth to the Eleventh of June, Inclusive* (Philadelphia: Published by order of the Committee of Arrangements, 1831), 7.

77. B. F. R., "Are Africans Americans?" *Liberator,* February 22, 1834.

78. B. F. R., "Bad Enough at Best," *Liberator,* December 6, 1834.

79. A word of caution with occupational information culled from census records. Because marshals received instruction to record men's occupations only, census records provide an incomplete picture of women's work. With that limitation in mind, it is possible to draw some broad conclusions about black men's vocational possibilities. As of 1850, the majority of black Bostonians performed unskilled and semiskilled manual labor, according to census takers. Individuals described as laborers made up most of this group, while some 46 of Ward 6's African American residents also supported themselves as seamen, a position that kept them away from family and friends for many months of the year. Because census schedules did not provide information about women's labor, the number of black Bostonians engaged in service positions, as waiters and domestics, for example, was in all likelihood much higher than the twenty-three individuals census takers identified. Unlike Baltimore's Ward 17, however, where close to one-half of black workers performed a skilled trade, less than 20 percent of African Americans working in Ward 6 labored in that capacity. As of 1850, Ward 6's African American community, nearly 1,200 strong, included just eighteen bakers, fourteen barbers, one book binder, two carpenters, two cigar makers, three shoemakers, and five tailors, for example. At the same time, however, in contrast to Baltimore, where African Americans were almost entirely shut out from nonmanual occupations, a significant—albeit still modest—proportion of black Bostonians in Ward 6 supported themselves with mental as opposed to manual labor.

80. "Benjamin Roberts to Amos A. Phelps," June 19, 1838, reprinted in the *Black Abolitionist Papers,* vol. 3, edited by C. Peter Ripley (Chapel Hill: University of North Carolina Press, 1991), 269–70.

81. George Price, "The Easton Family of Southeast Massachusetts," 119; "Amos Phelps to Whom It May Concern," May 16, 1838, Anti-Slavery Collection, Boston Public Library; B. F. R., "Meeting of the Colored Citizens," *Boston Daily Atlas,* October 8, 1844.

82. According to George Price, the school committee had agreed to enroll Sarah in the white Otis School but refused to allow Roberts's son Benjamin Jr. to attend any school other than the Smith School. When Roberts pointed to Sarah's success at the Otis School in an effort to dispute the school committee's decision regarding Benjamin Jr., the school committee chose to remove Sarah from the Otis School. Roberts, in response, then filed suit on Sarah's behalf. "The Easton Family of Southeast Massachusetts," 127–29.

83. On the Sarah Roberts case see, for example, Gerald Nelson Davis, "Massachusetts Blacks and the Quest for Education: 1638–1860" (Ed.D. dissertation, University of Massachusetts, 1977), 183–84; George Dargo, "The Sarah Roberts Case in Historical Perspective," *Massachusetts Legal History* 3 (1997): 37–51; and Stephen Kendrick and Paul Kendrick, *Sarah's Long Walk: The Free Blacks of Boston and How Their Struggle for Equality Changed America* (Boston: Beacon Press, 2004).

84. *Argument of Charles Sumner, Esq. against the Constitutionality of Separate Colored Schools, in the Case of Sarah C. Roberts vs. The City of Boston before the Supreme Court of Mass, Dec. 4, 1849* (Boston: B. F. Roberts, 1849), 4.

85. Secondary discussions linking *Roberts* and *Plessy* are numerous. See, for example, Kendrick and Kendrick, *Sarah's Long Walk;* Douglas J. Ficker, "From *Roberts* to *Plessy*: Educational Segregation and the 'Separate but Equal Doctrine,'" *Journal of Negro History* 84 (Autumn 1999): 301–14; Roderick T. Baltimore and Robert F. Williams, "The State Constitutional Roots of the 'Separate but Equal' Doctrine: *Roberts v. City of Boston*," *Rutgers Law Journal* 17 (1986): 537–52; Derrick A. Bell, Jr., *Race, Racism and American Law* (Boston: Little, Brown, and Co., 1973), 442–43; and Leonard W. Levy and Harlan B. Phillips, "The *Roberts* Case: Source of the 'Separate but Equal' Doctrine," *American Historical Review* 56 (April 1951): 510–18.

86. "Charges against a Schoolmaster," *Liberator,* May 31, 1844.

87. "Meeting of the Primary School Committee," *Liberator,* June 27, 1845.

88. "The Smith School," *Liberator,* June 28, 1844.

89. *Commonwealth on Complaint of Jona B. Wheelock vs. Julian B. McCrea et al.*

90. Roberts, "Letter to the Editor."

91. Benjamin H. Irvin, "Tar, Feathers, and the Enemies of American Liberties, 1768–1776," *New England Quarterly* 76 (June 2003): 197–238; Bertram Wyatt-Brown, *Honor and Violence in the Old South* (New York: Oxford University Press, 1986), 190–95; Alfred F. Young, *The Shoemaker and the Tea Party* (Boston: Beacon Press, 1999), 46–51; Richard Maxwell Brown, "Violence and the American

Revolution," in *Essays in the American Revolution,* edited by Stephen G. Kurtz and James H. Hutson (Chapel Hill: University of North Carolina Press, 1973), 81–120.

92. William Watkins to William Lloyd Garrison, September 30, 1835, Anti-Slavery Collection, BPL.

93. On this point see Manisha Sinha, "To 'Cast Just Obliquy' on Oppressors: Black Radicalism in the Age of Revolution," *William and Mary Quarterly* 64 (January 2007), 149–60.

94. David Waldstreicher, *In the Midst of Perpetual Fetes: The Making of American Nationalism, 1776–1820* (Chapel Hill: University of North Carolina Press, 1997), 312.

95. Waldstreicher, *In the Midst of Perpetual Fetes,* 327–28. For more on this practice, see Shane White, " 'It Was a Proud Day': African Americans, Festivals, and Parades in the North, 1741–1834," *Journal of American History* 81 (June 1994): 13–50; and Joanne Pope Melish, *Disowning Slavery: Gradual Emancipation and "Race" in New England, 1780–1860* (Ithaca, N.Y.: Cornell University Press, 1998), 163–65.

96. Leonard I. Sweet, "The Fourth of July and Black Americans in the Nineteenth Century: Northern Leadership Opinion within the Context of the Black Experience," *Journal of Negro History* 61 (July 1976), 263.

97. On African Americans and nationalist celebrations, see also Scott Hancock, " 'Tradition Informs Us': African Americans' Construction of Memory in the Antebellum North," in *Slavery, Resistance, Freedom,* edited by Gabor Boritt and Scott Hancock (New York: Oxford University Press, 2007), 40–69; Mitch A. Kachun, "Antebellum African Americans, Public Commemoration, and the Haitian Revolution: A Problem of Historical Mythmaking," *Journal of the Early Republic* 26 (Summer 2006): 249–73; Jeffrey Strickland, "African-American Public Rituals on the Fourth of July and Citizenship in South Carolina During Reconstruction," *Citizenship Studies* 10 (February 2006), 93–115; Len Travers, *Celebrating the Fourth: Independence Day and the Rites of Nationalism in the Early Republic* (Amherst: University of Massachusetts Press, 1997); and Benjamin Quarles, "Antebellum Free Blacks and the 'Spirit of '76,' " *Journal of Negro History* (July 1976): 229–42.

98. "The Fourth of July," *North Star,* July 7, 1848. For a thorough discussion of this address, see James A. Colaiaco, *Frederick Douglass and the Fourth of July* (New York: Palgrave Macmillan, 2006).

99. "Response to the above Petition: House . . . No. 100, Commonwealth of Massachusetts," reprinted in *William Cooper Nell: Selected Writings, 1832–1874,* edited by Dorothy Porter (Baltimore: Black Classic Press, 2002), 283–85; William C. Nell, *Service of Colored Americans in the Wars of 1776 and 1812* (Boston, 1851); William Nell, "Petition to the House of Representatives for an Appropriation of $1500 to Erect a Monument to Crispus Attucks, February 22, 1851," reprinted in William Nell, *The Colored Patriots of the American Revolution* (Boston: Robert F. Wallcut, 1855), 14; William C. Nell, "Colored Patriots of the American Revolution," *Liberator,* May 25, 1855.

100. "Declaration of Sentiments of the Colored Citizens of Boston, on the Fugitive Slave Bill," *Liberator,* October 11, 1850.

101. "Extract from Charles Sumner's Speech on Resisting the Fugitive Law," *Pittsfield Sun,* February 27, 1851.

102. "Flight of Fugitive Slaves from Boston," *Boston Evening Transcript,* October 8, 1850.

103. For this phrasing and observation, I am indebted to Adam R. Nelson.

104. Jack Tager, *Boston Riots: Three Centuries of Social Violence* (Boston: Northeastern University Press, 2001), 95; Leonard W. Levy, "Sims' Case: The Fugitive Slave Law in Boston in 1851," *Journal of Negro History* 35 (January 1950): 39–74; "Embarkation of Sims, the Fugitive Slave," *Pittsfield Sun,* April 17, 1851; "The Examination of T. P. Smith (Colored)," *Boston Evening Transcript,* March 1, 1851; "Ninth Arrest for the Slave Rescue," *Boston Evening Transcript,* March 1, 1851.

105. *Commonwealth of Massachusetts vs. McCrea et al.,* Boston Municipal Court Records (1851), bound vol., 2104–5, MSA; "The Colored Assault Cases," *Boston Evening Transcript,* June 14, 1851; "Criminal Proceedings," *Boston Daily Atlas,* June 17, 1851.

106. On violence in the antislavery movement, see, for example, John R. McKivigan and Stanley Harrold, eds. *Antislavery Violence: Sectional, Racial, and Cultural Conflict in Antebellum America* (Knoxville: University of Tennessee Press, 1999); James and Lois E. Horton, "Violence, Protest, and Identity: Black Manhood in Antebellum America," in *Free People of Color: Inside the African American Community,* edited by James O. Horton (Washington, D.C.: Smithsonian Institute Press, 1993), 80–97; William H. and Jane Pease, "Confrontation and Abolition in the 1850s," *Journal of American History* 58 (March 1972): 923–37; and John Demos, "The Antislavery Movement and the Problem of Violent Means," *New England Quarterly* 37 (December 1964): 501–26.

107. "The Northern Vocalists," *Liberator,* February 26, 1858; "Commemorative Meeting in Faneuil Hall," *Liberator,* February 19, 1858.

108. Eldrid Herrington, "Research Note: Poems by Charlotte Forten and Frances Watkins Harper Found in AAS Collections," *The Book* (November 2004): 5–6. Many thanks to Susan Cifaldi for this reference.

109. William C. Nell, "Fanueil Hall Commemorative Festival, Protest against the Dred Scott Decision," March 5, 1858, Broadsides, American Antiquarian Society, Worcester, Mass.

Conclusion

1. Horace Mann, *Twelfth Annual Report of the Secretary of the Massachusetts Board of Education* (Dutton and Wentworth: Boston, 1848), 59.

2. Mann, *Twelfth Annual Report,* 140.

3. Benj. F. Roberts, "Equal School Privileges," *Liberator*, April 4, 1851.

4. On the role of public education in the American Dream, see Jennifer Hochschild and Nathan Scovronick, *The American Dream and the Public Schools* (New York: Oxford University Press, 2003), 1–8.

5. Frederick Douglass, "Education among the Colored People," *North Star*, October 26, 1849.

6. "To the Senior Editor—No. 1," *Freedom's Journal*, August 3, 1827.

Index